BOLLINGEN SERIES XX

THE COLLECTED WORKS

OF

C. G. JUNG

VOLUME 7

EDITORS

SIR HERBERT READ

MICHAEL FORDHAM, M.D., M.R.C.P.

GERHARD ADLER, PH.D,

WILLIAM MCGUIRE, *executive editor*

TWO ESSAYS ON ANALYTICAL PSYCHOLOGY

C. G. JUNG

SECOND EDITION

TRANSLATED BY R. F. C. HULL

BOLLINGEN SERIES XX

PRINCETON UNIVERSITY PRESS

Second edition, revised and augmented, 1966
Second printing, 1970
Third printing, 1975

THIS EDITION IS BEING PUBLISHED IN THE
UNITED STATES OF AMERICA BY PRINCETON
UNIVERSITY PRESS AND IN ENGLAND BY
ROUTLEDGE AND KEGAN PAUL, LTD. IN THE
AMERICAN EDITION, ALL THE VOLUMES
COMPRISING THE COLLECTED WORKS CON-
STITUTE NUMBER XX IN BOLLINGEN SERIES.
THE PRESENT VOLUME IS NUMBER 7 OF THE
COLLECTED WORKS AND WAS THE SECOND
TO APPEAR.

The two principal works in this volume
are translated from *Über die Psychologie
des Unbewussten* (1943) and *Die Beziehungen zwischen dem Ich und dem
Unbewussten* (1928; 2nd edn., 1935),
published by Rascher Verlag, Zurich.

LIBRARY OF CONGRESS CATALOGUE CARD NUMBER: 75–156
ISBN 0–691–09776–3
MANUFACTURED IN THE U.S.A.

EDITORIAL NOTE TO THE FIRST EDITION

"The Structure of the Unconscious" and "New Paths in Psychology" together marked a turning point in the history of analytical psychology, for they revealed the foundations upon which the greater part of Professor Jung's later work was built.

Both these essays were considerably revised and expanded for the successive editions mentioned in the Prefaces to the present volume. These Prefaces indicate the extent of the changes which were made on each occasion. As C. F. and H. G. Baynes say in the introduction to their English translation of an intermediate version, where the title *Two Essays on Analytical Psychology* was used for the first time: "Of the first essay only the framework of its earlier form can be recognized, and so much new material has been added to the second essay that both works start afresh, so to speak, full of the amazing vitality of Jung's mind." The essays are indeed remarkable for the number of revisions to which they have been subjected, each reflecting a new development of thought based upon increasingly fruitful researches into the unconscious.

However interesting the intermediate versions may be in themselves, the original drafts of these essays are undoubtedly far more significant to the student of analytical psychology. They contain the first tentative formulations of Jung's concept of archetypes and the collective unconscious, as well as his germinating theory of types. This theory was put forward, partially at least, as an attempt to explain the conflicts within the psychoanalytic school, of which he had been so prominent a member and from which he had so recently seceded.

With these considerations in mind the Editors decided to include the original drafts of these two essays in separate Appendices. It was felt that their historical interest fully justified the duplication of reading matter which comparison of the texts would involve.

Acknowledgment is gratefully made of the kindness of Faber and Faber, Ltd., London, and the Oxford University Press, New York, in permitting quotation from the Louis MacNeice translation of Goethe's *Faust*.

EDITORIAL NOTE TO THE SECOND EDITION

When the stock of the first edition of this volume was exhausted, twelve years after its first publication, the publishers undertook a complete resetting of type rather than a corrected reprint, as the result of research among Professor Jung's posthumous papers.

The text of Appendix 1, "New Paths in Psychology," was found to be an incomplete version of what the author published in 1912, and it was decided to publish the complete version, with the earliest deletions indicated. For Appendix 2, "The Structure of the Unconscious," it had been necessary in the first edition to retranslate a French translation in the absence of the original German. Subsequently the author's holograph manuscript was discovered in his archives, and this furthermore contained several unpublished passages and variants of historical interest.

Both appendices have accordingly been re-edited and largely retranslated to take the new findings into account. (For details, see the editorial note at the beginning of each appendix.) Similar though not identical presentations were published in Volume 7 of the *Gesammelte Werke*, i.e., the Swiss edition, in 1964. Also on the model of the Swiss edition, the complete texts of the various forewords have been added. The title of the first essay has been modified to "On the Psychology of the Unconscious."

The texts of the two main essays have also been revised, for consistency, the reference apparatus has been brought up to date, a bibliography has been added, and a new index has been supplied.

TABLE OF CONTENTS

I

ON THE PSYCHOLOGY
OF THE UNCONSCIOUS

II

THE RELATIONS BETWEEN THE EGO AND THE UNCONSCIOUS

Part One

THE EFFECTS OF THE UNCONSCIOUS UPON CONSCIOUSNESS

Part Two

INDIVIDUATION

APPENDICES

I

ON THE PSYCHOLOGY
OF
THE UNCONSCIOUS

PREFACE TO THE FIRST EDITION (1917)

This essay* is the result of my attempt to revise, at the publisher's request, the paper which appeared in the Rascher Yearbook for 1912 under the title "Neue Bahnen der Psychologie." † The present work thus reproduces that earlier essay, though in altered and enlarged form. In my earlier paper I confined myself to the exposition of one essential aspect of the psychological views inaugurated by Freud. The manifold and important changes which recent years have brought in the psychology of the unconscious have compelled me to broaden considerably the framework of my earlier paper. On the one hand a number of passages on Freud were shortened, while on the other hand, Adler's psychology was taken into account; and, so far as was possible within the limits of this essay, a general survey of my own views was given.

I must warn the reader at the outset that he will be dealing with a study which, on account of its rather complicated subject-matter, will make considerable demands on his patience and attention. Nor can I associate this work with the idea that it is in any sense conclusive or adequately convincing. This requirement could be met only by comprehensive scientific treatises on each separate problem touched upon in the essay. The reader who wishes to probe more deeply into the questions at issue must therefore be referred to the specialist literature. My intention is simply to give a broad survey of the most recent views on the nature and psychology of the unconscious. I regard the problem of the unconscious as so important and so topical that it would, in my opinion, be a great loss if this question, which touches each one of us so closely, were to disappear from the orbit of the educated lay public by being banished to some inaccessible technical journal, there to lead a shadowy paper-existence on the shelves of libraries.

* [*Die Psychologie der unbewussten Prozesse* (Zurich, 1917). Trans. by Dora Hecht as "The Psychology of the Unconscious Processes" in *Collected Papers on Analytical Psychology* (2nd edn., London and New York, 1917).—EDITORS.]
† [Cf. below, pars. 407ff.: "New Paths in Psychology."]

The psychological concomitants of the present war—above all the incredible brutalization of public opinion, the mutual slanderings, the unprecedented fury of destruction, the monstrous flood of lies, and man's incapacity to call a halt to the bloody demon—are uniquely fitted to force upon the attention of every thinking person the problem of the chaotic unconscious which slumbers uneasily beneath the ordered world of consciousness. This war has pitilessly revealed to civilized man that he is still a barbarian, and has at the same time shown what an iron scourge lies in store for him if ever again he should be tempted to make his neighbour responsible for his own evil qualities. The psychology of the individual is reflected in the psychology of the nation. What the nation does is done also by each individual, and so long as the individual continues to do it, the nation will do likewise. Only a change in the attitude of the individual can initiate a change in the psychology of the nation. The great problems of humanity were never yet solved by general laws, but only through regeneration of the attitudes of individuals. If ever there was a time when self-reflection was the absolutely necessary and only right thing, it is now, in our present catastrophic epoch. Yet whoever reflects upon himself is bound to strike upon the frontiers of the unconscious, which contains what above all else he needs to know.

Küsnacht, Zurich, December 1916   C. G. JUNG

PREFACE TO THE SECOND EDITION (1918)

I am glad that it has been the lot of this little book to pass into a second edition in so short a time, despite the difficulties it must have presented to many readers. I am letting the second edition appear unaltered except for a few minor modifications and improvements, although I am aware that the last chapters in particular, owing to the extraordinary difficulty and the novelty of the material, really needed discussion on a much broader basis in order to be generally understood. But a more detailed treatment of the fundamental principles there outlined would far exceed the bounds of a more or less popular presentation, so that I preferred to treat these questions with due circumstantiality in a separate work which is now in preparation.*

From the many communications I received after the publication of the first edition I have discovered that, even among the wider public, interest in the problems of the human psyche is very much keener than I expected. This interest may be due in no small measure to the profound shock which our consciousness sustained through the World War. The spectacle of this catastrophe threw man back upon himself by making him feel his complete impotence; it turned his gaze inwards, and, with everything rocking about him, he must needs seek something that guarantees him a hold. Too many still look outwards, some believing in the illusion of victory and of victorious power, others in treaties and laws, and others again in the overthrow of the existing order. But still too few look inwards, to their own selves, and still fewer ask themselves whether the ends of human society might not best be served if each man tried to abolish the old order in himself, and to practise in his own person and in his own inward state those precepts, those victories which he preaches at every street-corner, instead of always expecting these things of his fellow men. Every individual needs revolution, inner division, overthrow of the existing order, and renewal, but not by forcing them upon his neighbours under the hypocritical cloak of Christian love or the sense of social responsibility or any of the other beautiful euphemisms for unconscious urges to personal power. Individual self-reflection, return of the individual to the ground of human nature, to his own deepest being with its individual and social destiny—here is the beginning of a cure for that blindness which reigns at the present hour.

Interest in the problem of the human psyche is a symptom of this instinctive return to oneself. It is to serve this interest that the present book was written.

Küsnacht, Zurich, October 1918   C. G. J.

* *Psychological Types.*

PREFACE TO THE THIRD EDITION * (1926)

This book was written during the World War, and it owes its existence primarily to the psychological repercussions of that great event. Now that the war is over, the waves are beginning to subside again. But the great psychological problems that the war threw up still occupy the mind and heart of every thinking and feeling person. It is probably thanks to this that my little book has survived the postwar period and now appears in a third edition.

In view of the fact that seven years have elapsed since the publication of the first edition, I have deemed it necessary to undertake fairly extensive alterations and improvements, particularly in the chapters on types and on the unconscious. The chapter on "The Development of Types in the Analytical Process" † I have omitted entirely, as this question has since received comprehensive treatment in my book *Psychological Types,* to which I must refer the interested reader.

Anyone who has tried to popularize highly complicated material that is still in the process of scientific development will agree with me that this is no easy task. It is even more difficult when many of the psychological processes and problems I have to discuss here are quite unknown to most people. Much of what I say may arouse their prejudices or may appear arbitrary; but they should bear in mind that the purpose of such a book can be, at most, to give them a rough idea of its subject and to provoke thought, but not to enter into all the details of the argument. I shall be quite satisfied if my book fulfils this purpose.

Küsnacht, Zurich, April 1925   C. G. J.

* [Zurich, 1926; title changed to *Das Unbewusste im normalen und kranken Seelenleben.* Trans. by H. G. and C. F. Baynes as "The Unconscious in the Normal and Pathological Mind" in *Two Essays on Analytical Psychology* (London and New York, 1928).]

† [*Collected Papers on Analytical Psychology* (2nd edn.), pp. 437–41.]

PREFACE TO THE FOURTH EDITION (1936)

Aside from a few improvements the fourth edition appears unchanged. From numerous reactions of the public I have seen that the idea of the collective unconscious, to which I have devoted one chapter in this book, has aroused particular interest. I cannot therefore omit calling the attention of my readers to the latest issues of the *Eranos-Jahrbuch*,* which contain important works by various authors on this subject. The present book makes no attempt to give a comprehensive account of the full range of analytical psychology; consequently, much is merely hinted at and some things are not mentioned at all. I hope, however, that it will continue to fulfil its modest purpose.

Küsnacht, Zurich, April 1936   C. G. J.

PREFACE TO THE FIFTH EDITION † (1943)

Since the last, unchanged edition, six years have gone by; hence it seemed to me advisable to submit the present, new edition of the book to a thorough revision. On this occasion a number of inadequacies could be eliminated or improved, and superfluous material deleted. A difficult and complicated matter like the psychology of the unconscious gives rise not only to many new insights but to errors as well. It is still a boundless expanse of virgin territory into which we make experimental incursions, and only by going the long way round do we strike the direct road. Although I have tried to introduce as many new viewpoints as possible into the text, my reader should not expect

* [For translations of several papers from the first three issues of the *Eranos-Jahrbuch* (1933–35), see *Spiritual Disciplines* (Papers from the Eranos Yearbooks, 4). Those issues also first published Jung's "A Study in the Process of Individuation," "Archetypes of the Collective Unconscious," and "Dream Symbols of the Individuation Process."]

† [Zurich, 1943; title changed to *Ueber die Psychologie des Unbewussten*. It is this edition which is translated in the present volume.]

anything like a complete survey of the fundamentals of our contemporary psychological knowledge in this domain. In this popular account I am presenting only a few of the most essential aspects of medical psychology and also of my own researches, and this only by way of an introduction. A solid knowledge cannot be acquired except through the study of the literature on the one hand and through practical experience on the other. In particular I would like to recommend to those readers who are desirous of gaining detailed knowledge of these matters that they should not only study the basic works of medical psychology and psychopathology, but also thoroughly digest the psychological text-books. So doing, they will acquire the requisite knowledge of the position and general significance of medical psychology in the most direct way.

From such a comparative study the reader will be able to judge how far Freud's complaint about the "unpopularity" of his psychoanalysis, and my own feeling that I occupy an isolated outpost, are justified. Although there have been a few notable exceptions, I do not think I exaggerate when I say that the views of modern medical psychology have still not penetrated far enough into the strongholds of academic science. New ideas, if they are not just a flash in the pan, generally require at least a generation to take root. Psychological innovations probably take much longer, since in this field more than in any other practically everybody sets himself up as an authority.

Küsnacht, Zurich, April 1942   C. G. J.

I

PSYCHOANALYSIS

1   If he wants to help his patient, the doctor and above all the "specialist for nervous diseases" must have psychological knowledge; for nervous disorders and all that is embraced by the terms "nervousness," hysteria, etc. are of psychic origin and therefore logically require psychic treatment. Cold water, light, fresh air, electricity, and so forth have at best a transitory effect and sometimes none at all. The patient is sick in mind, in the highest and most complex of the mind's functions, and these can hardly be said to belong any more to the province of medicine. Here the doctor must also be a psychologist, which means that he must have knowledge of the human psyche.

2   In the past, that is to say up to fifty years ago, the doctor's psychological training was still very bad. His psychiatric textbooks were wholly confined to clinical descriptions and the systematization of mental diseases, and the psychology taught in the universities was either philosophy or the so-called "experimental psychology" inaugurated by Wundt.[1] The first moves towards a psychotherapy of the neuroses came from the Charcot school, at the Salpetrière in Paris; Pierre Janet[2] began his epoch-making researches into the psychology of neurotic states, and Bernheim[3] in Nancy took up with great success Liébeault's[4] old and forgotten idea of treating the neuroses by suggestion. Sigmund Freud translated Bernheim's book and also derived valuable inspiration from it. At that time there was still no psychology of the neuroses and psychoses. To Freud belongs the

---

[1] *Principles of Physiological Psychology* (orig. 1893).

[2] *L'Automatisme psychologique* (1889); *Névroses et idées fixes* (1898).

[3] *De la suggestion et de ses applications à la thérapeutique* (1886); trans. by S. Freud as *Die Suggestion und ihre Heilwirkung*.

[4] Liébeault, *Du sommeil et des états analogues considérés au point de vue de l'action du moral sur le physique* (1866).

9

undying merit of having laid the foundations of a psychology of the neuroses. His teachings sprang from his experience in the practical treatment of the neuroses, that is, from the application of a method which he called *psychoanalysis*.

3   Before we enter upon a closer presentation of our subject, something must be said about its relation to science as known hitherto. Here we encounter a curious spectacle which proves yet again the truth of Anatole France's remark: "Les savants ne sont pas curieux." The first work of any magnitude[5] in this field awakened only the faintest echo, in spite of the fact that it introduced an entirely new conception of the neuroses. A few writers spoke of it appreciatively and then, on the next page, proceeded to explain their hysterical cases in the same old way. They behaved very much like a man who, having eulogized the idea or fact that the earth was a sphere, calmly continues to represent it as flat. Freud's next publications remained absolutely unnoticed, although they put forward observations which were of incalculable importance for psychiatry. When, in the year 1900, Freud wrote the first real psychology of dreams[6] (a proper Stygian darkness had hitherto reigned over this field), people began to laugh, and when he actually started to throw light on the psychology of sexuality in 1905,[7] laughter turned to insult. And this storm of learned indignation was not behindhand in giving Freudian psychology an unwanted publicity, a notoriety that extended far beyond the confines of scientific interest.

4   Accordingly we must look more closely into this new psychology. Already in Charcot's time it was known that the neurotic symptom is "psychogenic," i.e., originates in the psyche. It was also known, thanks mainly to the work of the Nancy school, that all hysterical symptoms can be produced through suggestion. Equally, something was known, thanks to the researches of Janet, about the psychological mechanisms that produce such hysterical phenomena as anaesthesia, paresia, paralysis, and amnesia. But it was not known *how* an hysterical symptom originates in the psyche; the psychic causal connections were completely unknown. In the early eighties Dr. Breuer, an old Viennese practitioner, made a discovery which became the real starting-point

[5] Breuer and Freud, *Studies on Hysteria* (orig. 1895).
[6] *The Interpretation of Dreams*.
[7] "Three Essays on the Theory of Sexuality."

for the new psychology. He had a young, very intelligent woman patient suffering from hysteria, who manifested the following symptoms among others: she had a spastic (rigid) paralysis of the right arm, and occasional fits of absentmindedness or twilight states; she had also lost the power of speech inasmuch as she could no longer command her mother tongue but could only express herself in English (systematic aphasia). They tried at that time to account for these disorders with anatomical theories, although the cortical centre for the arm function was as little disturbed here as with a normal person. The symptomatology of hysteria is full of anatomical impossibilities. One lady, who had completely lost her hearing because of an hysterical affection, often used to sing. Once, when she was singing, her doctor seated himself unobserved at the piano and softly accompanied her. In passing from one stanza to the next he made a sudden change of key, whereupon the patient, without noticing it, went on singing in the changed key. Thus she hears—and does not hear. The various forms of systematic blindness offer similar phenomena: a man suffering from total hysterical blindness recovered his power of sight in the course of treatment, but it was only partial at first and remained so for a long time. He could see everything with the exception of people's heads. He saw all the people round him without heads. Thus he sees—and does not see. From a large number of like experiences it had been concluded that only the conscious mind of the patient does not see and hear, but that the sense function is otherwise in working order. This state of affairs directly contradicts the nature of an organic disorder, which always affects the actual function as well.

5   After this digression, let us come back to the Breuer case. There were no organic causes for the disorder, so it had to be regarded as hysterical, i.e., psychogenic. Breuer had observed that if, during her twilight states (whether spontaneous or artificially induced), he got the patient to tell him of the reminiscences and fantasies that thronged in upon her, her condition was eased for several hours afterwards. He made systematic use of this discovery for further treatment. The patient devised the name "talking cure" for it or, jokingly, "chimney-sweeping."

6   The patient had become ill when nursing her father in his fatal illness. Naturally her fantasies were chiefly concerned with

these disturbing days. Reminiscences of this period came to the surface during her twilight states with photographic fidelity; so vivid were they, down to the last detail, that we can hardly assume the waking memory to have been capable of such plastic and exact reproduction. (The name "hypermnesia" has been given to this intensification of the powers of memory which not infrequently occurs in restricted states of consciousness.) Remarkable things now came to light. One of the many stories told ran somewhat as follows:

One night, watching by the sick man, who had a high fever, she was tense with anxiety because a surgeon was expected from Vienna to perform an operation. Her mother had left the room for a while, and Anna, the patient, sat by the sick-bed with her right arm hanging over the back of the chair. She fell into a sort of waking dream in which she saw a black snake coming, apparently out of the wall, towards the sick man as though to bite him. (It is quite likely that there really were snakes in the meadow at the back of the house, which had already given the girl a fright and which now provided the material for the hallucination.) She wanted to drive the creature away, but felt paralysed; her right arm, hanging over the back of the chair, had "gone to sleep": it had become anaesthetic and paretic, and, as she looked at it, the fingers changed into little serpents with death's-heads. Probably she made efforts to drive away the snake with her paralysed right hand, so that the anaesthesia and paralysis became associated with the snake hallucination. When the snake had disappeared, she was so frightened that she wanted to pray; but all speech failed her, she could not utter a word until finally she remembered an English nursery rhyme, and then she was able to go on thinking and praying in English.[8]

7   Such was the scene in which the paralysis and the speech disturbance originated, and with the narration of this scene the disturbance itself was removed. In this manner the case is said to have been finally cured.

8   I must content myself with this one example. In the book I have mentioned by Breuer and Freud there is a wealth of similar examples. It can readily be understood that scenes of this kind make a powerful impression, and people are therefore inclined to impute causal significance to them in the genesis of the symp-

[8] [Cf. Breuer and Freud, pp. 38f.]

tom. The view of hysteria then current, which derived from the English theory of the "nervous shock" energetically championed by Charcot, was well qualified to explain Breuer's discovery. Hence there arose the so-called trauma theory, which says that the hysterical symptom, and, in so far as the symptoms constitute the illness, hysteria in general, derive from psychic injuries or traumata whose imprint persists unconsciously for years. Freud, now collaborating with Breuer, was able to furnish abundant confirmation of this discovery. It turned out that none of the hundreds of hysterical symptoms arose by chance—they were always caused by psychic occurrences. So far the new conception opened up an extensive field for empirical work. But Freud's inquiring mind could not remain long on this superficial level, for already deeper and more difficult problems were beginning to emerge. It is obvious enough that moments of extreme anxiety such as Breuer's patient experienced may leave an abiding impression. But how did she come to experience them at all, since they already clearly bear a morbid stamp? Could the strain of nursing bring this about? If so, there ought to be many more occurrences of the kind, for there are unfortunately very many exhausting cases to nurse, and the nervous health of the nurse is not always of the best. To this problem medicine gives an excellent answer: "The x in the calculation is predisposition." One is just "predisposed" that way. But for Freud the problem was: what constitutes the predisposition? This question leads logically to an examination of the previous history of the psychic trauma. It is a matter of common observation that exciting scenes have quite different effects on the various persons involved, or that things which are indifferent or even agreeable to one person arouse the greatest horror in others—witness frogs, snakes, mice, cats, etc. There are cases of women who will assist at bloody operations without turning a hair, while they tremble all over with fear and loathing at the touch of a cat. I remember a young woman who suffered from acute hysteria following a sudden fright.[9] She had been to an evening party and was on her way home about midnight in the company of several acquaintances, when a cab came up behind them at full trot. The others got out of the way, but she, as though spellbound with terror,

[9] [For another presentation of this case, see "The Theory of Psychoanalysis," pars. 218ff., 297ff., and 355ff.—EDITORS.]

13

kept to the middle of the road and ran along in front of the horses. The cabman cracked his whip and swore; it was no good, she ran down the whole length of the road, which led across a bridge. There her strength deserted her, and to avoid being trampled on by the horses she would in her desperation have leapt into the river had not the passers-by prevented her. Now, this same lady had happened to be in St. Petersburg on the bloody twenty-second of January [1905], in the very street which was cleared by the volleys of the soldiers. All round her people were falling to the ground dead or wounded; she, however, quite calm and clear-headed, espied a gate leading into a yard through which she made her escape into another street. These dreadful moments caused her no further agitation. She felt perfectly well afterwards—indeed, rather better than usual.

9   This failure to react to an apparent shock can frequently be observed. Hence it necessarily follows that the intensity of a trauma has very little pathogenic significance in itself, but it must have a special significance for the patient. That is to say, it is not the shock as such that has a pathogenic effect under all circumstances, but, in order to have an effect, it must impinge on a special psychic disposition, which may, in certain circumstances, consist in the patient's unconsciously attributing a specific significance to the shock. Here we have a possible key to the "predisposition." We have therefore to ask ourselves: what are the particular circumstances of the scene with the cab? The patient's fear began with the sound of the trotting horses; for an instant it seemed to her that this portended some terrible doom—her death, or something as dreadful; the next moment she lost all sense of what she was doing.

10   The real shock evidently came from the horses. The patient's predisposition to react in so unaccountable a way to this unremarkable incident might therefore consist in the fact that horses have some special significance for her. We might conjecture, for instance, that she once had a dangerous accident with horses. This was actually found to be the case. As a child of about seven she was out for a drive with her coachman, when suddenly the horses took fright and at a wild gallop made for the precipitous bank of a deep river-gorge. The coachman jumped down and shouted to her to do likewise, but she was in such deadly fear that she could hardly make up her mind. Nevertheless she

jumped in the nick of time, while the horses crashed with the carriage into the depths below. That such an event would leave a very deep impression scarcely needs proof. Yet it does not explain why at a later date such an insensate reaction should follow the perfectly harmless hint of a similar situation. So far we know only that the later symptom had a prelude in childhood, but the pathological aspect of it still remains in the dark. In order to penetrate this mystery, further knowledge is needed. For it had become clear with increasing experience that in all the cases analysed so far, there existed, apart from the traumatic experiences, another, special class of disturbances which lie in the province of love. Admittedly "love" is an elastic concept that stretches from heaven to hell and combines in itself good and evil, high and low. With this discovery Freud's views underwent a considerable change. If, more or less under the spell of Breuer's trauma theory, he had formerly sought the cause of neurosis in traumatic experiences, now the centre of gravity of the problem shifted to an entirely different point. This is best illustrated by our case: we can understand well enough why horses should play a special part in the life of the patient, but we do not understand the later reaction, so exaggerated and uncalled for. The pathological peculiarity of this story lies in the fact that she is frightened of quite harmless horses. Remembering the discovery that besides the traumatic experience there is often a disturbance in the province of love, we might inquire whether perhaps there is something peculiar in this connection.

11   The lady knows a young man to whom she thinks of becoming engaged; she loves him and hopes to be happy with him. At first nothing more is discoverable. But it would never do to be deterred from investigation by the negative results of the preliminary questioning. There are indirect ways of reaching the goal when the direct way fails. We therefore return to that singular moment when the lady ran headlong in front of the horses. We inquire about her companions and what sort of festive occasion it was in which she had just taken part. It had been a farewell party for her best friend, who was going abroad to a health resort on account of her nerves. This friend is married and, we are told, happily; she is also the mother of a child. We may take leave to doubt the statement that she is happy; for, were she really so, she would presumably have no reason to be

15

"nervous" and in need of a cure. Shifting my angle of approach, I learned that after her friends had rescued her they brought the patient back to the house of her host—her best friend's husband —as this was the nearest shelter at that late hour of night. There she was hospitably received in her exhausted state. At this point the patient broke off her narrative, became embarrassed, fidgeted, and tried to change the subject. Evidently some disagreeable reminiscence had suddenly bobbed up. After the most obstinate resistance had been overcome, it appeared that yet another very remarkable incident had occurred that night: the amiable host had made her a fiery declaration of love, thus precipitating a situation which, in the absence of the lady of the house, might well be considered both difficult and distressing. Ostensibly this declaration of love came to her like a bolt from the blue, but these things usually have their history. It was now the task of the next few weeks to dig out bit by bit a long love story, until at last a complete picture emerged which I attempt to outline somewhat as follows:

As a child the patient had been a regular tomboy, caring only for wild boys' games, scorning her own sex, and avoiding all feminine ways and occupations. After puberty, when the erotic problem might have come too close, she began to shun all society, hated and despised everything that even remotely reminded her of the biological destiny of woman, and lived in a world of fantasies which had nothing in common with rude reality. Thus, until about her twenty-fourth year, she evaded all those little adventures, hopes, and expectations which ordinarily move a girl's heart at this age. Then she got to know two men who were destined to break through the thorny hedge that had grown up around her. Mr. A was her best friend's husband, and Mr. B was his bachelor friend. She liked them both. Nevertheless it soon began to look as though she liked Mr. B a vast deal better. An intimacy quickly sprang up between them and before long there was talk of a possible engagement. Through her relations with Mr. B and through her friend she often came into contact with Mr. A, whose presence sometimes disturbed her in the most unaccountable way and made her nervous. About this time the patient went to a large party. Her friends were also there. She became lost in thought and was dreamily playing with her ring when it suddenly slipped off her finger and rolled under the table. Both gentlemen looked for it and Mr. B succeeded in finding it. He placed the ring on her finger with an arch smile and said, "You know what that means!" Overcome by a strange and irresistible feeling, she tore the ring from her finger and flung it through the open window. A painful moment ensued, as may be imagined, and soon she left the party in deep dejection. Not long after this, so-called chance brought it about that she should spend her summer holidays at a health resort where Mr. and Mrs. A were also staying. Mrs. A then began to grow visibly nervous, and frequently stayed indoors because she felt out of sorts. The patient was thus in a position to go out for walks alone with Mr. A. On one occasion they went boating. So boisterous was she in her merriment that she suddenly fell overboard. She could not swim, and it was only with great difficulty that Mr. A pulled her half-unconscious into the boat. And then it was that he kissed her. With this romantic episode the bonds were tied fast. But the patient would not allow the depths of this passion to come to consciousness, evidently because she had long habituated herself to pass over such things or, better, to run away from them. To excuse herself in her own eyes she pursued her engagement to Mr. B all the more energetically, telling herself every day that it was Mr. B whom she loved. Naturally this curious little game had not escaped the keen glances of wifely jealousy. Mrs. A, her friend, had guessed the secret and fretted accordingly, so that her nerves only got worse. Hence it became necessary for Mrs. A to go abroad for a cure. At the farewell party the evil spirit stepped up to our patient and whispered in her ear, "Tonight he is alone. Something must happen to you so that you can go to his house." And so indeed it happened: through her own strange behaviour she came back to his house, and thus she attained her desire.

12   After this explanation everyone will probably be inclined to assume that only a devilish subtlety could devise such a chain of circumstances and set it to work. There is no doubt about the subtlety, but its moral evaluation remains a doubtful matter, because I must emphasize that the motives leading to this dramatic dénouement were in no sense conscious. To the patient, the whole story seemed to happen of itself, without her being conscious of any motive. But the previous history makes it perfectly clear that everything was unconsciously directed to this end, while the conscious mind was struggling to bring about the

engagement to Mr. B. The unconscious drive in the other direction was stronger.

13 So once more we return to our original question, namely, whence comes the pathological (i.e., peculiar or exaggerated) nature of the reaction to the trauma? On the basis of a conclusion drawn from analogous experiences, we conjectured that in this case too there must be, in addition to the trauma, a disturbance in the erotic sphere. This conjecture has been entirely confirmed, and we have learnt that the trauma, the ostensible cause of the illness, is no more than an occasion for something previously not conscious to manifest itself, i.e., an important erotic conflict. Accordingly the trauma loses its exclusive significance, and is replaced by a much deeper and more comprehensive conception which sees the pathogenic agent as an erotic conflict.

14 One often hears the question: why should the erotic conflict be the cause of the neurosis rather than any other conflict? To this we can only answer: no one asserts that it must be so, but in point of fact it frequently is so. In spite of all indignant protestations to the contrary, the fact remains that love,[10] its problems and its conflicts, is of fundamental importance in human life and, as careful inquiry consistently shows, is of far greater significance than the individual suspects.

15 The trauma theory has therefore been abandoned as antiquated; for with the discovery that not the trauma but a hidden erotic conflict is the root of the neurosis, the trauma loses its causal significance.[11]

[10] Using the word in the wider sense which belongs to it by right and embraces more than sexuality. This is not to say that love and its disturbances are the *only* source of neurosis. Such disturbances may be of secondary nature and conditioned by deeper-lying causes. There are other ways of becoming neurotic.

[11] Genuine shock-neuroses like shell-shock, "railway spine," etc. form an exception.

II

THE EROS THEORY

16   In the light of this discovery, the question of the trauma was answered in a most unexpected manner; but in its place the investigator was faced with the problem of the erotic conflict, which, as our example shows, contains a wealth of abnormal elements and cannot at first sight be compared with an ordinary erotic conflict. What is peculiarly striking and almost incredible is that only the pretence should be conscious, while the patient's real passion remained hidden from her. In this case certainly, it is beyond dispute that the real relationship was shrouded in darkness, while the pretended one dominated the field of consciousness. If we formulate these facts theoretically, we arrive at the following result: there are in a neurosis two tendencies standing in strict opposition to one another, one of which is unconscious. This proposition is formulated in very general terms on purpose, because I want to stress that although the pathogenic conflict is a personal matter it is also a broadly human conflict manifesting itself in the individual, for disunity with oneself is the hall-mark of civilized man. The neurotic is only a special instance of the disunited man who ought to harmonize nature and culture within himself.

17   The growth of culture consists, as we know, in a progressive subjugation of the animal in man. It is a process of domestication which cannot be accomplished without rebellion on the part of the animal nature that thirsts for freedom. From time to time there passes as it were a wave of frenzy through the ranks of men too long constrained within the limitations of their culture. Antiquity experienced it in the Dionysian orgies that surged over from the East and became an essential and characteristic ingredient of classical culture. The spirit of these orgies contributed not a little towards the development of the stoic ideal of asceticism in the innumerable sects and philosophical schools

of the last century before Christ, which produced from the polytheistic chaos of that epoch the twin ascetic religions of Mithraism and Christianity. A second wave of Dionysian licentiousness swept over the West at the Renaissance. It is difficult to gauge the spirit of one's own time; but in the succession of revolutionary questions to which the last half century gave birth, there was the "sexual question," and this has fathered a whole new species of literature. In this "movement" are rooted the beginnings of psychoanalysis, on whose theories it exerted a very one-sided influence. After all, nobody can be completely independent of the currents of his age. Since then the "sexual question" has largely been thrust into the background by political and spiritual problems. That, however, does nothing to alter the fundamental fact that man's instinctual nature is always coming up against the checks imposed by civilization. The names alter, but the facts remain the same. We also know today that it is by no means the animal nature alone that is at odds with civilized constraints; very often it is new ideas which are thrusting upwards from the unconscious and are just as much out of harmony with the dominating culture as the instincts. For instance, we could easily construct a political theory of neurosis, in so far as the man of today is chiefly excited by political passions to which the "sexual question" was only an insignificant prelude. It may turn out that politics are but the forerunner of a far deeper religious convulsion. Without being aware of it, the neurotic participates in the dominant currents of his age and reflects them in his own conflict.

18   Neurosis is intimately bound up with the problem of our time and really represents an unsuccessful attempt on the part of the individual to solve the general problem in his own person. Neurosis is self-division. In most people the cause of the division is that the conscious mind wants to hang on to its moral ideal, while the unconscious strives after its—in the contemporary sense—unmoral ideal which the conscious mind tries to deny. Men of this type want to be more respectable than they really are. But the conflict can easily be the other way about: there are men who are to all appearances very disreputable and do not put the least restraint upon themselves. This is at bottom only a pose of wickedness, for in the background they have their moral side which has fallen into the unconscious just as surely as

the immoral side in the case of the moral man. (Extremes should therefore be avoided as far as possible, because they always arouse suspicion of their opposite.)

19   This general discussion was necessary in order to clarify the idea of an "erotic conflict." Thence we can proceed to discuss firstly the technique of psychoanalysis and secondly the question of therapy.

20   Obviously the great question for this technique is: How are we to arrive by the shortest and best path at a knowledge of what is happening in the unconscious of the patient? The original method was hypnotism: either interrogation in a state of hypnotic concentration or else the spontaneous production of fantasies by the patient while in this state. This method is still occasionally employed, but compared with the present technique it is primitive and often unsatisfactory. A second method was evolved by the Psychiatric Clinic, in Zurich, the so-called association method.[1] It demonstrates very accurately the presence of conflicts in the form of "complexes" of feeling-toned ideas, as they are called, which betray themselves through characteristic disturbances in the course of the experiment.[2] But the most important method of getting at the pathogenic conflicts is, as Freud was the first to show, through the analysis of dreams.

21   Of the dream it can indeed be said that "the stone which the builders rejected, the same is become the the head of the corner." It is only in modern times that the dream, this fleeting and insignificant-looking product of the psyche, has met with such profound contempt. Formerly it was esteemed as a harbinger of fate, a portent and comforter, a messenger of the gods. Now we see it as the emissary of the unconscious, whose task it is to reveal the secrets that are hidden from the conscious mind, and this it does with astounding completeness. The "manifest" dream, i.e., the dream as we remember it, is in Freud's view only a façade which gives us no idea of the interior of the house, but, on the contrary, carefully conceals it with the help of the "dream censor." If, however, while observing certain technical rules, we induce the dreamer to talk about the details of his dream, it soon becomes evident that his associations tend in a particular direc-

[1] Jung and others, *Studies in Word Association*, trans. by M. D. Eder. [In the *Coll. Works*, Vol. 2.]
[2] Jung, "A Review of the Complex Theory."

tion and group themselves round particular topics. These are of personal significance and yield a meaning which could never have been conjectured to lie behind the dream, but which, as careful comparison has shown, stands in an extremely delicate and meticulously exact relationship to the dream façade. This particular complex of ideas wherein are united all the threads of the dream is the conflict we are looking for, or rather a variation of it conditioned by circumstances. According to Freud, the painful and incompatible elements in the conflict are in this way so covered up or obliterated that we we may speak of a "wish-fulfilment." However, it is only very seldom that dreams fulfil obvious wishes, as for instance in the so-called body-stimulus dreams, e.g., the sensation of hunger during sleep, when the desire for food is satisfied by dreaming about delicious meals. Likewise the pressing idea that one ought to get up, conflicting with the desire to go on sleeping, leads to the wish-fulfilling dream-idea that one has already got up, etc. In Freud's view there are also unconscious wishes whose nature is incompatible with the ideas of the waking mind, painful wishes which one prefers not to admit, and these are precisely the wishes that Freud regards as the real architects of the dream. For instance, a daughter loves her mother tenderly, but dreams to her great distress that her mother is dead. Freud argues that there exists in this daughter, unbeknown to herself, the exceedingly painful wish to see her mother removed from this world with all speed, because she has secret resistances to her. Even in the most blameless daughter such moods may occur, but they would be met with the most violent denial if one tried to saddle her with them. To all appearances the manifest dream contains no trace of wish-fulfilment, rather of apprehension or alarm, consequently the direct opposite of the supposed unconscious impulse. But we know well enough that *exaggerated* alarm can often and rightly be suspected of the contrary. (Here the critical reader may justifiably ask: When is the alarm in a dream exaggerated?) Such dreams, in which there is apparently no trace of wish-fulfilment, are innumerable: the conflict worked out in the dream is unconscious, and so is the attempted solution. Actually, there does exist in our dreamer the tendency to be rid of her mother; expressed in the language of the unconscious, she wants her mother to die. But the dreamer should certainly not be saddled

22

with this tendency because, strictly speaking, it was not she who fabricated the dream, but the unconscious. The unconscious has this tendency, most unexpected from the dreamer's point of view, to get rid of the mother. The very fact that she can dream such a thing proves that she does not consciously think it. She has no notion why her mother should be got rid of. Now we know that a certain layer of the unconscious contains everything that has passed beyond the recall of memory, including all those infantile instinctual impulses which could find no outlet in adult life. We can say that the bulk of what comes out of the unconscious has an infantile character at first, as for instance this wish, which is simplicity itself: "When Mummy dies you will marry me, won't you, Daddy?" This expression of an infantile wish is the substitute for a recent desire to marry, a desire in this case painful to the dreamer, for reasons still to be discovered. The idea of marriage, or rather the seriousness of the corresponding impulse, is, as they say, "repressed into the unconscious" and from there must necessarily express itself in an infantile fashion, because the material at the disposal of the unconscious consists largely of infantile reminiscences.

22   Our dream is apparently concerned with a twinge of infantile jealousy. The dreamer is more or less in love with her father, and for that reason she wants to get rid of her mother. But her real conflict lies in the fact that on the one hand she wants to marry, and on the other hand is unable to make up her mind: for one never knows what it will be like, whether he will make a suitable husband, etc. Again, it is so nice at home, and what will happen when she has to part from darling Mummy and be all independent and grown up? She fails to notice that the marriage question is now a serious matter for her and has her in its grip, so that she can no longer creep home to father and mother without bringing the fateful question into the bosom of the family. She is no longer the child she once was; she is the woman who wants to get married. As such she comes back, complete with her wish for a husband. But in the family the father is the husband and, without her being aware of it, it is on him that the daughter's desire for a husband falls. But that is *incest!* In this way there arises a secondary incest-intrigue. Freud assumes that the tendency to incest is primary and the real reason why the dreamer cannot make up her mind to marry. Compared with that, the

other reasons we have cited count for little. With regard to this view I have long adopted the standpoint that the occasional occurrence of incest is no proof of a universal tendency to incest, any more than the fact of murder proves the existence of a universal homicidal mania productive of conflict. I would not go so far as to say that the germs of every kind of criminality are not present in each of us. But there is a world of difference between the presence of such a germ and an actual conflict with its resulting cleavage of the personality, such as exists in a neurosis.

23   If we follow the history of a neurosis with attention, we regularly find a critical moment when some problem emerged that was evaded. This evasion is just as natural and just as common a reaction as the laziness, slackness, cowardice, anxiety, ignorance, and unconsciousness which are at the back of it. Whenever things are unpleasant, difficult, and dangerous, we mostly hesitate and if possible give them a wide berth. I regard these reasons as entirely sufficient. The symptomatology of incest, which is undoubtedly there and which Freud rightly saw, is to my mind a secondary phenomenon, already pathological.

24   The dream is often occupied with apparently very silly details, thus producing an impression of absurdity, or else it is on the surface so unintelligible as to leave us thoroughly bewildered. Hence we always have to overcome a certain resistance before we can seriously set about disentangling the intricate web through patient work. But when at last we penetrate to its real meaning, we find ourselves deep in the dreamer's secrets and discover with astonishment that an apparently quite senseless dream is in the highest degree significant, and that in reality it speaks only of important and serious matters. This discovery compels rather more respect for the so-called superstition that dreams have a meaning, to which the rationalistic temper of our age has hitherto given short shrift.

25   As Freud says, dream-analysis is the *via regia* to the unconscious. It leads straight to the deepest personal secrets, and is, therefore, an invaluable instrument in the hand of the physician and educator of the soul.

26   The analytical method in general, and not only the specifically Freudian psychoanalysis, consists in the main of numerous dream-analyses. In the course of treatment, the dreams successively throw up the contents of the unconscious in order to ex-

pose them to the disinfecting power of daylight, and in this way much that is valuable and believed lost is found again. It is only to be expected that for many people who have false ideas about themselves the treatment is a veritable torture. For, in accordance with the old mystical saying, "Give up what thou hast, then shalt thou receive!" they are called upon to abandon all their cherished illusions in order that something deeper, fairer, and more embracing may arise within them. It is a genuine old wisdom that comes to light again in the treatment, and it is especially curious that this kind of psychic education should prove necessary in the heyday of our culture. In more than one respect it may be compared with the Socratic method, though it must be said that analysis penetrates to far greater depths.

27   The Freudian mode of investigation sought to prove that an overwhelming importance attaches to the erotic or sexual factor as regards the origin of the pathogenic conflict. According to this theory there is a collision between the trend of the conscious mind and the unmoral, incompatible, unconscious wish. The unconscious wish is infantile, i.e., it is a wish from the childish past that will no longer fit the present, and is therefore repressed on moral grounds. The neurotic has the soul of a child who bears ill with arbitrary restrictions whose meaning he does not see; he tries to make this morality his own, but falls into disunity with himself: one side of him wants to suppress, the other longs to be free—and this struggle goes by the name of neurosis. Were the conflict clearly conscious in all its parts, presumably it would never give rise to neurotic symptoms; these occur only when we cannot see the other side of our nature and the urgency of its problems. Only under these conditions does the symptom appear, and it helps to give expression to the unrecognized side of the psyche. The symptom is therefore, in Freud's view, the fulfilment of unrecognized desires which, when conscious, come into violent conflict with our moral convictions. As already observed, this shadow-side of the psyche, being withdrawn from conscious scrutiny, cannot be dealt with by the patient. He cannot correct it, cannot come to terms with it, nor yet disregard it; for in reality he does not "possess" the unconscious impulses at all. Thrust out from the hierarchy of the conscious psyche, they have become autonomous complexes which it is the task of analysis, not without great resistances, to bring under control again.

There are patients who boast that for them the shadow-side does not exist; they assure us that they have no conflict, but they do not see that other things of unknown origin cumber their path— hysterical moods, underhand tricks which they play on themselves and their neighbours, a nervous catarrh of the stomach, pains in various places, irritability for no reason, and a whole host of nervous symptoms.

28   Freudian psychoanalysis has been accused of liberating man's (fortunately) repressed animal instincts and thus causing incalculable harm. This apprehension shows how little trust we place in the efficacy of our moral principles. People pretend that only the morality preached from the pulpit holds men back from unbridled licence; but a much more effective regulator is necessity, which sets bounds far more real and persuasive than any moral precepts. It is true that psychoanalysis makes the animal instincts conscious, though not, as many would have it, with a view to giving them boundless freedom, but rather to incorporating them in a purposeful whole. It is under all circumstances an advantage to be in full possession of one's personality, otherwise the repressed elements will only crop up as a hindrance elsewhere, not just at some unimportant point, but at the very spot where we are most sensitive. If people can be educated to see the shadow-side of their nature clearly, it may be hoped that they will also learn to understand and love their fellow men better. A little less hypocrisy and a little more self-knowledge can only have good results in respect for our neighbour; for we are all too prone to transfer to our fellows the injustice and violence we inflict upon our own natures.

29   The Freudian theory of repression certainly does seem to say that there are, as it were, only hypermoral people who repress their unmoral, instinctive natures. Accordingly the unmoral man, who lives a life of unrestrained instinct, should be immune to neurosis. This is obviously not the case, as experience shows. Such a man can be just as neurotic as any other. If we analyse him, we simply find that his morality is repressed. The neurotic immoralist presents, in Nietzsche's striking phrase, the picture of the "pale felon" who does not live up to his acts.

30   We can of course take the view that the repressed remnants of decency are in this case only a traditional hang-over from in-

fancy, which imposes an unnecessary check on instinctual nature and should therefore be eradicated. The principle of *écrasez l'infâme* would end in a theory of absolute libertinism. Naturally, that would be quite fantastic and nonsensical. It should never be forgotten—and of this the Freudian school must be reminded—that morality was not brought down on tables of stone from Sinai and imposed on the people, but is a function of the human soul, as old as humanity itself. Morality is not imposed from outside; we have it in ourselves from the start—not the law, but our moral nature without which the collective life of human society would be impossible. That is why morality is found at all levels of society. It is the instinctive regulator of action which also governs the collective life of the herd. But moral laws are valid only within a compact human group. Beyond that, they cease. There the old truth runs: *Homo homini lupus*. With the growth of civilization we have succeeded in subjecting ever larger human groups to the rule of the same morality, without, however, having yet brought the moral code to prevail beyond the social frontiers, that is, in the free space between mutually independent societies. There, as of old, reign lawlessness and licence and mad immorality—though of course it is only the enemy who dares to say it out loud.

31   The Freudian school is so convinced of the fundamental, indeed exclusive, importance of sexuality in neurosis that it has drawn the logical conclusion and valiantly attacked the sexual morality of our day. This was beyond a doubt useful and necessary, for in this field there prevailed and still prevail ideas which in view of the extremely complicated state of affairs are too undifferentiated. Just as in the early Middle Ages finance was held in contempt because there was as yet no differentiated financial morality to suit each case, but only a mass morality, so today there is only a mass sexual morality. A girl who has an illegitimate baby is condemned and nobody asks whether she is a decent human being or not. Any form of love not sanctioned by law is considered immoral, whether between worth-while people or bounders. We are still so hypnotized by *what* happens that we forget *how* and *to whom* it happens, just as for the Middle Ages finance was nothing but glittering gold, fiercely coveted and therefore the devil.

27

32   Yet things are not quite so simple as that. Eros is a questionable fellow and will always remain so, whatever the legislation of the future may have to say about it. He belongs on one side to man's primordial animal nature which will endure as long as man has an animal body. On the other side he is related to the highest forms of the spirit. But he thrives only when spirit and instinct are in right harmony. If one or the other aspect is lacking to him, the result is injury or at least a lopsidedness that may easily veer towards the pathological. Too much of the animal distorts the civilized man, too much civilization makes sick animals. This dilemma reveals the vast uncertainty that Eros holds for man. For, at bottom, Eros is a superhuman power which, like nature herself, allows itself to be conquered and exploited as though it were impotent. But triumph over nature is dearly paid for. Nature requires no explanations of principle, but asks only for tolerance and wise measure.

33   "Eros is a mighty daemon," as the wise Diotima said to Socrates. We shall never get the better of him, or only to our own hurt. He is not the whole of our inward nature, though he is at least one of its essential aspects. Thus Freud's sexual theory of neurosis is grounded on a true and factual principle. But it makes the mistake of being one-sided and exclusive; also it commits the imprudence of trying to lay hold of unconfinable Eros with the crude terminology of sex. In this respect Freud is a typical representative of the materialistic epoch,[3] whose hope it was to solve the world riddle in a test-tube. Freud himself, with advancing years, admitted this lack of balance in his theory, and he opposed to Eros, whom he called libido, the destructive or death instinct.[4] In his posthumous writings he says:

After long hesitancies and vacillations we have decided to assume the the existence of only two basic instincts, *Eros* and *the destructive instinct*. . . . The aim of the first of these basic instincts is to establish ever greater unities and to preserve them thus—in short, to bind together; the aim of the second is, on the contrary, to undo connec-

[3] Cf. Jung, "Sigmund Freud in His Historical Setting."
[4] This idea came originally from my pupil S. Spielrein: cf. "Die Destruktion als Ursache des Werdens" (1912). This work is mentioned by Freud, who introduces the destructive instinct in "Beyond the Pleasure Principle" (orig. 1920), Ch. V. [More fully in Ch. VI, which contains the Spielrein reference: Standard Edn., XVIII, p. 55.—EDITORS.]

tions and so to destroy things. . . . For this reason we also call it the *death instinct*.[5]

34   I must content myself with this passing reference, without entering more closely into the questionable nature of the conception. It is sufficiently obvious that life, like any other process, has a beginning and an end and that every beginning is also the beginning of the end. What Freud probably means is the essential fact that every process is a phenomenon of energy, and that all energy can proceed only from the tension of opposites.

5 ["An Outline of Psycho-Analysis" (orig. 1940), Standard Edn., XXIII, p. 148.]

III

THE OTHER POINT OF VIEW:
THE WILL TO POWER

35   So far we have considered the problem of this new psychology
essentially from the Freudian point of view. Undoubtedly it has
shown us a very real truth to which our pride, our civilized consciousness, may say no, though something else in us says yes.
Many people find this fact extremely irritating; it arouses their
hostility or even their fear, and consequently they are unwilling
to recognize the conflict. And indeed it is a frightening thought
that man also has a shadow-side to him, consisting not just of
little weaknesses and foibles, but of a positively demonic dynamism. The individual seldom knows anything of this; to him, as
an individual, it is incredible that he should ever in any circumstances go beyond himself. But let these harmless creatures form
a mass, and there emerges a raging monster; and each individual
is only one tiny cell in the monster's body, so that for better or
worse he must accompany it on its bloody rampages and even
assist it to the utmost. Having a dark suspicion of these grim
possibilities, man turns a blind eye to the shadow-side of human
nature. Blindly he strives against the salutary dogma of original
sin, which is yet so prodigiously true. Yes, he even hesitates to
admit the conflict of which he is so painfully aware. It can readily be understood that a school of psychology—even if it be
biased and exaggerated in this or that respect—which insists on
the seamy side, is unwelcome, not to say frightening, because it
forces us to gaze into the bottomless abyss of this problem. A
dim premonition tells us that we cannot be whole without this
negative side, that we have a body which, like all bodies, casts
a shadow, and that if we deny this body we cease to be three-
dimensional and become flat and without substance. Yet this
body is a beast with a beast's soul, an organism that gives un-
questioning obedience to instinct. To unite oneself with this

shadow is to say yes to instinct, to that formidable dynamism lurking in the background. From this the ascetic morality of Christianity wishes to free us, but at the risk of disorganizing man's animal nature at the deepest level.

36   Has anyone made clear to himself what that means—a yea-saying to instinct? That was what Nietzsche desired and taught, and he was in deadly earnest. With a rare passion he sacrificed himself, his whole life, to the idea of the Superman—to the idea of the man who through obedience to instinct transcends himself. And what was the course of that life? It was as Nietzsche himself prophesied in *Zarathustra*, in that foreboding vision of the fatal fall of the rope-dancer, the man who would not be "surpassed." To the dying rope-dancer Zarathustra says: "Thy soul will sooner be dead than thy body!" and later the dwarf says to Zarathustra, "O Zarathustra, stone of wisdom! High thou flingest thyself, but every stone that is flung must fall! Condemned to thyself and to thine own stoning: O Zarathustra, far indeed thou flingest the stone—but upon thyself will it fall." And when he cried his "Ecce Homo" over himself, again it was too late, as once before when this saying was uttered, and the crucifixion of the soul began before the body was dead.

37   We must look very critically at the life of one who taught such a yea-saying, in order to examine the effects of this teaching on the teacher's own life. When we scrutinize his life with this aim in view we are bound to admit that Nietzsche lived beyond instinct, in the lofty heights of heroic sublimity—heights that he could maintain only with the help of the most meticulous diet, a carefully selected climate, and many aids to sleep—until the tension shattered his brain. He talked of yea-saying and lived the nay. His loathing for man, for the human animal that lived by instinct, was too great. Despite everything, he could not swallow the toad he so often dreamed of and which he feared had to be swallowed. The roaring of the Zarathustrian lion drove back into the cavern of the unconscious all the "higher" men who were clamouring to live. Hence his life does not convince us of his teaching. For the "higher" man wants to be able to sleep without chloral, to live in Naumburg and Basel despite "fogs and shadows." He desires wife and offspring, standing and esteem among the herd, innumerable commonplace realities, and not least those of the Philistine. Nietzsche failed to live this in-

stinct, the animal urge to life. For all his greatness and importance, Nietzsche's was a pathological personality.

38   But what was it that he lived, if not the life of instinct? Can Nietzsche really be accused of having denied his instincts in practice? He would scarcely have agreed to that. He could even show without much difficulty that he lived his instinctual life in the highest sense. But how is it possible, we may ask in astonishment, for man's instinctual nature to drive him into separation from his kind, into absolute isolation from humanity, into an aloofness from the herd upheld by loathing? We think of instinct as uniting man, causing him to mate, to beget, to seek pleasure and good living, the satisfaction of all sensuous desires. We forget that this is only one of the possible directions of instinct. There exists not only the instinct for the preservation of the species, but also the instinct of *self*-preservation.

39   It is of this last instinct, the *will to power,* that Nietzsche obviously speaks. Whatever else is instinctual only follows, for him, in the train of the will to power. From the standpoint of Freud's sexual psychology, this is an error of the most glaring kind, a misconception of biology, the bungling of a decadent neurotic. For it is a very simple matter for any adherent of sexual psychology to prove that everything lofty and heroic in Nietzsche's view of life and the world is nothing but a consequence of the repression and misunderstanding of that other instinct which *this* psychology regards as fundamental.

40   The case of Nietzsche shows, on the one hand, the consequences of neurotic one-sidedness, and, on the other hand, the dangers that lurk in this leap beyond Christianity. Nietzsche undoubtedly felt the Christian denial of animal nature very deeply indeed, and therefore he sought a higher human wholeness beyond good and evil. But he who seriously criticizes the basic attitudes of Christianity also forfeits the protection which these bestow upon him. He delivers himself up unresistingly to the animal psyche. That is the moment of Dionysian frenzy, the overwhelming manifestation of the "blond beast," [1] which seizes the unsuspecting soul with nameless shudderings. The seizure transforms him into a hero or into a godlike being, a super-

---

1 [Cf. Jung, "The Role of the Unconscious," par. 17.—EDITORS.]

human entity. He rightly feels himself "six thousand feet beyond good and evil."

41   The psychological observer knows this state as "identification with the shadow," a phenomenon which occurs with great regularity at such moments of collision with the unconscious. The only thing that helps here is cautious self-criticism. Firstly and before all else, it is exceedingly unlikely that one has just discovered a world-shattering truth, for such things happen extremely seldom in the world's history. Secondly, one must carefully inquire whether something similar might not have happened elsewhere—for instance Nietzsche, as a philologist, could have adduced a few obvious classical parallels which would certainly have calmed his mind. Thirdly, one must reflect that a Dionysian experience may well be nothing more than a relapse into a pagan form of religion, so that in reality nothing new is discovered and the same story only repeats itself from the beginning. Fourthly, one cannot avoid foreseeing that this joyful intensification of mood to heroic and godlike heights is dead certain to be followed by an equally deep plunge into the abyss. These considerations would put one in a position of advantage: the whole extravaganza could then be reduced to the proportions of a somewhat exhausting mountaineering expedition, to which succeed the eternal commonplaces of day. Just as every stream seeks the valley and the broad river that hastens towards the flatlands, so life not only flows along in commonplaces, but makes everything else commonplace. The uncommon, if it is not to end in catastrophe, may steal in alongside the commonplace, but not often. If heroism becomes chronic, it ends in a cramp, and the cramp leads to catastrophe or to neurosis or both. Nietzsche got stuck in a state of high tension. But with this ecstasy he could just as well have borne up under Christianity. Not that this answers the question of the animal psyche in the least—for an ecstatic animal is a monstrosity. An animal fulfils the law of its own life, neither more nor less. We can call it obedient and "good." But the ecstatic by-passes the law of his own life and behaves, from the point of view of nature, improperly. This impropriety is the exclusive prerogative of man, whose consciousness and free will can occasionally loose themselves *contra naturam* from their roots in animal nature. It is the indispensable

foundation of all culture, but also of spiritual sickness if exaggerated. Man can suffer only a certain amount of culture without injury. The endless dilemma of culture and nature is always a question of too much or too little, never of either-or.

42   The case of Nietzsche faces us with the question: What did the collision with the shadow, namely the will to power, reveal to him? Is it to be regarded as something bogus, a symptom of repression? Is the will to power genuine or merely secondary? If the conflict with the shadow had let loose a flood of sexual fantasies, the matter would be perfectly clear; but it happened otherwise. The "Kern des Pudels" was not Eros but the power of the ego. From this we would have to conclude that what was repressed was not Eros but the will to power. There is in my opinion no ground for the assumption that Eros is genuine and the will to power bogus. The will to power is surely just as mighty a daemon as Eros, and just as old and original.

43   A life like Nietzsche's, lived to its fatal end with rare consistency in accordance with the underlying instinct for power, cannot simply be explained away as bogus. Otherwise one would make oneself guilty of the same unfair judgment that Nietzsche passed on his polar opposite, Wagner: "Everything about him is false. What is genuine is hidden or decorated. He is an actor, in every good and bad sense of the word." Why this prejudice? Because Wagner embodies that other elemental urge which Nietzsche overlooked, and upon which Freud's psychology is built. If we inquire whether Freud knew of that other instinct, the urge to power, we find that he conceived it under the name of "ego-instinct." But these "ego-instincts" occupy a rather pokey little corner in his psychology compared with the broad, all too broad, development of the sexual factor. In reality human nature bears the burden of a terrible and unending conflict between the principle of the ego and the principle of instinct: the ego all barriers and restraint, instinct limitless, and both principles of equal might. In a certain sense man may count himself happy that he is "conscious only of the single urge," and therefore it is only prudent to guard against ever knowing the other. But if he does learn to know the other, it is all up with him: he then enters upon the Faustian conflict. In the first part of *Faust* Goethe has shown us what it means to accept instinct and in the second part what it means to accept the ego and its weird uncon-

scious world. All that is insignificant, paltry, and cowardly in us cowers and shrinks from this acceptance—and there is an excellent pretext for this: we discover that the "other" in us is indeed "another," a real man, who actually thinks, does, feels, and desires all the things that are despicable and odious. In this way we can seize hold of the bogey and declare war on him to our satisfaction. Hence those chronic idiosyncrasies of which the history of morals has preserved some fine examples. A particularly transparent example is that already cited—"Nietzsche *contra* Wagner, *contra* Paul," etc. But daily life abounds in such cases. By this ingenious device a man may save himself from the Faustian catastrophe, before which his courage and his strength might well fail him. A whole man, however, knows that his bitterest foe, or indeed a host of enemies, does not equal that one worst adversary, the "other self" who dwells in his bosom. Nietzsche had Wagner *in himself,* and that is why he envied him *Parsifal;* but, what was worse, he, Saul, also had Paul in him. Therefore Nietzsche became one stigmatized by the spirit; like Saul he had to experience Christification, when the "other" whispered the "Ecce Homo" in his ear. Which of them "broke down before the cross"—Wagner or Nietzsche?

44   Fate willed it that one of Freud's earliest disciples, Alfred Adler, should formulate a view of neurosis[2] based exclusively on the power principle. It is of no little interest, indeed singularly fascinating, to see how utterly different the same things look when viewed in a contrary light. To take the main contrast first: with Freud everything follows from antecedent circumstances according to a rigorous causality, with Adler everything is a teleological "arrangement." Here is a simple example: A young woman begins to have attacks of anxiety. At night she wakes up from a nightmare with a blood-curdling cry, is scarcely able to calm herself, clings to her husband and implores him not to leave her, demanding assurance that he really loves her, etc. Gradually a nervous asthma develops, the attacks also coming on during the day.

45   The Freudian method at once begins burrowing into the inner causality of the sickness and its symptoms. What were the first anxiety dreams about? Ferocious bulls, lions, tigers, and evil men were attacking her. What are the patient's associations? A

2 *The Neurotic Constitution.*

story of something that happened to her before she was married. She was staying at a health resort in the mountains. She played a good deal of tennis and the usual acquaintances were made. There was a young Italian who played particularly well and also knew how to handle a guitar in the evening. An innocent flirtation developed, leading once to a moonlight stroll. On this occasion the Italian temperament "unexpectedly" broke loose, much to the alarm of the unsuspecting girl. He gave her "such a look" that she could never forget it. This look follows her even in her dreams: the wild animals that pursue her look at her just like that. But does this look in fact come only from the Italian? Another reminscence is instructive. The patient had lost her father through an accident when she was about fourteen years old. Her father was a man of the world and travelled a good deal. Not long before his death he took her with him to Paris, where they visited, among other places, the Folies Bergères. There something happened that made an indelible impression on her. On leaving the theatre, a painted hussy jostled her father in an incredibly brazen way. Looking in alarm to see what he would do, she saw this same look, this animal glare, in his eyes. This inexplicable something followed her day and night. From then on her relations with her father changed. Sometimes she was irritable and subject to venomous moods, sometimes she loved him extravagantly. Then came sudden fits of weeping for no reason, and for a time, whenever her father was at home, she suffered at table from a horrible gulping accompanied by what looked like choking-fits, generally followed by loss of voice for one or two days. When the news of the sudden death of her father reached her, she was seized by uncontrollable grief, which gave way to fits of hysterical laughter. However, she soon calmed down; her condition quickly improved, and the neurotic symptoms practically vanished. A veil of forgetfulness was drawn over the past. Only the episode with the Italian stirred something in her of which she was afraid. She then abruptly broke off all connection with the young man. A few years later she married. The first appearance of her present neurosis was after the birth of her second child, just when she made the discovery that her husband had a certain tender interest in another woman.

46   This history gives rise to many questions: for example, what

about the mother? Concerning the mother the relevant facts are that she was very nervous and spent her time trying every kind of sanatorium and method of cure. She too suffered from nervous asthma and anxiety symptoms. The marriage had been of a very distant kind as far back as the patient could remember. Her mother did not understand the father properly; the patient always had the feeling that she understood him much better. She was her father's confessed darling and was correspondingly cool at heart towards her mother.

47   These hints may suffice to give us an over-all picture of the illness. Behind the present symptoms lie fantasies which are immediately related to the experience with the Italian, but which clearly point back to the father, whose unhappy marriage gave the little daughter an early opportunity to secure for herself the place that should properly have been filled by the mother. Behind this conquest there lies, of course, the fantasy of being the really suitable wife for the father. The first attack of neurosis broke out at a moment when this fantasy received a severe shock, probably the same shock that the mother had also received, though this would be unknown to the child. The symptoms are easily understandable as an expression of disappointed and slighted love. The choking is due to that feeling of constriction in the throat, a well-known concomitant of violent affects which cannot be quite "swallowed down." (The metaphors of common speech, as we know, frequently relate to such physiological phenomena.) When the father died, her conscious mind was grieved to death, but her shadow laughed, after the manner of Till Eulenspiegel, who was doleful when things went downhill, but full of merry pranks on the weary way up, always on the look-out for what lay ahead. When her father was at home, she was dejected and ill; when he was away, she always felt much better, like the innumerable husbands and wives who hide from each other the sweet secret that neither is altogether indispensable to the other.

48   That the unconscious had at this juncture some justification for laughing is shown by the supervening period of good health. She succeeded in letting her whole past sink into oblivion. Only the episode with the Italian threatened to resurrect the underworld. But with a quick gesture she flung the door to and remained healthy until the dragon of neurosis came creeping

37

back, just when she imagined herself safely over the mountain, in the perfect state, so to speak, of wife and mother.

49   Sexual psychology says: the cause of the neurosis lies in the patient's fundamental inability to free herself from her father. That is why that experience came up again when she discovered in the Italian the mysterious "something" which had previously made such an overwhelming impression on her in connection with her father. These memories were naturally revived by the analogous experience with her husband, the immediate cause of the neurosis. We could therefore say that the content of and reason for the neurosis was the conflict between the infantile-erotic relation to her father and her love for her husband.

50   If, however, we look at the same clinical picture from the point of view of the "other" instinct, the will to power, it assumes quite a different aspect. Her parents' unhappy marriage afforded an excellent opportunity for the childish urge to power. The power-instinct wants the ego to be "on top" under all circumstances, by fair means or foul. The "integrity of the personality" must be preserved at all costs. Every attempt, be it only an apparent attempt, of the environment to obtain the slightest ascendency over the subject is met, to use Adler's expression, by the "masculine protest." The disillusionment of the mother and her withdrawal into neurosis created the desired opportunity for a display of power and for gaining the ascendency. Love and good behaviour are, from the standpoint of the power-instinct, known to be a choice means to this end. Virtuousness often serves to *compel* recognition from others. Already as a child the patient knew how to secure a privileged position with her father through especially ingratiating and affectionate behaviour, and to get the better of her mother—not out of love for her father, but because love was a good method of gaining the upper hand. The laughing-fit at the time of her father's death is striking proof of this. We are inclined to regard such an explanation as a horrible depreciation of love, not to say a malicious insinuation, until we reflect for a moment and look at the world as it is. Have we not seen countless people who love and believe in their love, and then, when their purpose is accomplished, turn away as though they had never loved? And finally, is not this the way of nature herself? Is "disinterested" love at all pos-

sible? If so, it belongs to the highest virtues, which in point of fact are exceedingly rare. Perhaps there is in general a tendency to think as little as possible about the purpose of love; otherwise we might make discoveries which would show the worth of our love in a less favourable light.

51 The patient, then, had a laughing-fit at the death of her father—she had finally arrived on top. It was an hysterical laughter, a psychogenic symptom, something that sprang from unconscious motives and not from those of the conscious ego. That is a difference not to be made light of, and one that also tells us whence and how certain human virtues arise. Their opposites went down to hell—or, in modern parlance, into the unconscious—where the counterparts of our conscious virtues have long been accumulating. Hence for very virtue we wish to know nothing of the unconscious; indeed it is the acme of virtuous sagacity to declare that there is no such thing as the unconscious. But alas! it fares with us all as with Brother Medardus in Hoffmann's tale *The Devil's Elixir:* somewhere we have a sinister and frightful brother, our own flesh-and-blood counterpart, who holds and maliciously hoards everything that we would so willingly hide under the table.

52 The first outbreak of neurosis in our patient occurred the moment she realized that there was something in her father which she could not dominate. And then a great light dawned: she now knew what was the purpose of her mother's neurosis, namely that when you encounter an obstacle which cannot be overcome by rational methods and charm, there is still another method, hitherto unknown to her, which her mother had already discovered beforehand, i.e., neurosis. So from now on she imitates her mother's neurosis. But what, we may ask in astonishment, is the good of a neurosis? What can it do? Anyone who has in his neighbourhood a definite case of neurosis knows well enough what it can "do." There is no better method of tyrannizing over the entire household. Heart-attacks, choking-fits, spasms of all kinds, produce an enormous effect that can hardly be surpassed. Oceans of sympathy are let loose, there is the anguish of worried parents, the running to and fro of servants, telephone bells, hurrying doctors, difficult diagnoses, elaborate examinations, lengthy treatments, heavy expenses, and there in

the midst of all the hubbub lies the innocent sufferer, with everybody overflowing with gratitude when at last she recovers from her "spasms."

53   This unsurpassable "arrangement"—to use Adler's expression—was discovered by the little one and applied with success whenever her father was there. It became superfluous when the father died, for now she was finally on top. The Italian was dropped overboard when he laid too much emphasis on her femininity by an appropriate reminder of his virility. But when a suitable chance of marriage presented itself, she loved, and resigned herself without a murmur to the fate of wife and mother. So long as her revered superiority was maintained, everything went swimmingly. But once her husband had a little bit of interest outside, she had recourse as before to that exceedingly effective "arrangement" for the indirect exercise of her power, because she had again encountered the obstacle—this time in her husband—which previously in her father's case had escaped her mastery.

54   This is how things look from the point of view of power psychology. I fear the reader must feel like the *cadi* who, having heard the counsel for the one party, said, "Thou hast well spoken. I perceive that thou art right." Then came the other party, and when he had finished, the *cadi* scratched himself behind the ear and said, "Thou hast well spoken. I perceive that thou also art right." It is unquestionable that the urge to power plays an extraordinarily important part. It is correct that neurotic symptoms and complexes are also elaborate "arrangements" which inexorably pursue their aims, with incredible obstinacy and cunning. Neurosis is teleologically oriented. In establishing this Adler has won for himself no small credit.

55   Which of the two points of view is right? That is a question that might lead to much brain-racking. One simply cannot lay the two explanations side by side, for they contradict each other absolutely. In the one, the chief and decisive fact is Eros and its destiny; in the other, it is the power of the ego. In the first case, the ego is merely a sort of appendage to Eros; in the second, love is just a means to the end, which is ascendency. Those who have the power of the ego most at heart will revolt against the first conception, but those who care most for love will never be reconciled to the second.

IV

THE PROBLEM OF THE ATTITUDE-TYPE

1

56   The incompatibility of the two theories discussed in the preceding chapters requires a standpoint superordinate to both, in
which they could come together in unison. We are certainly not
entitled to discard one in favour of the other, however conven-
ient this expedient might be. For, if we examine the two theories without prejudice, we cannot deny that both contain significant truths, and, contradictory as these are, they should not be
regarded as mutually exclusive. The Freudian theory is attrac-
tively simple, so much so that it almost pains one if anybody
drives in the wedge of a contrary assertion. But the same is true
of Adler's theory. It too is of illuminating simplicity and explains just as much as the Freudian theory. No wonder, then,
that the adherents of both schools obstinately cling to their one-
sided truths. For humanly understandable reasons they are unwilling to give up a beautiful, rounded theory in exchange for a
paradox, or, worse still, lose themselves in the confusion of contradictory points of view.

57   Now, since both theories are in a large measure correct—that
is to say, since they both appear to explain their material—it follows that a neurosis must have two opposite aspects, one of
which is grasped by the Freudian, the other by the Adlerian theory. But how comes it that each investigator sees only one side,
and why does each maintain that he has the only valid view? It
must come from the fact that, owing to his psychological peculiarity, each investigator most readily sees that factor in the neurosis which corresponds to his peculiarity. It cannot be assumed
that the cases of neurosis seen by Adler are totally different from
those seen by Freud. Both are obviously working with the same
material; but because of personal peculiarities they each see

things from a different angle, and thus they evolve fundamentally different views and theories. Adler sees how a subject who feels suppressed and inferior tries to secure an illusory superiority by means of "protests," "arrangements," and other appropriate devices directed equally against parents, teachers, regulations, authorities, situations, institutions, and such. Even sexuality may figure among these devices. This view lays undue emphasis upon the subject, before which the idiosyncrasy and significance of objects entirely vanish. Objects are regarded at best as vehicles of suppressive tendencies. I shall probably not be wrong in assuming that the love relation and other desires directed upon objects exist equally in Adler as essential factors; yet in his theory of neurosis they do not play the principal role assigned to them by Freud.

58   Freud sees his patient in perpetual dependence on, and in relation to, significant objects. Father and mother play a large part here; whatever other significant influences or conditions enter into the life of the patient go back in a direct line of causality to these prime factors. The *pièce de résistance* of his theory is the concept of transference, i.e., the patient's relation to the doctor. Always a specifically qualified object is either desired or met with resistance, and this reaction always follows the pattern established in earliest childhood through the relation to father and mother. What comes from the subject is essentially a blind striving after pleasure; but this striving always acquires its quality from specific objects. With Freud objects are of the greatest significance and possess almost exclusively the determining power, while the subject remains remarkably insignificant and is really nothing more than the source of desire for pleasure and a "seat of anxiety." As already pointed out, Freud recognizes ego-instincts, but this term alone is enough to show that his conception of the subject differs *toto coelo* from Adler's, where the subject figures as the determining factor.

59   Certainly both investigators see the subject in relation to the object; but how differently this relation is seen! With Adler the emphasis is placed on a subject who, no matter what the object, seeks his own security and supremacy; with Freud the emphasis is placed wholly upon objects, which, according to their specific character, either promote or hinder the subject's desire for pleasure.

60   This difference can hardly be anything else but a difference of temperament, a contrast between two types of human mentality, one of which finds the determining agency pre-eminently in the subject, the other in the object. A middle view, it may be that of common sense, would suppose that human behaviour is conditioned as much by the subject as by the object. The two investigators would probably assert, on the other hand, that their theory does not envisage a psychological explanation of the normal man, but is a theory of neurosis. But in that case Freud would have to explain and treat some of his patients along Adlerian lines, and Adler condescend to give earnest consideration in certain instances to his former teacher's point of view—which has occurred neither on the one side nor on the other.

61   The spectacle of this dilemma made me ponder the question: are there at least two different human types, one of them more interested in the object, the other more interested in himself? And does that explain why the one sees only the one and the other only the other, and thus each arrives at totally different conclusions? As we have said, it was hardly to be supposed that fate selected the patients so meticulously that a definite group invariably reached a definite doctor. For some time it had struck me, in connection both with myself and with my colleagues, that there are some cases which make a distinct appeal, while others somehow refuse to "click." It is of crucial importance for the treatment whether a good relationship between doctor and patient is possible or not. If some measure of natural confidence does not develop within a short period, then the patient will do better to choose another doctor. I myself have never shrunk from recommending to a colleague a patient whose peculiarities were not in my line or were unsympathetic to me, and indeed this is in the patient's own interests. I am positive that in such a case I would not do good work. Everyone has his personal limitations, and the psychotherapist in particular is well advised never to disregard them. Excessive personal differences and incompatibilities cause resistances that are disproportionate and out of place, though they are not altogether unjustified. The Freud-Adler controversy is simply a paradigm and one single instance among many possible attitude-types.

62   I have long busied myself with this question and have finally, on the basis of numerous observations and experiences, come to

43

postulate two fundamental attitudes, namely *introversion* and *extraversion*. The first attitude is normally characterized by a hesitant, reflective, retiring nature that keeps itself to itself, shrinks from objects, is always slightly on the defensive and prefers to hide behind mistrustful scrutiny. The second is normally characterized by an outgoing, candid, and accommodating nature that adapts easily to a given situation, quickly forms attachments, and, setting aside any possible misgivings, will often venture forth with careless confidence into unknown situations. In the first case obviously the subject, and in the second the object, is all-important.

63   Naturally these remarks sketch the two types only in the roughest outlines.[1] As a matter of empirical fact the two attitudes, to which I shall come back shortly, can seldom be observed in their pure state. They are infinitely varied and compensated, so that often the type is not at all easy to establish. The reason for variation—apart from individual fluctuations—is the predominance of one of the conscious functions, such as thinking or feeling, which then gives the basic attitude a special character. The numerous compensations of the basic type are generally due to experiences which teach a man, perhaps in a very painful way, that he cannot give free rein to his nature. In other cases, for instance with neurotics, one frequently does not know whether one is dealing with a conscious or an unconscious attitude because, owing to the dissociation of the personality, sometimes one half of it and sometimes the other half occupies the foreground and confuses one's judgment. This is what makes it so excessively trying to live with neurotic persons.

64   The actual existence of far-reaching type-differences, of which I have described eight groups[2] in the above-mentioned book, has enabled me to conceive the two controversial theories of neurosis as manifestations of a type-antagonism.

65   This discovery brought with it the need to rise above the opposition and to create a theory which should do justice not

[1] A complete study of the type problem is to be found in my *Psychological Types.*

[2] Naturally this does not include all the existing types. Further points of difference are age, sex, activity, emotionality, and level of development. My type-psychology is based on the four orienting functions of consciousness: thinking, feeling, sensation, and intuition. See ibid., pars. 577ff.

merely to one or the other side, but to both equally. For this purpose a critique of both the aforementioned theories is essential. Both are painfully inclined to reduce high-flown ideals, heroic attitudes, nobility of feeling, deep convictions, to some banal reality, if applied to such things as these. On no account should they be so applied, for both theories are properly therapeutic instruments from the armoury of the doctor, whose knife must be sharp and pitiless for excising what is diseased and injurious. This was what Nietzsche wanted with his destructive criticism of ideals, which he held to be morbid overgrowths in the soul of humanity (as indeed they sometimes are). In the hand of a good doctor, of one who really knows the human soul —who, to use Nietzsche's phrase, has a "finger for nuances"— both theories, when applied to the really sick part of a soul, are wholesome caustics, of great help in dosages measured to the individual case, but harmful and dangerous in the hand that knows not how to measure and weigh. They are critical methods, having, like all criticism, the power to do good when there is something that must be destroyed, dissolved, or reduced, but capable only of harm when there is something to be built.

66   Both theories may therefore be allowed to pass with no ill consequences provided that, like medical poisons, they are entrusted to the sure hand of the physician, for it requires an uncommon knowledge of the human psyche to apply these caustics with advantage. One must be capable of distinguishing the pathological and the useless from what is valuable and worth preserving, and that is one of the most difficult things. Anyone who wishes to get a vivid impression of how irresponsibly a psychologizing doctor can falsify his subject through narrow, pseudo-scientific prejudice, should turn to the writings of Möbius on Nietzsche, or, better still, to the various "psychiatric" writings on the "case" of Christ. He will not hesitate to cry a "threefold lamentation" over the patient who meets with such "understanding."

67   The two theories of neurosis are not universal theories: they are caustic remedies to be applied, as it were, locally. They are destructive and reductive. They say to everything, "You are nothing but. . . ." They explain to the sufferer that his symptoms come from here and from there and are nothing but this or that. It would be unjust to assert that this reduction is wrong in

45

a given case; but, exalted to the status of a general explanation of the healthy psyche as well as the sick, a reductive theory by itself is impossible. For the human psyche, be it sick or healthy, cannot be explained *solely* by reduction. Eros is certainly always and everywhere present, the urge to power certainly pervades the heights and depths of the psyche, but the psyche is not *just* the one or the other, nor for that matter both together. It is *also* what it has made and will make out of them. A man is only half understood when we know how everything in him came into being. If that were all, he could just as well have been dead years ago. As a living being he is not understood, for life does not have only a yesterday, nor is it explained by reducing today to yesterday. Life has also a tomorrow, and today is understood only when we can add to our knowledge of what was yesterday the beginnings of tomorrow. This is true of all life's psychological expressions, even of pathological symptoms. The symptoms of a neurosis are not simply the effects of long-past causes, whether "infantile sexuality" or the infantile urge to power; they are also attempts at a new synthesis of life—unsuccessful attempts, let it be added in the same breath, yet attempts nevertheless, with a core of value and meaning. They are seeds that fail to sprout owing to the inclement conditions of inner and outer nature.

68   The reader will doubtless ask: What in the world is the value and meaning of a neurosis, this most useless and pestilent curse of humanity? To be neurotic—what good can that do? As much good, possibly, as flies and other pests, which the good Lord created so that man might exercise the useful virtue of patience. However stupid this thought is from the point of view of natural science, it may yet be sensible enough from the point of view of psychology, if we put "nervous symptoms" instead of "pests." Even Nietzsche, a rare one for scorning stupid and banal thoughts, more than once acknowledged how much he owed to his malady. I myself have known more than one person who owed his entire usefulness and reason for existence to a neurosis, which prevented all the worst follies in his life and *forced* him to a mode of living that developed his valuable potentialities. These might have been stifled had not the neurosis, with iron grip, held him to the place where he belonged. There are actually people who have the whole meaning of their life, their true significance, in the unconscious, while in the conscious mind is

nothing but inveiglement and error. With others the case is reversed, and here neurosis has a different meaning. In these cases, but not in the former, a thoroughgoing reduction is indicated.

69   At this point the reader may be inclined to grant the possibility that the neurosis has such a meaning in certain cases, while denying it so far-reaching a purposiveness in ordinary everyday cases. What, for instance, could be the value of a neurosis in the above-mentioned case of asthma with its hysterical anxiety-states? I admit that the value is not so obvious here, especially when the case is considered from the theoretical reductive standpoint, that is, from the shadow-side of individual development.

70   The two theories we have been discussing evidently have this much in common: they pitilessly unveil everything that belongs to man's shadow-side. They are theories or, more correctly, hypotheses which explain in what the pathogenic factor consists. They are accordingly concerned not with a man's positive values, but with his negative values which make themselves so disturbingly conspicuous.

71   A "value" is a possibility for the display of energy. But in so far as a negative value is likewise a possibility for the display of energy—which can be seen most clearly in the notable manifestations of neurotic energy—it too is properly a "value," but one that brings about useless and harmful manifestations of energy. Energy in itself is neither good nor bad, neither useful nor harmful, but neutral, since everything depends on the *form* into which energy passes. Form gives energy its quality. On the other hand, mere form without energy is equally neutral. For the creation of a real value, therefore, both energy and valuable form are needed. In neurosis psychic energy[3] is present, but undoubtedly it is there in an inferior and unserviceable form. The two reductive theories act as solvents of this inferior form. They are approved caustic remedies, by means of which we obtain free but neutral energy. Now, it has hitherto been supposed that this newly disengaged energy is at the conscious disposal of the patient, so that he can apply it at his pleasure. Since it was thought that the energy is nothing but the instinctual power of sex, people talked of a "sublimated" application of it, on the assumption that the patient could, with the help of analysis, canalize the

[3] Cf. my essay "On Psychic Energy."

sexual energy into a "sublimation," in other words, could apply it non-sexually, in the practice of an art, perhaps, or in some other good or useful activity. According to this view, it is possible for the patient, from free choice or inclination, to achieve the sublimation of his instinctual forces.

72   We may allow that this view has a certain justification in so far as man is at all capable of marking out a definite line along which his life has to go. But we know that there is no human foresight or wisdom that can prescribe direction to our life, except for small stretches of the way. This is of course true only of the "ordinary" type of life, not of the "heroic" type. The latter kind also exists, though it is much rarer. Here we are certainly not entitled to say that no marked direction can be given to life, or only for short distances. The heroic style of life is absolute—that is, it is oriented by fateful decisions, and the decision to go in a certain direction holds, sometimes, to the bitter end. Admittedly the doctor has to do, in the main, only with human beings, seldom with voluntary heroes, and then they are mostly of a type whose surface heroism is an infantile defiance of a fate greater than they, or else a pomposity meant to cover up some touchy inferiority. In this overpoweringly humdrum existence, alas, there is little out of the ordinary that is healthy, and not much room for conspicuous heroism. Not that heroic demands are never put to us: on the contrary—and this is just what is so irritating and irksome—the banal everyday makes banal demands upon our patience, our devotion, perseverance, self-sacrifice; and for us to fulfil these demands (as we must) humbly and without courting applause through heroic gestures, a heroism is needed that cannot be seen from the outside. It does not glitter, is not belauded, and it always seeks concealment in everyday attire. These are the demands which, if not fulfilled, are the cause of neurosis. In order to evade them, many a man has dared the *great* decision of his life and carried it through, even if in the common human estimation it was a great error. Before a fate such as this one can only bow one's head. But, as I say, such cases are rare; the others are in the vast majority. For them the direction of their life is not a simple, straight line; fate confronts them like an intricate labyrinth, all too rich in possibilities, and yet of these many possibilities only one is their own right way. Who would presume—even though armed with the completest

knowledge of his own character—to designate in advance that single possibility? Much indeed can be attained by the will, but, in view of the fate of certain markedly strong-willed personalities, it is a fundamental error to try to subject our own fate at all costs to our will. Our will is a function regulated by reflection; hence it is dependent on the quality of that reflection. This, if it really is reflection, is supposed to be rational, i.e., in accord with reason. But has it ever been shown, or will it ever be, that life and fate are in accord with reason, that they too are rational? We have on the contrary good grounds for supposing that they are irrational, or rather that in the last resort they are grounded beyond human reason. The irrationality of events is shown in what we call chance, which we are obviously compelled to deny because we cannot in principle think of any process that is not causal and necessary, whence it follows that it cannot happen by chance.[4] In practice, however, chance reigns everywhere, and so obtrusively that we might as well put our causal philosophy in our pocket. The plenitude of life is governed by law and yet not governed by law, rational and yet irrational. Hence reason and the will that is grounded in reason are valid only up to a point. The further we go in the direction selected by reason, the surer we may be that we are excluding the irrational possibilities of life which have just as much right to be lived. It was indeed highly expedient for man to become somewhat more capable of directing his life. It may justly be maintained that the acquisition of reason is the greatest achievement of humanity; but that is not to say that things must or will always continue in that direction. The frightful catastrophe of the first World War drew a very thick line through the calculations of even the most optimistic rationalizers of culture. In 1913, Wilhelm Ostwald wrote:

The whole world is agreed that the present state of armed peace is untenable and is gradually becoming impossible. It demands tremendous sacrifices from each single nation, far exceeding the expenditure for cultural purposes, yet without securing any positive values. If mankind could discover ways and means for doing away with

4 Modern physics has put an end to this strict causality. Now there is only "statistical probability." As far back as 1916, I had pointed out the limitations of the causal view in psychology, for which I was heavily censured at the time. See my preface to the second edition of *Collected Papers on Analytical Psychology*, in *Freud and Psychoanalysis*, pp. 293ff.

these preparations for wars *which never take place,* together with the immobilization of a large part of the nation's manhood, at the age of maximum strength and efficiency, for the furtherance of war-like aims, and all the other innumerable evils which the present state of affairs creates, such an immense economy of energy would be effected that from this moment onwards we could look forward to a blossoming of culture hitherto undreamed of. For war, like personal combat, although the oldest of all possible means of settling contests of will, is on that very account the most inept, and entails the most grievous waste of energy. Hence the complete abolition of warfare, potential no less than actual, is the categorical imperative of efficiency and one of the supremely important cultural tasks of our day.[5]

73   The irrationality of fate, however, did not concur with the rationality of well-meaning thinkers; it ordained not only the destruction of the accumulated arms and armies, but, far beyond that, a mad and monstrous devastation, a mass murder without parallel—from which humanity may possibly draw the conclusion that only one side of fate can be mastered with rational intentions.

74   What is true of humanity in general is also true of each individual, for humanity consists only of individuals. And as is the psychology of humanity so also is the psychology of the individual. The World War brought a terrible reckoning with the rational intentions of civilization. What is called "will" in the individual is called "imperialism" in nations; for all will is a demonstration of power over fate, i.e., the exclusion of chance. Civilization is the rational, "purposeful" sublimation of free energies, brought about by will and intention. It is the same with the individual; and just as the idea of a world civilization received a fearful correction at the hands of war, so the individual must often learn in his life that so-called "disposable" energies are not his to dispose.

75   Once, in America, I was consulted by a business man of about forty-five, whose case is a good illustration of what has been said. He was a typical American self-made man who had worked his way up from the bottom. He had been very successful and had founded an immense business. He had also succeeded in organizing it in such a way that he was able to think of

[5] Ostwald, *Die Philosophie der Werte,* pp. 312f.

retiring. Two years before I saw him he had in fact taken his farewell. Until then he had lived entirely for his business and concentrated all his energies on it with the incredible intensity and one-sidedness peculiar to successful American business men. He had purchased a splendid estate where he thought of "living," by which he meant horses, automobiles, golf, tennis, parties and what not. But he had reckoned without his host. The energy which should have been at his disposal would not enter into these alluring prospects, but went capering off in quite another direction. A few weeks after the initiation of the longed-for life of bliss, he began brooding over peculiar, vague sensations in his body, and a few weeks more sufficed to plunge him into a state of extreme hypochondria. He had a complete nervous collapse. From a healthy man, of uncommon physical strength and abounding energy, he became a peevish child. That was the end of all his glories. He fell from one state of anxiety to the next and worried himself almost to death with hypochondriacal mopings. He then consulted a famous specialist, who recognized at once that there was nothing wrong with the man but lack of work. The patient saw the sense of this, and returned to his former position. But, to his immense disappointment, no interest in the business could be aroused. Neither patience nor resolution was of any use. His energy could not by any means be forced back into the business. His condition naturally became worse than before. All that had formerly been living, creative energy in him now turned against him with terrible destroying force. His creative genius rose up, as it were, in revolt against him; and just as before he had built up great organizations in the world, so now his daemon spun equally subtle systems of hypochondriacal delusion that completely annihilated him. When I saw him he was already a hopeless moral ruin. Nevertheless I tried to make clear to him that though such colossal energy might be withdrawn from the business, the question remained, where should it go? The finest horses, the fastest cars, and the most amusing parties may very likely fail to allure the energy, although it would be rational enough to think that a man who had devoted his whole life to serious work had a sort of natural right to enjoy himself. Yes, if fate behaved in a humanly rational way, it would certainly be so: first work, then well-earned rest. But fate behaves irrationally, and the energy

51

of life inconveniently demands a gradient agreeable to itself; otherwise it simply gets dammed up and turns destructive. It regresses to former situations—in the case of this man, to the memory of a syphilitic infection contracted twenty-five years before. Yet even this was only a stage on the way to the resuscitation of infantile reminiscences which had all but vanished in the meantime. It was the original relation to his mother that mapped the course of his symptoms: they were an "arrangement" whose purpose it was to compel the attention and interest of his long-dead mother. Nor was this stage the last; for the ultimate goal was to drive him back, as it were, into his own body, after he had lived since his youth only in his head. He had differentiated one side of his being; the other side remained in an inert physical state. He would have needed this other side in order to "live." The hypochondriacal "depression" pushed him down into the body he had always overlooked. Had he been able to follow the direction indicated by his depression and hypochondriacal illusion, and make himself conscious of the fantasies which proceed from such a condition, that would have been the road to salvation. My arguments naturally met with no response, as was to be expected. A case so far advanced can only be cared for until death; it can hardly be cured.

76   This example clearly shows that it does not lie in our power to transfer "disposable" energy at will to a rationally chosen object. The same is true in general of the apparently disposable energy which is disengaged when we have destroyed its unserviceable forms through the corrosive of reductive analysis. This energy, as we have said, can at best be applied voluntarily for only a short time. But in most cases it refuses to seize hold, for any length of time, of the possibilities rationally presented to it. Psychic energy is a very fastidious thing which insists on fulfilment of its own conditions. However much energy may be present, we cannot make it serviceable until we have succeeded in finding the right gradient.

77   This question of the gradient is an eminently practical problem which crops up in most analyses. For instance, when in a favourable case the disposable energy, the so-called libido,[6] does

---

[6] From the foregoing it will have become clear to the reader that the term "libido," coined by Freud and very suitable for practical usage, is used by me in a much wider sense. Libido for me means psychic energy, which is equivalent

seize hold of a rational object, we think we have brought about the transformation through conscious exertion of the will. But in that we are deluded, because even the most strenuous exertions would not have sufficed had there not been present at the same time a gradient in that direction. How important the gradient is can be seen in cases when, despite the most desperate exertions, and despite the fact that the object chosen or the form desired impresses everybody with its reasonableness, the transformation still refuses to take place, and all that happens is a new repression.

78   It has become abundantly clear to me that life can flow forward only along the path of the gradient. But there is no energy unless there is a tension of opposites; hence it is necessary to discover the opposite to the attitude of the conscious mind. It is interesting to see how this compensation by opposites also plays its part in the historical theories of neurosis: Freud's theory espoused Eros, Adler's the will to power. Logically, the opposite of love is hate, and of Eros, Phobos (fear); but psychologically it is the will to power. Where love reigns, there is no will to power; and where the will to power is paramount, love is lacking. The one is but the shadow of the other: the man who adopts the standpoint of Eros finds his compensatory opposite in the will to power, and that of the man who puts the accent on power is Eros. Seen from the one-sided point of view of the conscious attitude, the shadow is an inferior component of the personality and is consequently repressed through intensive resistance. But the repressed content must be made conscious so as to produce a tension of opposites, without which no forward movement is pos-

---

to the intensity with which psychic contents are charged. Freud, in accordance with his theoretical assumptions, identifies libido with Eros and tries to distinguish it from psychic energy in general. Thus he says ("Three Essays on the Theory of Sexuality" [orig. 1908], p. 217): "We have defined the concept of libido as a quantitatively variable force which could serve as a measure of processes and transformations occurring in the field of sexual excitation. We distinguish this libido in respect of its special origin from the energy which must be supposed to underlie mental processes in general." Elsewhere Freud remarks that in respect of the destructive instinct he lacks "a term analogous to libido." Since the so-called destructive instinct is also a phenomenon of energy, it seems to me simpler to define libido as an inclusive term for psychic intensities, and consequently as sheer psychic energy. Cf. my *Symbols of Transformation*, pars. 190ff.; also "On Psychic Energy," pars. 4ff.

sible. The conscious mind is on top, the shadow underneath, and just as high always longs for low and hot for cold, so all consciousness, perhaps without being aware of it, seeks its unconscious opposite, lacking which it is doomed to stagnation, congestion, and ossification. Life is born only of the spark of opposites.

79 It was a concession to intellectual logic on the one hand and to psychological prejudice on the other that impelled Freud to name the opposite of Eros the destructive or death instinct. For in the first place, Eros is not equivalent to life; but for anyone who thinks it is, the opposite of Eros will naturally appear to be death. And in the second place, we all feel that the opposite of our own highest principle must be purely destructive, deadly, and evil. We refuse to endow it with any positive life-force; hence we avoid and fear it.

80 As I have already indicated, there are many highest principles both of life and of philosophy, and accordingly there are just as many different forms of compensation by opposites. Earlier on I singled out the two—as it seems to me—main opposite types, which I have called introverted and extraverted. William James[7] had already been struck by the existence of both these types among thinkers. He distinguished them as "tender-minded" and "tough-minded." Similarly Ostwald[8] found an analogous division into "classic" and "romantic" types among men of learning. So I am not alone in my idea of types, to mention only these two well-known names among many others. Inquiries into history have shown me that not a few of the great spiritual controversies rest upon the opposition of the two types. The most significant case of this kind was the opposition between nominalism and realism which, beginning with the difference between the Platonic and Megarian schools, became the heritage of scholastic philosophy, and it was Abelard's great merit to have hazarded at least the attempt to unite the two opposed standpoints in his "conceptualism."[9] This controversy has continued right into our own day, as is shown in the opposition between idealism and materialism. And again, not only the human mind in general, but each individual has a share in this

7 *Pragmatism.*
8 *Grosse Männer.*
9 *Psychological Types*, pars. 68ff.

opposition of types. It has come to light on closer investigation that either type has a predilection to marry its opposite, each being unconsciously complementary to the other. The reflective nature of the introvert causes him always to think and consider before acting. This naturally makes him slow to act. His shyness and distrust of things induce hesitation, and so he always has difficulty in adapting to the external world. Conversely the extravert has a positive relation to things. He is, so to speak, attracted to them. New, unknown situations fascinate him. In order to make closer acquaintance with the unknown he will jump into it with both feet. As a rule he acts first and thinks afterwards. Thus his action is swift, subject to no misgivings and hesitations. The two types therefore seem created for a symbiosis. The one takes care of reflection and the other sees to the initiative and practical action. When the two types marry they may effect an ideal union. So long as they are fully occupied with their adaptation to the manifold external needs of life they fit together admirably. But when the man has made enough money, or if a fine legacy should drop from the skies and external necessity no longer presses, then they have time to occupy themselves with one another. Hitherto they stood back to back and defended themselves against necessity. But now they turn face to face and look for understanding—only to discover that they have never understood one another. Each speaks a different language. Then the conflict between the two types begins. This struggle is envenomed, brutal, full of mutual depreciation, even when conducted quietly and in the greatest intimacy. For the value of the one is the negation of value for the other. It might reasonably be supposed that each, conscious of his own value, could peaceably recognize the other's value, and that in this way any conflict would be superfluous. I have seen a good number of cases where this line of argument was adopted, without, however, arriving at a satisfactory goal. Where it is a question of normal people, such critical periods of transition will be overcome fairly smoothly. By "normal" I mean a person who can somehow exist under all circumstances which afford him the minimum needs of life. But many people cannot do this; therefore not so very many people are normal. What we commonly mean by a "normal person" is actually an ideal person whose happy blend of character is a rare occurrence. By far the greater number of more or less differentiated persons demand conditions of life which offer considerably more than the certainty of food and sleep. For these the ending of a symbiotic relationship comes as a severe shock.

81   It is not easy to understand why this should be so. Yet if we consider that no man is simply introverted or simply extraverted, but has both attitudes potentially in him—although he has developed only one of them as a function of adaptation—we shall immediately conjecture that with the introvert extraversion lies dormant and undeveloped somewhere in the background, and that introversion leads a similar shadowy existence in the extravert. And this is indeed the case. The introvert does possess an extraverted attitude, but it is unconscious, because his conscious gaze is always turned to the subject. He sees the object, of course, but has false or inhibiting ideas about it, so that he keeps his distance as much as possible, as though the object were something formidable and dangerous. I will make my meaning clear by a simple illustration:

Let us suppose two youths rambling in the country. They come to a fine castle; both want to see inside it. The introvert says, "I'd like to know what it's like inside." The extravert answers, "Right, let's go in," and makes for the gateway. The introvert draws back—"Perhaps we aren't allowed in," says he, with visions of policemen, fines, and fierce dogs in the background. Whereupon the extravert answers, "Well, we can ask. They'll let us in all right"—with visions of kindly old watchmen, hospitable seigneurs, and the possibility of romantic adventures. On the strength of extraverted optimism they at length find themselves in the castle. But now comes the dénouement. The castle has been rebuilt inside, and contains nothing but a couple of rooms with a collection of old manuscripts. As it happens, old manuscripts are the chief joy of the introverted youth. Hardly has he caught sight of them than he becomes as one transformed. He loses himself in contemplation of the treasures, uttering cries of enthusiasm. He engages the caretaker in conversation so as to extract from him as much information as possible, and when the result is disappointing he asks to see the curator in order to propound his questions to him. His shyness has vanished, objects have taken on a seductive glamour, and the world wears a new face. But meanwhile the spirits of the extraverted

56

youth are ebbing lower and lower. His face grows longer and he begins to yawn. No kindly watchmen are forthcoming here, no knightly hospitality, not a trace of romantic adventure—only a castle made over into a museum. There are manuscripts enough to be seen at home. While the enthusiasm of the one rises, the spirits of the other fall, the castle bores him, the manuscripts remind him of a library, library is associated with university, university with studies and menacing examinations. Gradually a veil of gloom descends over the once so interesting and enticing castle. The object becomes negative. "Isn't it marvellous," cries the introvert, "to have stumbled on this wonderful collection?" "The place bores me to extinction," replies the other with undisguised ill humour. This annoys the introvert, who secretly vows never again to go rambling with an extravert. The latter is annoyed with the other's annoyance, and he thinks to himself that he always knew the fellow was an inconsiderate egotist who would, in his own selfish interest, waste all the lovely spring day that could be enjoyed so much better out of doors.

82   What has happened? Both were wandering together in happy symbiosis until they discovered the fatal castle. Then the forethinking, or Promethean, introvert said it might be seen from the inside, and the after-thinking, or Epimethean, extravert opened the door.[10] At this point the types invert themselves: the introvert, who at first resisted the idea of going in, cannot now be induced to go out, and the extravert curses the moment when he set foot inside the castle. The former is now fascinated by the object, the latter by his negative thoughts. When the introvert spotted the manuscripts, it was all up with him. His shyness vanished, the object took possession of him, and he yielded himself willingly. The extravert, however, felt a growing resistance to the object and was eventually made the prisoner of his own ill-humoured subjectivity. The introvert became extraverted, the extravert introverted. But the extraversion of the introvert is different from the extraversion of the extravert, and vice versa. So long as both were wandering along in joyous harmony, neither fell foul of the other, because each was in his natural character. Each was positive to the other, because their attitudes were complementary. They were complementary, how-

10 Cf. my discussion of Carl Spitteler's *Prometheus und Epimetheus* in *Psychological Types*, pars. 275ff.

ever, only because the attitude of the one included the other. We can see this from the short conversation at the gateway. Both wanted to enter the castle. The doubt of the introvert as to whether an entry were possible also held good for the other. The initiative of the extravert likewise held good for the other. Thus the attitude of the one includes the other, and this is always in some degree true if a person happens to be in the attitude natural to him, for this attitude has some degree of collective adaptation. The same is true of the introvert's attitude, although this always starts from the subject. It simply goes from subject to object, while the extravert's attitude goes from object to subject.

83   But the moment when, in the case of the introvert, the object overpowers and attracts the subject, his attitude loses its social character. He forgets the presence of his friend, he no longer includes him, he becomes absorbed into the object and does not see how very bored his friend is. In the same way the extravert loses all consideration for the other as soon as his expectations are disappointed and he withdraws into subjectivity and moodiness.

84   We can therefore formulate the occurrence as follows: in the introvert the influence of the object produces an inferior extraversion, while in the extravert an inferior introversion takes the place of his social attitude. And so we come back to the proposition from which we started: "The value of the one is the negation of value for the other."

85   Positive as well as negative occurrences can constellate the inferior counter-function. When this happens, sensitiveness appears. Sensitiveness is a sure sign of the presence of inferiority. This provides the psychological basis for discord and misunderstanding, not only as between two people, but also in ourselves. The essence of the inferior function[11] is autonomy: it is independent, it attacks, it fascinates and so spins us about that we are no longer masters of ourselves and can no longer rightly distinguish between ourselves and others.

86   And yet it is necessary for the development of character that we should allow the other side, the inferior function, to find expression. We cannot in the long run allow one part of our personality to be cared for symbiotically by another; for the moment when we might have need of the other function may come

11 *Psychological Types,* Def. 30.

at any time and find us unprepared, as the above example shows. And the consequences may be bad: the extravert loses his indispensable relation to the object, and the introvert loses his to the subject. Conversely, it is equally indispensable for the introvert to arrive at some form of action not constantly bedevilled by doubts and hesitations, and for the extravert to reflect upon himself, yet without endangering his relationships.

87   In extraversion and introversion it is clearly a matter of two antithetical, natural attitudes or trends, which Goethe once referred to as diastole and systole. They ought, in their harmonious alternation, to give life a rhythm, but it seems to require a high degree of art to achieve such a rhythm. Either one must do it quite unconsciously, so that the natural law is not disturbed by any conscious act, or one must be conscious in a much higher sense, to be capable of willing and carrying out the antithetical movements. Since we cannot develop backwards into animal unconsciousness, there remains only the more strenuous way forwards into higher consciousness. Certainly that consciousness, which would enable us to live the great Yea and Nay of our own free will and purpose, is an altogether superhuman ideal. Still, it is a goal. Perhaps our present mentality only allows us consciously to will the Yea and to bear with the Nay. When that is the case, much is already achieved.

88   The problem of opposites, as an inherent principle of human nature, forms a further stage in our process of realization. As a rule it is one of the problems of maturity. The practical treatment of a patient will hardly ever begin with this problem, especially not in the case of young people. The neuroses of the young generally come from a collision between the forces of reality and an inadequate, infantile attitude, which from the causal point of view is characterized by an abnormal dependence on the real or imaginary parents, and from the teleological point of view by unrealizable fictions, plans, and aspirations. Here the reductive methods of Freud and Adler are entirely in place. But there are many neuroses which either appear only at maturity or else deteriorate to such a degree that the patients become incapable of work. Naturally one can point out in these cases that an unusual dependence on the parents existed even in youth, and that all kinds of infantile illusions were present; but all that did not prevent them from taking up a profession, from practising it

successfully, from keeping up a marriage of sorts until that moment in riper years when the previous attitude suddenly failed. In such cases it is of little help to make them conscious of their childhood fantasies, dependence on the parents, etc., although this is a necessary part of the procedure and often has a not unfavourable result. But the real therapy only begins when the patient sees that it is no longer father and mother who are standing in his way, but himself—i.e., an unconscious part of his personality which carries on the role of father and mother. Even this realization, helpful as it is, is still negative; it simply says, "I realize that it is not father and mother who are against me, but I myself." But *who* is it in him that is against him? What is this mysterious part of his personality that hides under the father- and mother-imagos, making him believe for years that the cause of his trouble must somehow have got into him from outside? This part is the counterpart of his conscious attitude, and it will leave him no peace and will continue to plague him until it has been accepted. For young people a liberation from the past may be enough: a beckoning future lies ahead, rich in possibilities. It is sufficient to break a few bonds; the life-urge will do the rest. But we are faced with another task in the case of people who have left a large part of their life behind them, for whom the future no longer beckons with marvellous possibilities, and nothing is to be expected but the endless round of familiar duties and the doubtful pleasures of old age.

89   If ever we succeed in liberating young people from the past, we see that they always transfer the imagos of their parents to more suitable substitute figures. For instance, the feeling that clung to the mother now passes to the wife, and the father's authority passes to respected teachers and superiors or to institutions. Although this is not a fundamental solution, it is yet a practical road which the normal man treads unconsciously and therefore with no notable inhibitions and resistances.

90   The problem for the adult is very different. He has put this part of the road behind him with or without difficulty. He has cut loose from his parents, long since dead perhaps, and has sought and found the mother in the wife, or, in the case of a woman, the father in the husband. He has duly honoured his fathers and their institutions, has himself become a father, and, with all this in the past, has possibly come to realize that what

originally meant advancement and satisfaction has now become a boring mistake, part of the illusion of youth, upon which he looks back with mingled regret and envy, because nothing now awaits him but old age and the end of all illusions. Here there are no more fathers and mothers; all the illusions he projected upon the world and upon things gradually come home to him, jaded and way-worn. The energy streaming back from these manifold relationships falls into the unconscious and activates all the things he had neglected to develop.

91   In a young man, the instinctual forces tied up in the neurosis give him, when released, buoyancy and hope and the chance to extend the scope of his life. To the man in the second half of life the development of the function of opposites lying dormant in the unconscious means.a renewal; but this development no longer proceeds via the dissolution of infantile ties, the destruction of infantile illusions and the transference of old imagos to new figures: it proceeds via the problem of opposites.

92   The principle of opposition is, of course, fundamental even in adolescence, and a psychological theory of the adolescent psyche is bound to recognize this fact. Hence the Freudian and Adlerian viewpoints contradict each other only when they claim to be generally applicable theories. But so long as they are content to be technical, auxiliary concepts, they do not contradict or exclude one another. A psychological theory, if it is to be more than a technical makeshift, must base itself on the principle of opposition; for without this it could only re-establish a neurotically unbalanced psyche. There is no balance, no system of self-regulation, without opposition. The psyche is just such a self-regulating system.

2

93   If at this point we take up the thread we let fall earlier, we shall now see clearly why it is that the values which the individual lacks are to be found in the neurosis itself. At this point, too, we can return to the case of the young woman and apply the insight we have gained. Let us suppose that this patient is "analysed," i.e., she has, through the treatment, come to understand the nature of the unconscious thoughts lurking behind her symptoms, and has thus regained possession of the unconscious energy which constituted the strength of those symptoms. The

question then arises: what to do with the so-called disposable energy? In accordance with the psychological type of the patient, it would be rational to transfer this energy to an object—to philanthropic work, for example, or some useful activity. With exceptionally energetic natures that are not afraid of wearing themselves to the bone, if need be, or with people who delight in the toil and moil of such activities, this way is possible, but mostly it is impossible. For—do not forget—the libido, as this psychic energy is technically called, already possesses its object unconsciously, in the form of the young Italian or some equally real human substitute. In these circumstances a sublimation is as impossible as it is desirable, because the real object generally offers the energy a much better gradient than do the most admirable ethical activities. Unfortunately far too many of us talk about a man only as it would be desirable for him to be, never about the man as he really is. But the doctor has always to do with the real man, who remains obstinately himself until all sides of his reality are recognized. True education can only start from naked reality, not from a delusive ideal.

94 It is unhappily the case that no man can direct the so-called disposable energy at will. It follows its own gradient. Indeed, it had already found that gradient even before we set the energy free from the unserviceable form to which it was linked. For we discover that the patient's fantasies, previously occupied with the young Italian, have now transferred themselves to the doctor.[12] The doctor has himself become the object of the unconscious libido. If the patient altogether refuses to recognize the fact of the transference,[13] or if the doctor fails to understand it,

---

[12] Freud introduced the concept of transference as a designation for the projection of unconscious contents.

[13] Contrary to certain views I am not of the opinion that the "transference to the doctor" is a regular phenomenon indispensable to the success of the treatment. Transference is projection, and projection is either there or not there. But it is not *necessary*. In no sense can it be "made," for by definition it springs from unconscious motivations. The doctor may be a suitable object for the projection, or he may not. There is absolutely no saying that he will in all circumstances correspond to the natural gradient of the patient's libido; for it is quite on the cards that the libido is envisaging a much more important object for its projections. The absence of projections to the doctor may in fact considerably facilitate the treatment, because the real personal values can then come more clearly to the forefront.

or interprets it falsely, vigorous resistances supervene, directed towards making the relation with the doctor completely impossible. Then the patient goes away and looks for another doctor, or for someone who understands; or, if he gives up the search, he gets stuck in his problem.

95   If, however, the transference to the doctor takes place, and is accepted, a natural form is found which supplants the earlier one and at the same time provides the energy with an outlet relatively free from conflict. Hence if the libido is allowed to run its natural course, it will find its own way to the destined object. Where this does not happen, it is always a question of wilful defiance of the laws of nature, or of some disturbing influence.

96   In the transference all kinds of infantile fantasies are projected. They must be cauterized, i.e., resolved by reductive analysis, and this is generally known as "resolving the transference." Thereby the energy is again released from an unserviceable form, and again we are faced with the problem of its disposability. Once more we shall put our trust in nature, hoping that, even before it is sought, an object will have been chosen which will provide a favourable gradient.

V

THE PERSONAL AND THE COLLECTIVE
(OR TRANSPERSONAL) UNCONSCIOUS

97   At this point a new stage in our process of realization begins.
We carried the analysis of infantile transference fantasies to the
point where it became sufficiently clear, even to the patient, that
he was making the doctor his father, mother, uncle, guardian,
and teacher, and all the rest of the parental authorities. But, as
experience has repeatedly shown, still other fantasies appear
which represent the doctor as a saviour or godlike being—naturally in complete contradiction to healthy conscious reasoning.
Moreover it transpires that these godlike attributes go far beyond the framework of Christianity in which we have grown up;
they take on a pagan glamour and indeed very often appear in
animal form.

98   The transference is in itself no more than a projection of
unconscious contents. At first the so-called superficial contents
of the unconscious are projected, as can be seen from symptoms,
dreams, and fantasies. In this state the doctor is interesting as a
possible lover (rather like the young Italian in the case we were
discussing). Then he appears more in the role of the father:
either the good, kind father or the "thunderer," depending on
the qualities which the real father had for the patient. Sometimes the doctor has a maternal significance, a fact that seems
somewhat peculiar, but is still within the bounds of possibility.
All these fantasy projections are founded on personal memories.

99   Finally there appear forms of fantasy that possess an extravagant character. The doctor is then endowed with uncanny powers: he is a magician or a wicked demon, or else the corresponding personification of goodness, a saviour. Again, he may appear
as a mixture of both. Of course it is to be understood that he
need not necessarily appear like this to the patient's conscious

mind; it is only the fantasies coming to the surface which picture him in this guise. Such patients often cannot get it into their heads that their fantasies really come from themselves and have little or nothing to do with the character of the doctor. This delusion rests on the fact that there are no personal grounds in the memory for this kind of projection. It can sometimes be shown that similar fantasies had, at a certain period in childhood, attached themselves to the father or mother, although neither father nor mother provided any real occasion for them.

100   Freud has shown in a little essay[1] how Leonardo da Vinci was influenced in his later life by the fact that he had two mothers. The fact of the two mothers, or of a double descent, was real enough in Leonardo's case, but it plays a role in the lives of other artists as well. Benvenuto Cellini had this fantasy of a double descent. Generally speaking it is a mythological motif. Many heroes in legend have two mothers. The fantasy does not arise from the actual fact that the heroes have two mothers; it is a widespread "primordial" image belonging not to the domain of personal memory but to the secrets of the mental history of mankind.

101   There are present in every individual, besides his personal memories, the great "primordial" images, as Jacob Burckhardt once aptly called them, the inherited possibilities of human imagination as it was from time immemorial. The fact of this inheritance explains the truly amazing phenomenon that certain motifs from myths and legends repeat themselves the world over in identical forms. It also explains why it is that our mental patients can reproduce exactly the same images and associations that are known to us from the old texts. I give some examples of this in my book *Symbols of Transformation*.[2] In so doing I do not by any means assert the inheritance of ideas, but only of the possibility of such ideas, which is something very different.

102   In this further stage of treatment, then, when fantasies are produced which no longer rest on personal memories, we have to do with the manifestations of a deeper layer of the unconscious where the primordial images common to humanity lie sleeping. I have called these images or motifs "archetypes," also

---

1 "Leonardo da Vinci and a Memory of His Childhood" (orig. 1910).
2 Cf. also "The Concept of the Collective Unconscious."

"dominants" of the unconscious. For a further elucidation of the idea I must refer the reader to the relevant literature.[3]

103   This discovery means another step forward in our understanding: the recognition, that is, of two layers in the unconscious. We have to distinguish between a personal unconscious and an *impersonal* or *transpersonal unconscious*. We speak of the latter also as the *collective unconscious*,[4] because it is detached from anything personal and is common to all men, since its contents can be found everywhere, which is naturally not the case with the personal contents. The personal unconscious contains lost memories, painful ideas that are repressed (i.e., forgotten on purpose), subliminal perceptions, by which are meant sense-perceptions that were not strong enough to reach consciousness, and finally, contents that are not yet ripe for consciousness. It corresponds to the figure of the shadow so frequently met with in dreams.[5]

104   The primordial images are the most ancient and the most universal "thought-forms" of humanity. They are as much feelings as thoughts; indeed, they lead their own independent life rather in the manner of part-souls,[6] as can easily be seen in those philosophical or Gnostic systems which rely on perception of the unconscious as the source of knowledge. The idea of angels, archangels, "principalities and powers" in St. Paul, the archons of the Gnostics, the heavenly hierarchy of Dionysius the Areopagite, all come from the perception of the relative autonomy of the archetypes.

105   We have now found the object which the libido chooses when it is freed from the personal, infantile form of transference. It follows its own gradient down into the depths of the unconscious, and there activates what has lain slumbering from

[3] *Symbols of Transformation; Psychological Types,* Def. 26; *The Archetypes and the Collective Unconscious;* Commentary on *The Secret of the Golden Flower.*
[4] The collective unconscious stands for the objective psyche, the personal unconscious for the subjective psyche.
[5] By shadow I mean the "negative" side of the personality, the sum of all those unpleasant qualities we like to hide, together with the insufficiently developed functions and the contents of the personal unconscious. A comprehensive account is to be found in T. Wolff, "Einführung in die Grundlagen der komplexen Psychologie," pp. 107ff.
[6] Cf. "A Review of the Complex Theory."

the beginning. It has discovered the hidden treasure upon which mankind ever and anon has drawn, and from which it has raised up its gods and demons, and all those potent and mighty thoughts without which man ceases to be man.

106   Let us take as an example one of the greatest thoughts which the nineteenth century brought to birth: the idea of the conservation of energy. Robert Mayer, the real creator of this idea, was a physician, and not a physicist or natural philosopher, for whom the making of such an idea would have been more appropriate. But it is very important to realize that the idea was not, strictly speaking, "made" by Mayer. Nor did it come into being through the fusion of ideas or scientific hypotheses then extant, but grew in its creator like a plant. Mayer wrote about it in the following way to Griesinger, in 1844:

> I am far from having hatched out the theory at my writing desk. [He then reports certain physiological observations he had made in 1840 and 1841 as ship's doctor.] Now, if one wants to be clear on matters of physiology, some knowledge of physical processes is essential, unless one prefers to work at things from the metaphysical side, which I find infinitely disgusting. I therefore held fast to physics and stuck to the subject with such fondness that, although many may laugh at me for this, I paid but little attention to that remote quarter of the globe in which we were, preferring to remain on board where I could work without intermission, and where I passed many an hour as though *inspired,* the like of which I cannot remember either before or since. Some flashes of thought that passed through me while in the roads of Surabaya were at once assiduously followed up, and in their turn led to fresh subjects. Those times have passed, but the quiet examination of that which then came to the surface in me has taught me that it is a truth, which can not only be subjectively felt, but objectively proved. It remains to be seen whether this can be accomplished by a man so little versed in physics as I am.[7]

107   In his book on energetics,[8] Helm expresses the view that "Robert Mayer's new idea did not detach itself gradually from the traditional concepts of energy by deeper reflection on them, but belongs to those intuitively apprehended ideas which, aris-

---

[7] Mayer, *Kleinere Schriften und Briefe,* p. 213 (letter to Wilhelm Griesinger, June 16, 1844).
[8] Helm, *Die Energetik nach ihrer geschichtlichen Entwicklung,* p. 20.

ing in other realms of a spiritual nature, as it were take possession of the mind and compel it to reshape the traditional conceptions in their likeness."

108   The question now arises: Whence came this new idea that
thrust itself upon consciousness with such elemental force? And
whence did it derive the power that could so seize upon consciousness that it completely eclipsed the multitudinous impressions of a first voyage to the tropics? These questions are not so
easy to answer. But if we apply our theory here, the explanation
can only be this: the idea of energy and its conservation must be
a primordial image that was dormant in the collective unconscious. Such a conclusion naturally obliges us to prove that a
primordial image of this kind really did exist in the mental history of mankind and was operative through the ages. As a matter
of fact, this proof can be produced without much difficulty: the
most primitive religions in the most widely separated parts of
the earth are founded upon this image. These are the so-called
dynamistic religions whose sole and determining thought is that
there exists a universal magical power[9] about which everything
revolves. Tylor, the well-known English investigator, and Frazer
likewise, misunderstood this idea as animism. In reality primitives do not mean, by their power-concept, souls or spirits at all,
but something which the American investigator Lovejoy has appropriately termed "primitive energetics."[10] This concept is
equivalent to the idea of soul, spirit, God, health, bodily
strength, fertility, magic, influence, power, prestige, medicine,
as well as certain states of feeling which are characterized by the
release of affects. Among certain Polynesians mulungu—this
same primitive power-concept—means spirit, soul, daemonism,
magic, prestige; and when anything astonishing happens, the
people cry out "Mulungu!" This power-concept is also the earliest form of a concept of God among primitives, and is an image
which has undergone countless variations in the course of history. In the Old Testament the magic power glows in the burning bush and in the countenance of Moses; in the Gospels it
descends with the Holy Ghost in the form of fiery tongues from
heaven. In Heraclitus it appears as world energy, as "ever-living

[9] Generally called mana. Cf. Söderblom, Das Werden des Gottesglaubens (trans.
from the Swedish Gudstrons uppkomst).
[10] Lovejoy, "The Fundamental Concept of the Primitive Philosophy," p. 361.

fire"; among the Persians it is the fiery glow of *haoma,* divine grace; among the Stoics it is the original heat, the power of fate. Again, in medieval legend it appears as the aura or halo, and it flares up like a flame from the roof of the hut in which the saint lies in ecstasy. In their visions the saints behold the sun of this power, the plenitude of its light. According to the old view, the soul itself is this power; in the idea of the soul's immortality there is implicit its conservation, and in the Buddhist and primitive notion of metempsychosis—transmigration of souls—is implicit its unlimited changeability together with its constant duration.

109   So this idea has been stamped on the human brain for aeons. That is why it lies ready to hand in the unconscious of every man. Only, certain conditions are needed to cause it to appear. These conditions were evidently fulfilled in the case of Robert Mayer. The greatest and best thoughts of man shape themselves upon these primordial images as upon a blueprint. I have often been asked where the archetypes or primordial images come from. It seems to me that their origin can only be explained by assuming them to be deposits of the constantly repeated experiences of humanity. One of the commonest and at the same time most impressive experiences is the apparent movement of the sun every day. We certainly cannot discover anything of the kind in the unconscious, so far as the known physical process is concerned. What we do find, on the other hand, is the myth of the sun-hero in all its countless variations. It is this myth, and not the physical process, that forms the sun archetype. The same can be said of the phases of the moon. The archetype is a kind of readiness to produce over and over again the same or similar mythical ideas. Hence it seems as though what is impressed upon the unconscious were exclusively the subjective fantasy-ideas aroused by the physical process. We may therefore assume that the archetypes are recurrent impressions made by subjective reactions.[11] Naturally this assumption only pushes the problem further back without solving it. There is nothing to prevent us from assuming that certain archetypes exist even in animals, that they are grounded in the peculiarities of the living organism itself and are therefore direct expressions of life whose nature cannot be further explained. Not only are the

11 Cf. "The Structure of the Psyche," pp. 152ff.

archetypes, apparently, impressions of ever-repeated typical experiences, but, at the same time, they behave empirically like agents that tend towards the repetition of these same experiences. For when an archetype appears in a dream, in a fantasy, or in life, it always brings with it a certain influence or power by virtue of which it either exercises a numinous or a fascinating effect, or impels to action.

110   Having shown, in this example, how new ideas arise out of the treasure-house of primordial images, we will proceed to the further discussion of the transference process. We saw that the libido had, for its new object, seized upon those seemingly absurd and singular fantasies, the contents of the collective unconscious. As I have already said, the projection of primordial images upon the doctor is a danger not to be underrated at this stage of the treatment. The images contain not only all the fine and good things that humanity has ever thought and felt, but the worst infamies and devilries of which men have been capable. Owing to their specific energy—for they behave like highly charged autonomous centres of power—they exert a fascinating and possessive influence upon the conscious mind and can thus produce extensive alterations in the subject. One can see this in religious conversions, in cases of influence by suggestion, and particularly at the onset of certain forms of schizophrenia.[12] Now, if the patient is unable to distinguish the personality of the doctor from these projections, all hope of an understanding is finally lost and a human relationship becomes impossible. But if the patient avoids this Charybdis, he is wrecked on the Scylla of *introjecting* these images—in other words, he ascribes their peculiarities not to the doctor but to himself. This is just as disastrous. In projection, he vacillates between an extravagant and pathological deification of the doctor, and a contempt bristling with hatred. In introjection, he gets involved in a ridiculous self-deification, or else in a moral self-laceration. The mistake he makes in both cases comes from attributing to a *person* the contents of the collective unconscious. In this way he makes himself or his partner either god or devil. Here we see the characteristic effect of the archetype: it seizes hold of the psyche with a kind of

12 One such case is analysed in detail in *Symbols of Transformation*. Cf. also Nelken, "Analytische Beobachtungen über Phantasien eines Schizophrenen" (1912), p. 504.

primeval force and compels it to transgress the bounds of humanity. It causes exaggeration, a puffed-up attitude (inflation), loss of free will, delusion, and enthusiasm in good and evil alike. This is the reason why men have always needed demons and cannot live without gods, except for a few particularly clever specimens of *homo occidentalis* who lived yesterday or the day before, supermen for whom "God is dead" because they themselves have become gods—but tin-gods with thick skulls and cold hearts. The idea of God is an absolutely necessary psychological function of an irrational nature, which has nothing whatever to do with the question of God's existence. The human intellect can never answer this question, still less give any proof of God. Moreover such proof is superfluous, for the idea of an all-powerful divine Being is present everywhere, unconsciously if not consciously, because it is an archetype. There is in the psyche some superior power, and if it is not consciously a god, it is the "belly" at least, in St. Paul's words. I therefore consider it wiser to acknowledge the idea of God consciously; for, if we do not, something else is made God, usually something quite inappropriate and stupid such as only an "enlightened" intellect could hatch forth. Our intellect has long known that we can form no proper idea of God, much less picture to ourselves in what manner he really exists, if at all. The existence of God is once and for all an unanswerable question. The *consensus gentium* has been talking of gods for aeons and will still be talking of them aeons hence. No matter how beautiful and perfect man may believe his reason to be, he can always be certain that it is only one of the possible mental functions, and covers only that one side of the phenomenal world which corresponds to it. But the irrational, that which is not agreeable to reason, rings it about on all sides. And the irrational is likewise a psychological function—in a word, it is the collective unconscious; whereas the rational is essentially tied to the conscious mind. The conscious mind must have reason, firstly to discover some order in the chaos of disorderly individual events occurring in the world, and secondly to create order, at least in human affairs. We are moved by the laudable and useful ambition to extirpate the chaos of the irrational both within and without to the best of our ability. Apparently the process has gone pretty far. As a mental patient once told me: "Doctor, last night I disinfected the whole heavens with bichloride of mercury, but I found no God." Something of the sort has happened to us as well.

111   Old Heraclitus, who was indeed a very great sage, discovered the most marvellous of all psychological laws: the regulative function of opposites. He called it *enantiodromia*, a running contrariwise, by which he meant that sooner or later everything runs into its opposite. (Here I would remind you of the case above of the American business man, a beautiful example of enantiodromia.) Thus the rational attitude of culture necessarily runs into its opposite, namely the irrational devastation of culture.[13] We should never identify ourselves with reason, for man is not and never will be a creature of reason alone, a fact to be noted by all pedantic culture-mongers. The irrational cannot be and must not be extirpated. The gods cannot and must not die. I said just now that there seems to be something, a kind of superior power, in the human psyche, and that if this is not the idea of God, then it is the "belly." I wanted to express the fact that one or other basic instinct, or complex of ideas, will invariably concentrate upon itself the greatest sum of psychic energy and thus force the ego into its service. As a rule the ego is drawn into this focus of energy so powerfully that it identifies with it and thinks it desires and needs nothing further. In this way a craze develops, a monomania or possession, an acute one-sidedness which most seriously imperils the psychic equilibrium. Without doubt the capacity for such one-sidedness is the secret of success— of a sort, for which reason our civilization assiduously strives to foster it. The passion, the piling up of energy in these monomanias, is what the ancients called a "god," and in common speech we still do the same. Do we not say, "He makes a god of this or that"? A man thinks that he wills and chooses, and does not notice that he is already possessed, that his interest has become the master, arrogating all power to itself. Such interests are indeed gods of a kind which, once recognized by the many, gradually form a "church" and gather a herd of believers about them.

---

[13] This sentence was written during the first World War. I have let it stand in its original form because it contains a truth which has been confirmed more than once in the course of history. (Written in 1925.) As present events show, the confirmation did not have to wait very long. Who wants this blind destruction? But we all help the daemon to our last gasp. *O sancta simplicitas!* (Written in 1942.)

This we then call an "organization." It is followed by a dis-organizing reaction which aims to drive out the devil with Beelzebub. The enantiodromia that always threatens when a movement attains to undisputed power offers no solution of the problem, for it is just as blind in its disorganization as it was in its organization.

112   The only person who escapes the grim law of enantiodromia is the man who knows how to separate himself from the uncon-scious, not by repressing it—for then it simply attacks him from the rear—but by putting it clearly before him as *that which he is not.*

113   This prepares the way for the solution of the Scylla and Charybdis problem described above. The patient must learn to differentiate what is ego and what is non-ego, i.e., collective psyche. In this way he finds the material to which he will hence-forth have to accommodate himself. His energy, until now laid up in unserviceable and pathological forms, has come into its proper sphere. It is essential, in differentiating the ego from the non-ego, that a man should be firmly rooted in his ego-function; that is, he must fulfil his duty to life, so as to be in every respect a viable member of the community. All that he neglects in this respect falls into the unconscious and reinforces its position, so that he is in danger of being swallowed up by it. But the penal-ties for this are heavy. As Synesius opined of old, it is just the "inspired soul" (πνευματικὴ ψυχή) that becomes god and de-mon, and as such suffers the divine punishment of being torn asunder like Zagreus. This was what Nietzsche experienced at the onset of his malady. Enantiodromia means being torn asun-der into pairs of opposites, which are the attributes of "the god" and hence also of the godlike man, who owes his godlikeness to overcoming his gods. As soon as we speak of the collective un-conscious we find ourselves in a sphere, and concerned with a problem, which is altogether precluded in the practical analysis of young people or of those who have remained infantile too long. Wherever the father and mother imagos have still to be overcome, wherever there is a little bit of life still to be con-quered, which is the natural possession of the average man, then we had better make no mention of the collective unconscious and the problem of opposites. But once the parental transfer-ences and the youthful illusions have been mastered, or are at

73

least ripe for mastery, then we must speak of these things. We are here outside the range of Freudian and Adlerian reductions; we are no longer concerned with how to remove the obstacles to a man's profession, or to his marriage, or to anything that means a widening of his life, but are confronted with the task of finding a meaning that will enable him to continue living at all—a meaning more than blank resignation and mournful retrospect.

114   Our life is like the course of the sun. In the morning it gains continually in strength until it reaches the zenith-heat of high noon. Then comes the enantiodromia: the steady forward movement no longer denotes an increase, but a decrease, in strength. Thus our task in handling a young person is different from the task of handling an older person. In the former case, it is enough to clear away all the obstacles that hinder expansion and ascent; in the latter, we must nurture everything that assists the descent. An inexperienced youth thinks one can let the old people go, because not much more can happen to them anyway: they have their lives behind them and are no better than petrified pillars of the past. But it is a great mistake to suppose that the meaning of life is exhausted with the period of youth and expansion; that, for example, a woman who has passed the menopause is "finished." The afternoon of life is just as full of meaning as the morning; only, its meaning and purpose are different.[14] Man has two aims: the first is the natural aim, the begetting of children and the business of protecting the brood; to this belongs the acquisition of money and social position. When this aim has been reached a new phase begins: the cultural aim. For the attainment of the former we have the help of nature and, on top of that, education; for the attainment of the latter, little or nothing helps. Often, indeed, a false ambition survives, in that an old man wants to be a youth again, or at least feels he must behave like one, although in his heart he can no longer make believe. This is what makes the transition from the natural to the cultural phase so terribly difficult and bitter for many people; they cling to the illusion of youth or to their children, hoping to salvage in this way a last little scrap of youth. One sees it especially in mothers, who find their sole meaning in their children and imagine they will sink into a bottomless void when they have to give them up. No wonder that many bad neu-

[14] Cf. "The Stages of Life."

roses appear at the onset of life's afternoon. It is a sort of second puberty, another "storm and stress" period, not infrequently accompanied by tempests of passion—the "dangerous age." But the problems that crop up at this age are no longer to be solved by the old recipes: the hand of this clock cannot be put back. What youth found and must find outside, the man of life's afternoon must find within himself. Here we face new problems which often cause the doctor no light headache.

115   The transition from morning to afternoon means a revaluation of the earlier values. There comes the urgent need to appreciate the value of the opposite of our former ideals, to perceive the error in our former convictions, to recognize the untruth in our former truth, and to feel how much antagonism and even hatred lay in what, until now, had passed for love. Not a few of those who are drawn into the conflict of opposites jettison everything that had previously seemed to them good and worth striving for; they try to live in complete opposition to their former ego. Changes of profession, divorces, religious convulsions, apostasies of every description, are the symptoms of this swing over to the opposite. The snag about a radical conversion into one's opposite is that one's former life suffers repression and thus produces just as unbalanced a state as existed before, when the counterparts of the conscious virtues and values were still repressed and unconscious. Just as before, perhaps, neurotic disorders arose because the opposing fantasies were unconscious, so now other disorders arise through the repression of former idols. It is of course a fundamental mistake to imagine that when we see the non-value in a value or the untruth in a truth, the value or the truth ceases to exist. It has only become *relative*. Everything human is relative, because everything rests on an inner polarity; for everything is a phenomenon of energy. Energy necessarily depends on a pre-existing polarity, without which there could be no energy. There must always be high and low, hot and cold, etc., so that the equilibrating process—which is energy— can take place. Therefore the tendency to deny all previous values in favour of their opposites is just as much of an exaggeration as the earlier one-sidedness. And in so far as it is a question of rejecting universally accepted and indubitable values, the result is a fatal loss. One who acts in this way empties himself out with his values, as Nietzsche has already said.

116   The point is not conversion into the opposite but conservation of previous values together with recognition of their opposites. Naturally this means conflict and self-division. It is understandable enough that one should shrink from it, philosophically as well as morally; hence the alternative sought, more often than conversion into the opposite, is a convulsive stiffening of the previous attitude. It must be admitted that, in the case of elderly men, this is a phenomenon of no little merit, however disagreeable it may be: at least they do not become renegades, they remain upright, they do not fall into muddle-headedness nor yet into the mud; they are no defaulters, but are merely dead wood or, to put it more politely, pillars of the past. But the accompanying symptoms, the rigidity, the narrow-mindedness, the stand-offishness of these *laudatores temporis acti* are unpleasant, not to say harmful; for their method of espousing a truth or any other value is so inflexible and violent that their unmannerliness repels more than the truth attracts, so that the result is the opposite of the intended good. The fundamental cause of their rigidity is fear of the problem of opposites: they have a foreboding and secret dread of the "sinister brother of Medardus." Therefore there must be only one truth and one guiding principle of action, and that must be absolute; otherwise it affords no protection against the impending disaster, which is sensed everywhere save in themselves. But actually the most dangerous revolutionary is within ourselves, and all must realize this who wish to pass over safely into the second half of life. Certainly this means exchanging the apparent security we have so far enjoyed for a condition of insecurity, of internal division, of contradictory convictions. The worst feature of all is that there appears to be no way out of this condition. *Tertium non datur,* says logic—there is no middle way.

117   The practical necessities of treatment have therefore forced us to look for ways and means that might lead out of this intolerable situation. Whenever a man is confronted by an apparently insurmountable obstacle, he draws back: he makes what is technically called a regression. He goes back to the times when he found himself in similar situations, and he tries to apply again the means that helped him then. But what helped in youth is of no use in age. What good did it do that American business man to return to his former position? It simply wouldn't work. So the

regression continues right back into childhood (hence the child-
ishness of many elderly neurotics) and ends up in the time before childhood. That may sound strange, but in point of fact it is
not only logical but altogether possible.

118   We mentioned earlier that the unconscious contains, as it
were, two layers: the personal and the collective. The personal
layer ends at the earliest memories of infancy, but the collective
layer comprises the pre-infantile period, that is, the residues of
ancestral life. Whereas the memory-images of the personal unconscious are, as it were, filled out, because they are images personally experienced by the individual, the archetypes of the collective unconscious are not filled out because they are forms not
personally experienced. When, on the other hand, psychic energy regresses, going beyond even the period of early infancy,
and breaks into the legacy of ancestral life, the mythological images are awakened: these are the archetypes.[15] An interior spiritual world whose existence we never suspected opens out and displays contents which seem to stand in sharpest contrast to all our
former ideas. These images are so intense that it is quite understandable why millions of cultivated persons should be taken in
by theosophy and anthroposophy. This happens simply because
such modern gnostic systems meet the need for expressing and
formulating the wordless occurrences going on within ourselves
better than any of the existing forms of Christianity, not ex-
cepting Catholicism. The latter is certainly able to express, far
more comprehensively than Protestantism, the facts in question
through its dogma and ritual symbolism. But neither in the past
nor in the present has even Catholicism attained anything like
the richness of the old pagan symbolism, which is why this
symbolism persisted far into Christianity and then gradually
went underground, forming currents that, from the early Middle

15 The reader will note the admixture here of a new element in the idea of the
archetypes, not previously mentioned. This admixture is not a piece of unintentional obscurantism, but a deliberate extension of the archetype by means of
the *karmic* factor, which is so very important in Indian philosophy. The *karma*
aspect is essential to a deeper understanding of the nature of an archetype.
Without entering here into a closer description of this factor, I would like at
least to mention its existence. I have been severely attacked by critics for my
idea of archetypes. I admit at once that it is a controversial idea and more than
a little perplexing. But I have always wondered what sort of idea my critics
would have used to characterize the empirical material in question.

Ages to modern times, have never quite lost their vitality. To a large extent they vanished from the surface; but, changing their form, they come back again to compensate the one-sidedness of our conscious mind with its modern orientation.[16] Our consciousness is so saturated with Christianity, so utterly moulded by it, that the unconscious counter-position can discover no foothold there, for the simple reason that it seems too much the antithesis of our ruling ideas. The more one-sidedly, rigidly, and absolutely the one position is held, the more aggressive, hostile, and incompatible will the other become, so that at first sight there would seem to be little prospect of reconciling the two. But once the conscious mind admits at least the *relative* validity of all human opinion, then the opposition loses something of its irreconcilable character. In the meantime the conflict casts round for appropriate expression in, for instance, the oriental religions—Buddhism, Hinduism, Taoism. The syncretism of theosophy goes a long way towards meeting this need, and that explains its numerous successes.

119   The work involved in analytical treatment gives rise to experiences of an archetypal nature which require to be expressed and shaped. Obviously this is not the only occasion for experiences of such a kind; often they occur quite spontaneously, and by no means only in the case of "psychological-minded" people. I have heard the most curious dreams and visions from the lips of people whose mental sanity not even the professional psychologist could doubt. The experience of the archetype is frequently guarded as the closest personal secret, because it is felt to strike into the very core of one's being. It is like a primordial experience of the non-ego, of an interior opponent who throws down a challenge to the understanding. Naturally enough we then look round for helpful parallels, and it happens all too easily that the original occurrence is interpreted in terms of derivative ideas. A typical instance of this kind is the Trinity vision of Brother Nicholas of Flüe,[17] or again, St. Ignatius' vision of the snake with multiple eyes, which he interpreted first as a divine apparition and then as a visitation from the devil. Through these periphrastic interpretations the authentic experience is replaced by images and words borrowed from a foreign source, and by views,

16 Cf. "Paracelsus as a Spiritual Phenomenon" and *Psychology and Alchemy*.
17 Cf. "Brother Klaus."

ideas, and forms that have not grown on our soil and have no ties with our hearts, but only with our heads. Indeed, not even our thought can clearly grasp them, because it never invented them. It is a case of stolen goods that bring no prosperity. Such substitutes make men shadowy and unreal; they put empty words in the place of living realities, and slip out of the painful tension of opposites into a wan, two-dimensional, phantasmal world where everything vital and creative withers and dies.

120　　The wordless occurrences which are called forth by regression to the pre-infantile period need no substitutes; they demand to be individually shaped in and by each man's life and work. They are images sprung from the life, the joys and sorrows, of our ancestors; and to life they seek to return, not in experience only, but in deed. Because of their opposition to the conscious mind they cannot be translated straight into our world; hence a way must be found that can mediate between conscious and unconscious reality.

VI

THE SYNTHETIC OR
CONSTRUCTIVE METHOD

121   The process of coming to terms with the unconscious is a
true labour, a work which involves both action and suffering. It
has been named the "transcendent function" [1] because it represents a function based on real and "imaginary," or rational and
irrational, data, thus bridging the yawning gulf between conscious and unconscious. It is a natural process, a manifestation of
the energy that springs from the tension of opposites, and it consists in a series of fantasy-occurrences which appear spontaneously in dreams and visions.[2] The same process can also be observed in the initial stages of certain forms of schizophrenia. A
classical account of such a proceeding is to be found, for example, in Gérard de Nerval's autobiographical fragment, *Aurelia*.
But the most important literary example is Part II of *Faust*. The
natural process by which the opposites are united came to serve
me as the model and basis for a method consisting essentially in
this: everything that happens at the behest of nature, unconsciously and spontaneously, is deliberately summoned forth and
integrated into the conscious mind and its outlook. Failure in
many cases is due precisely to the fact that they lack the mental
and spiritual equipment to master the events taking place in
them. Here medical help must intervene in the form of a special
method of treatment.

122   As we have seen, the theories discussed at the beginning of
this book rest on an exclusively causal and reductive procedure
which resolves the dream (or fantasy) into its memory compo-

---

[1] I discovered only subsequently that the idea of the transcendent function also
occurs in the higher mathematics, and is actually the name of the function of
real and imaginary numbers. See also my essay "The Transcendent Function."
[2] For an analysis of one such dream-series see *Psychology and Alchemy*.

nents and the underlying instinctual processes. I have indicated above the justification as well as the limitation of this procedure. It breaks down at the point where the dream symbols can no longer be reduced to personal reminiscences or aspirations, that is, when the images of the collective unconscious begin to appear. It would be quite senseless to try to reduce these collective ideas to anything personal—not only senseless but positively harmful, as painful experience has taught me. Only with much difficulty, after long hesitation and disabuse by many failures, was I able to decide to abandon the purely personalistic attitude of medical psychology in the sense indicated. I had first to come to the fundamental realization that analysis, in so far as it is reduction and nothing more, must necessarily be followed by synthesis, and that certain kinds of psychic material mean next to nothing if simply broken down, but display a wealth of meaning if, instead of being broken down, that meaning is reinforced and extended by all the conscious means at our disposal—by the so-called method of amplification.[3] The images or symbols of the collective unconscious yield their distinctive values only when subjected to a synthetic mode of treatment. Just as analysis breaks down the symbolical fantasy-material into its components, so the synthetic procedure integrates it into a general and intelligible statement. The procedure is not exactly simple, so I will give an example which will help to explain the whole process.

123   A woman patient, who had just reached the critical borderline between the analysis of the personal unconscious and the emergence of contents from the collective unconscious, had the following dream: *She is about to cross a wide river. There is no bridge, but she finds a ford where she can cross. She is on the point of doing so, when a large crab that lay hidden in the water seizes her by the foot and will not let her go.* She wakes up in terror.

Associations:

124   *River:* "Forms a boundary that is difficult to get across—I have to overcome an obstacle—probably to do with the fact that I'm progressing so slowly—I ought to reach the other side."

3 [For an account of amplification see "The Theory of Psychoanalysis," pars. 326ff.—EDITORS.]

125   *Ford:* "An opportunity to cross in safety—a possible way, otherwise the river would be too broad—in the treatment lies the possibility of surmounting the obstacle."

126   *Crab:* "The crab was quite hidden in the water, I did not see it before—cancer [German *Krebs* = crab] is a terrible disease, incurable [reference to Mrs. X, who died of carcinoma]—I am afraid of this disease—the crab is an animal that walks backwards—and obviously wants to drag me into the river—it caught hold of me in a horrible way and I was terribly frightened—what keeps stopping me from getting across? Oh yes, I had another row with my friend [a woman]."

127   There is something peculiar about her relations with this friend. It is a sentimental attachment, bordering on the homosexual, that has lasted for years. The friend is like the patient in many ways, and equally nervy. They have marked artistic interests in common. The patient is the stronger personality of the two. Because their mutual relationship is too intimate and excludes too many of the other possibilities of life, both are nervy and, despite their ideal friendship, have violent scenes due to mutual irritability. The unconscious is trying in this way to put a distance between them, but they refuse to listen. The quarrel usually begins because one of them finds that she is still not sufficiently understood, and urges that they should speak more plainly to one another; whereupon both make enthusiastic efforts to unbosom themselves. Naturally a misunderstanding comes about in next to no time, and a worse scene than ever ensues. *Faute de mieux,* this quarrelling had long been for both of them a pleasure substitute which they were unwilling to relinquish. My patient in particular could not do without the sweet pain of being misunderstood by her best friend, although every scene "tired her to death." She had long since realized that this friendship had become moribund, and that only false ambition led her to believe that something ideal could still be made of it. She had formerly had an exaggerated, fantastic relation to her mother and after her mother's death had transferred her feelings to her friend.

Analytical (causal-reductive) interpretation:[4]

128   This interpretation can be summed up in one sentence: "I
see well enough that I ought to cross the river (that is, give up
relations with my friend), but I would much rather that my
friend did not let me out of her clutches (i.e., embraces)—
which, as an infantile wish, means that I want Mother to draw
me to her in the exuberant embrace I know so well." The incompatibility of the wish lies in the strong undercurrent of homosexuality, abundantly proved by the facts. The crab seizes her
by the foot. The patient has large "masculine" feet, she plays the
masculine role with her friend and has corresponding sexual
fantasies. The foot has a notoriously phallic significance.[5] Thus
the over-all interpretation would be: The reason why she does
not want to leave her friend is because she has repressed sexual
desires for her. As these desires are morally and aesthetically incompatible with the tendency of the conscious personality, they
are repressed and therefore more or less unconscious. Her anxiety corresponds to her repressed desire.

129   This interpretation is a severe depreciation of the patient's
exalted ideal of friendship. To be sure, at this point in the analysis she would no longer have taken exception to such an interpretation. Some time earlier certain facts had amply convinced
her of her homosexual tendency, so that she could freely admit
this inclination, although it was by no means agreeable to her.
If, then, I had given her this interpretation at the present stage
of treatment, I would have not encountered any resistance. She
had already overcome the painfulness of this unwelcome tendency by understanding it. But she would have said to me, "Why
are we still analysing this dream? It only reiterates what I have
known for a long time." The interpretation, in fact, tells the
patient nothing new; it is therefore uninteresting and ineffective. Such an interpretation would have been impossible at the
beginning of the treatment, because the unusual prudery of the
patient would not under any circumstances have admitted any-

---

[4] A parallel view of the two kinds of interpretation is to be found in Herbert
Silberer's commendable book, *Problems of Mysticism and Its Symbolism.*

[5] Aigremont (pseud. of Siegmar Baron von Schultze-Galléra), *Fuss- und Schuhsymbolik und -Erotik* [1909].

thing of that kind. The "poison" of understanding had to be injected with extreme care, and in very small doses, until she gradually became more reasonable. Now, when the analytical or causal-reductive interpretation ceases to bring to light anything new, but only the same thing in different variations, the moment has come to look out for possible archetypal motifs. If such a motif comes clearly to the forefront, it is high time to change the interpretative procedure. The causal-reductive procedure has in this particular case certain disadvantages. Firstly, it does not take accurate account of the patient's associations, e.g., the association of "crab" with "cancer." Secondly, the peculiar choice of the symbol remains unexplained. Why should the mother-friend appear as a crab? A prettier and more graphic representation would have been a water-nymph. ("Half drew she him, half sank he under," etc.) An octopus, a dragon, a snake, or a fish would have served as well. Thirdly, the causal-reductive procedure forgets that the dream is a subjective phenomenon, and that consequently an exhaustive interpretation can never refer the crab to the friend or the mother alone, but must refer it also to the subject, the dreamer herself. The dreamer is the whole dream; she is the river, the ford, and the crab, or rather these details express conditions and tendencies in the unconscious of the subject.

130   I have therefore introduced the following terminology: I call every interpretation which equates the dream images with real objects an *interpretation on the objective level.* In contrast to this is the interpretation which refers every part of the dream and all the actors in it back to the dreamer himself. This I call *interpretation on the subjective level.* Interpretation on the objective level is analytic, because it breaks down the dream content into memory-complexes that refer to external situations. Interpretation on the subjective level is synthetic, because it detaches the underlying memory-complexes from their external causes, regards them as tendencies or components of the subject, and reunites them with that subject. (In any experience I experience not merely the object but first and foremost myself, provided of course that I render myself an account of the experience.) In this case, therefore, all the contents of the dream are treated as symbols for subjective contents.

84

131   Thus the synthetic or constructive process of interpretation[6] is interpretation on the subjective level.

The synthetic (constructive) interpretation:
132   The patient is unconscious of the fact that the obstacle to be overcome lies in herself: namely, a boundary-line that is difficult to cross and hinders further progress. Nevertheless it is possible to pass the barrier. But a special and unexpected danger looms up just at this moment—something "animal" (non-human or subhuman), which moves backwards and downwards, threatening to drag with it the whole personality of the dreamer. This danger is like a deadly disease that begins in some secret place and is incurable (overpowering). The patient imagines that her friend is hindering her and trying to drag her down. So long as she believes this, she must go on trying to "uplift" her friend, educate and improve her; she has to make futile and senselessly idealistic efforts to stop herself from being dragged down. Naturally her friend makes similar efforts too, for she is in the same pass as the patient. So the two keep jumping at each other like fighting cocks, each trying to get the upper hand. And the higher the pitch the one screws herself up to, the fiercer become the self-torments of the other. Why? Because each thinks the fault lies in the other, in the object. Interpretation on the subjective level brings release from this folly; for the dream shows the patient that she has something in herself which prevents her from crossing the boundary, i.e., from getting out of one situation or attitude into another. The interpretation of a change of place as a change of attitude is corroborated by forms of speech in certain primitive languages, where, for example, "I am thinking of going" is expressed as "I am at the place of (on the point of) going." To make the language of dreams intelligible we need numerous parallels from the psychology of primitive and historical symbolism, because dreams spring essentially from the unconscious, which contains remnants of the functional possibilities of all preceding epochs of evolution. A classical example of this is the "Crossing of the Great Water" in the oracles of the *I Ching*.

6 Cf. "On Psychological Understanding." Elsewhere I have called this procedure the "hermeneutic" method; cf. infra, pars. 493ff.

133   Obviously, everything now depends on what is meant by the crab. We know in the first place that it is something connected with the friend (since the patient associates it with her friend), and also something connected with her mother. Whether mother and friend really have this quality is irrelevant so far as the patient is concerned. The situation can be changed only by the patient changing herself. Nothing can be changed in the mother, for she is dead. And the friend cannot be nagged into changing. If she wants to change, that is her own affair. The fact that the quality in question is connected with the mother points to something infantile. What, then, is there in common in the patient's relation to her mother and to her friend? The common factor is a violent, sentimental demand for love, so impassioned that she feels herself overwhelmed. This demand has the character of an overpowering infantile craving which, as we know, is blind. So we are dealing with an undisciplined, undifferentiated, and not yet humanized part of the libido which still possesses the compulsive character of an instinct, a part still untamed by domestication. For such a part some kind of *animal* is an entirely appropriate symbol. But why should the animal be a crab? The patient associates it with cancer, of which disease Mrs. X died at about the same age as that now reached by the patient herself. So there may be a hint of identification with Mrs. X. We must therefore follow this up. The patient relates the following facts about her: Mrs. X was widowed early; she was very merry and full of life; she had a series of adventures with men, and one in particular with an extremely gifted artist whom the patient knew personally and who always impressed her as remarkably fascinating and strange.

134   An identification can occur only on the basis of some unrealized, i.e., unconscious, similarity. Now in what way is our patient similar to Mrs. X? Here I was able to remind the patient of a series of earlier fantasies and dreams which had plainly shown that she too had a frivolous streak in her, and one which she always anxiously repressed, because she feared this dimly apprehended tendency in herself might betray her into leading an immoral life. With this we have made a further important contribution towards understanding the "animal" element; for once more we come upon the same untamed, instinctual craving, but

86

this time directed towards men. And we have also discovered another reason why she cannot let go of her friend: she must cling to her so as not to fall victim to this other tendency, which seems to her much more dangerous. Accordingly she remains at the infantile, homosexual level, because it serves her as a defence. (Experience shows that this is one of the most potent motives for clinging to unsuitable infantile relationships.) In this animal element, however, also lies her health, the germ of a future sound personality which will not shrink from the hazards of life.

135   But the patient had drawn quite a different conclusion from the fate of Mrs. X. She had taken the latter's sudden grave illness and early death as the punishment of fate for the gay life which, without admitting it, the patient had always envied. When Mrs. X died, the patient made a very long moral face which concealed an all-too-human malicious satisfaction. To punish herself for this, she continually used the example of Mrs. X to scare herself away from life and all further development, and burdened herself with the misery of an unsatisfying friendship. Naturally this whole sequence of events had never been clear to her, otherwise she would never have acted as she did. The rightness of this surmise was easily verified from the material.

136   The story of this identification by no means ends here. The patient subsequently emphasized that Mrs. X possessed a not inconsiderable artistic capacity which developed only after her husband's death and then led to her friendship with the artist. This fact seems to be one of the essential reasons for the identification, if we remember that the patient had remarked what a strong and peculiarly fascinating impression the artist had made upon her. A fascination of this kind is never exercised exclusively by one person upon another; it is always a phenomenon of relationship, which requires two people in so far as the person fascinated necessarily has a corresponding disposition. But the disposition must be unconscious, or no fascination will take place. Fascination is a compulsive phenomenon in the sense that it lacks a conscious motive; it is not a voluntary process, but something that rises up from the unconscious and forcibly obtrudes itself upon the conscious mind.

137   It must therefore be assumed that the patient has an uncon-

87

scious disposition similar to that of the artist. Accordingly she is also identified with a man.[7] We recall the analysis of the dream, where we met an allusion to the "masculine" foot. And in fact the patient does play a masculine role with her friend; she is the active one who always sets the tone, who bosses her friend and sometimes actually forces her to do something she alone wants. Her friend is distinctly feminine, even in external appearance, while the patient is clearly of a somewhat masculine type. Her voice too is strong and deeper than her friend's. Mrs. X is described as a very feminine woman, comparable to her friend, so the patient thinks, in gentleness and affectionateness. This gives us another clue: in relation to her friend, the patient obviously plays the same role that the artist played with Mrs. X. Thus she unconsciously completes her identification with Mrs. X and her lover, and thus, in spite of all, she gives expression to the frivolous streak in her which she had so anxiously repressed. But she is not living it consciously, she is rather the plaything of this unconscious tendency; in other words, she is possessed by it, and has become the unconscious exponent of her complex.

138   We now know very much more about the crab: it contains the inner psychology of this untamed bit of libido. The unconscious identifications keep drawing her down further and further. They have this power because, being unconscious, they are not open to insight or correction. The crab is therefore the symbol for the unconscious contents. These contents are always trying to draw the patient back into her relations with her friend. (The crab walks backwards.) But the connection with her friend is synonymous with disease, for through it she became neurotic.

139   Strictly speaking, all this really belongs to the analysis on the objective level. But we must not forget that we came into possession of this knowledge only by making use of the subjective level, which thus proves to be an important heuristic principle. For practical purposes we might rest content with the results so far reached; but we have to satisfy the demands of theory: not all the associations have yet been evaluated, nor has the significance of the choice of symbol yet been sufficiently explained.

140   We shall now take up the patient's remark that the crab lay

[7] I am not overlooking the fact that the deeper reason for her identification with the artist lies in a certain creative aptitude on the part of the patient.

hidden in the water and that she did not see it at first. Nor did she see, at first, the unconscious relations which we have just discussed; they too lay hidden in the water. The river is the obstacle that prevents her from crossing to the other side. It is precisely these unconscious relations, binding her to her friend, that prevented her. The unconscious was the obstacle. Thus the water signifies the unconscious, or rather, the state of unconsciousness, of concealment; for the crab too is something unconscious, in fact it is the dynamic content that lies concealed in its depths.

VII

THE ARCHETYPES OF THE COLLECTIVE UNCONSCIOUS

141   We are now faced with the task of raising to the subjective level the phenomena which have so far been understood on the objective level. For this purpose we must detach them from the object and take them as symbolical exponents of the patient's subjective complexes. If we try to interpret the figure of Mrs. X on the subjective level, we must regard it as the personification of a part-soul, or rather of a certain aspect of the dreamer. Mrs. X then becomes an image of what the patient would like to be, and yet fears to be. She represents, as it were, a partial picture of the patient's future character. The fascinating artist cannot so easily be raised to the subjective level, because the unconscious artistic capacity lying dormant in the patient is already taken up by Mrs. X. It would, however, be correct to say that the artist is the image of the patient's masculinity which is not consciously realized and therefore lies in the unconscious.[1] This is true in the sense that the patient does in fact delude herself in this matter. In her own eyes she is quite remarkably fragile, sensitive, and feminine, and not in the least masculine. She was therefore indignantly amazed when I pointed out her masculine traits. But the strange, fascinating element is out of keeping with these traits. It seems to be entirely lacking to them. Yet it must be hiding somewhere, since she produced this feeling out of herself.

142   Whenever such an element is not to be found in the dreamer himself, experience tells us that it is always projected. But upon whom? Is it still attached to the artist? He has long since disappeared from the patient's purview and cannot very well have taken the projection with him, since it lies anchored in the un-

1 I have called this masculine element in woman the animus and the corresponding feminine element in man the anima. See infra, pars. 296–340; also Emma Jung, "On the Nature of the Animus."

conscious of the patient, and moreover she had no personal relation with this man despite his fascination. For her he was more a figure of fantasy. No, a projection of this kind is always topical, that is, somewhere there must be somebody upon whom this content is projected, otherwise she would be palpably aware of it in herself.

143   At this point we come back to the objective level, for without it we cannot locate the projection. The patient does not know any man who means anything special to her, apart from myself; and as her doctor I mean a good deal. Presumably therefore this content is projected on to me, though I had certainly noticed nothing of the sort. But these subtler contents never appear on the surface; they always come to light outside the consulting hour. I therefore asked her cautiously, "Tell me, how do I seem to you when you are not with me? Am I just the same?" She said, "When I am with you, you are quite pleasant, but when I am by myself, or have not seen you for some time, the picture I have of you changes in a remarkable way. Sometimes you seem quite idealized, and then again different." Here she hesitated, and I prompted her: "In what way different?" Then she said, "Sometimes you seem rather dangerous, sinister, like an evil magician or a demon. I don't know how I ever get such ideas—you are not a bit like that."

144   So the content was fixed on me as part of the transference, and that is why it was missing from her psychic inventory. Here we recognize another important fact: I was contaminated (identified) with the artist, so in her unconscious fantasy she naturally plays the role of Mrs. X with me. I could easily prove this to her with the help of the material—sexual fantasies—previously brought to light. But I myself am then the obstacle, the crab that prevents her from getting across. If, in this particular case, we were to confine ourselves to the objective level, the position would be very tricky. What would be the good of my explaining, "But I am not this artist in any sense, I am not in the least sinister, nor am I an evil magician!" That would leave the patient quite cold, for she knows that just as well as I do. The projection continues as before, and I really am the obstacle to her further progress.

145   It is at this point that many a treatment comes to a standstill. There is no way of getting out of the toils of the unconscious,

except for the doctor to raise himself to the subjective level and to acknowledge himself as an image. But an image of what? Here lies the greatest difficulty of all. "Well now," the doctor will say, "an image of something in the unconscious of the patient." Whereupon she will say, "What, so I am a man, and a sinister, fascinating man at that, a wicked magician or demon? Not on your life! I cannot accept that, it's all nonsense. I'd sooner believe this of you!" She is right: it is preposterous to transfer such things to her. She cannot accept being turned into a demon any more than the doctor can. Her eyes flash, an evil expression creeps into her face, the gleam of an unknown resistance never seen before. I am suddenly faced by the possibility of a painful misunderstanding. What is it? Disappointed love? Does she feel offended, depreciated? In her glance there lurks something of the beast of prey, something really demoniacal. Is she a demon after all? Or am I the beast of prey, the demon, and is this a terrified victim sitting before me, trying to defend herself with the brute strength of despair against my wicked spells? All this must surely be nonsense—fantastic delusion. What have I touched? What new chord is vibrating? Yet it is only a passing moment. The expression on the patient's face clears, and she says, as though relieved, "It is queer, but just now I had a feeling you had touched the point I could never get over in relation to my friend. It's a horrible feeling, something inhuman, evil, cruel. I simply cannot describe how queer this feeling is. It makes me hate and despise my friend when it comes, although I struggle against it with all my might."

146   This remark throws an explanatory light on what has happened: I have taken the place of the friend. The friend has been overcome. The ice of the repression is broken and the patient has entered a new phase of life without knowing it. Now I know that all that was painful and bad in her relation with her friend will devolve upon me, as well as all the good, but it will be in violent conflict with the mysterious x which the patient has never been able to master. A new phase of the transference has started, although it does not as yet clearly reveal the nature of the x that has been projected upon me.

147   One thing is certain: if the patient gets stuck in this form of transference, the most troublesome misunderstandings lie ahead, for she will be bound to treat me as she treated her friend

—in other words, the x will be continually in the air giving rise to misunderstandings. It will inevitably turn out that she will see the demon in me, since she cannot accept it in herself. All insoluble conflicts come about in this fashion. And an insoluble conflict means bringing life to a standstill.

148   Or another possibility: the patient could use her old defence mechanism against this new difficulty and could simply ignore the point of obscurity. That is to say, she could begin repressing again, instead of keeping things conscious, which is the necessary and obvious demand of the whole method. But nothing would be gained by this; on the contrary, the x now threatens from the unconscious, and that is far more unpleasant.

149   Whenever such an unacceptable content appears, we must consider carefully whether it is a personal quality at all. "Magician" and "demon" may well represent qualities whose very names make it instantly clear that these are not human and personal qualities but mythological ones. Magician and demon are mythological figures which express the unknown, "inhuman" feeling that swept over the patient. They are attributes not in any sense applicable to a human personality, although, as intuitive judgments not subjected to closer criticism, they are constantly being projected upon our fellow men, to the very great detriment of human relations.

150   These attributes always indicate that contents of the transpersonal or collective unconscious are being projected. Personal memories cannot account for "demons," or for "wicked magicians," although everyone has, of course, at one time or another heard or read of these things. We have all heard of rattlesnakes, but we do not call a lizard or a blindworm a rattlesnake and display the corresponding emotions merely because we have been startled by the rustling of a lizard or a blindworm. Similarly, we do not call one of our fellows a demon unless there really is something demonic in his effect upon us. But if this effect were truly a part of his personal character, it would show itself everywhere, and then the man would be a demon indeed, a sort of werewolf. But that is mythology, i.e., collective psyche, and not individual psyche. In so far as through our unconscious we have a share in the historical collective psyche, we live naturally and unconsciously in a world of werewolves, demons, magicians, etc., for these are things which all previous ages have in-

vested with tremendous affectivity. Equally we have a share in gods and devils, saviours and criminals; but it would be absurd to attribute these potentialities of the unconscious to ourselves personally. It is therefore absolutely essential to make the sharpest possible demarcation between the personal and the impersonal attributes of the psyche. This is not to deny the sometimes very formidable existence of the contents of the collective unconscious, but only to stress that, as contents of the collective psyche, they are opposed to and different from the individual psyche. Simple-minded folk have never, of course, separated these things from their individual consciousness, because the gods and demons were not regarded as psychic projections and hence as contents of the unconscious, but as self-evident realities. Only in the age of enlightenment did people discover that the gods did not really exist, but were simply projections. Thus the gods were disposed of. But the corresponding psychological function was by no means disposed of; it lapsed into the unconscious, and men were thereupon poisoned by the surplus of libido that had once been laid up in the cult of divine images. The devaluation and repression of so powerful a function as the religious function naturally have serious consequences for the psychology of the individual. The unconscious is prodigiously strengthened by this reflux of libido, and, through its archaic collective contents, begins to exercise a powerful influence on the conscious mind. The period of the Enlightenment closed, as we know, with the horrors of the French Revolution. And at the present time, too, we are once more experiencing this uprising of the unconscious destructive forces of the collective psyche. The result has been mass-murder on an unparalleled scale.[2] This is precisely what the unconscious was after. Its position had been immeasurably strengthened beforehand by the rationalism of modern life, which, by depreciating everything irrational, precipitated the function of the irrational into the unconscious. But once this function finds itself in the unconscious, it works unceasing havoc, like an incurable disease whose focus cannot be eradicated because it is invisible. Individual and nation alike are then compelled to live the irrational in their own lives, even devoting their loftiest ideals and their best wits to expressing its madness in the most perfect form. We see the same thing in

2 Written in 1916; superfluous to remark that it is still true today [1943].

miniature in our patient, who fled from a course of life that seemed to her irrational—Mrs. X—only to act it out in pathological form, and with the greatest sacrifices, in her relations with her friend.

151 There is nothing for it but to recognize the irrational as a necessary, because ever-present, psychological function, and to take its contents not as concrete realities—that would be a regression!—but as psychic realities, real because they *work*. The collective unconscious, being the repository of man's experience and at the same time the prior condition of this experience, is an image of the world which has taken aeons to form. In this image certain features, the archetypes or dominants, have crystallized out in the course of time. They are the ruling powers, the gods, images of the dominant laws and principles, and of typical, regularly occurring events in the soul's cycle of experience.[3] In so far as these images are more or less faithful replicas of psychic events, their archetypes, that is, their general characteristics which have been emphasized through the accumulation of similar experiences, also correspond to certain general characteristics of the physical world. Archetypal images can therefore be taken metaphorically, as intuitive concepts for physical phenomena. For instance, *aether*, the primordial breath or soul-substance, is a concept found all over the world, and *energy*, or magical power, is an intuitive idea that is equally widespread.

152 On account of their affinity with physical phenomena,[4] the archetypes usually appear in projection; and, because projections are unconscious, they appear on persons in the immediate environment, mostly in the form of abnormal over- or undervaluations which provoke misunderstandings, quarrels, fanaticisms, and follies of every description. Thus we say, "He makes a god of so-and-so," or, "So-and-so is Mr. X's *bête noire.*" In this way, too, there grow up modern myth-formations, i.e., fantastic rumours, suspicions, prejudices. The archetypes are therefore exceedingly important things with a powerful effect, meriting our closest attention. They must not be suppressed out of hand, but must be very carefully weighed and considered, if only be-

[3] As indicated earlier (par. 109), the archetypes may be regarded as the effect and deposit of experiences that have already taken place, but equally they appear as the factors which cause such experiences.

[4] Cf. "The Structure of the Psyche," pars. 325ff.

cause of the danger of psychic infection they carry with them. Since they usually occur as projections, and since these only attach themselves where there is a suitable hook, their evaluation and assessment is no light matter. Thus, when somebody projects the devil upon his neighbour, he does so because this person has something about him which makes the attachment of such an image possible. But this is not to say that the man is on that account a devil; on the contrary, he may be a particularly good fellow, but antipathetic to the maker of the projection, so that a "devilish" (i.e., *dividing*) effect arises between them. Nor need the projector necessarily be a devil, although he has to recognize that he has something just as devilish in himself, and has only stumbled upon it by projecting it. But that does not make him a devil; indeed he may be just as decent as the other man. The appearance of the devil in such a case simply means that the two people are at present incompatible: for which reason the unconscious forces them apart and keeps them away from each other. The devil is a variant of the "shadow" archetype, i.e., of the dangerous aspect of the unrecognized dark half of the personality.

153   One of the archetypes that is almost invariably met with in the projection of unconscious collective contents is the "magic demon" with mysterious powers. A good example of this is Gustav Meyrink's *Golem,* also the Tibetan wizard in the same author's *Fledermäuse,* who unleashes world war by magic. Naturally Meyrink learned nothing of this from me; he brought it independently out of his unconscious by clothing in words and imagery a feeling not unlike the one which my patient had projected upon me. The magician type also figures in *Zarathustra,* while in *Faust* he is the actual hero.

154   The image of this demon forms one of the lowest and most ancient stages in the conception of God. It is the type of primitive tribal sorcerer or medicine-man, a peculiarly gifted personality endowed with magical power.[5] This figure often appears as dark-skinned and of mongoloid type, and then it represents a negative and possibly dangerous aspect. Sometimes it can hardly

---

[5] The idea of the medicine-man who communes with spirits and wields magical powers is so deeply ingrained in many primitives that they even believe "doctors" are to be found among animals. Thus the Achomawi of northern California speak of ordinary coyotes and of "doctor" coyotes.

be distinguished, if at all, from the shadow; but the more the magical note predominates, the easier it is to make the distinction, and this is not without relevance in so far as the demon can also have a very positive aspect as the "wise old man." [6]

155   The recognition of the archetypes takes us a long step forwards. The magical or daemonic effect emanating from our neighbour disappears when the mysterious feeling is traced back to a definite entity in the collective unconscious. But now we have an entirely new task before us: the question of how the ego is to come to terms with this psychological non-ego. Can we rest content with establishing the real existence of the archetypes, and simply let things take care of themselves?

156   That would be to create a permanent state of dissociation, a split between the individual and the collective psyche. On the one side we should have the differentiated modern ego, and on the other a sort of negroid culture, a very primitive state of affairs. We should have, in fact, what actually exists—a veneer of civilization over a dark-skinned brute; and the cleavage would be clearly demonstrated before our eyes. But such a dissociation requires immediate synthesis and the development of what has remained undeveloped. There must be a union of the two parts; for, failing that, there is no doubt how the matter would be decided: the primitive man would inevitably lapse back into repression. But that union is possible only where a still valid and therefore living religion exists, which allows the primitive man adequate means of expression through a richly developed symbolism. In other words, in its dogmas and rites, this religion must possess a mode of thinking and acting that harks back to the most primitive level. Such is the case in Catholicism, and this is its special advantage as well as its greatest danger.

157   Before we go into this new question of a possible union, let us return to the dream from which we started. This whole discussion has given us a wider understanding of the dream, and particularly of one essential part of it—the feeling of fear. This fear is a primitive dread of the contents of the collective unconscious. As we have seen, the patient identifies herself with Mrs. X, thereby showing that she also has some relation to the mysterious artist. It proved that the doctor was identified with the artist, and further we saw that on the subjective level I became

[6] Cf. "Archetypes of the Collective Unconscious," pars. 74ff.

an image for the figure of the magician in the collective unconscious.

158   All this is covered in the dream by the symbol of the crab, which walks backwards. The crab is the living content of the unconscious, and it cannot be exhausted or made ineffective by analysis on the objective level. We can, however, separate the mythological or collective psychic contents from the objects of consciousness, and consolidate them as psychological realities outside the individual psyche. Through the act of cognition we "posit" the reality of the archetypes, or, more precisely, we postulate the psychic existence of such contents on a cognitive basis. It must emphatically be stated that it is not just a question of cognitive contents, but of transubjective, largely autonomous psychic systems which on that account are only very conditionally under the control of the conscious mind and for the most part escape it altogether.

159   So long as the collective unconscious and the individual psyche are coupled together without being differentiated, no progress can be made; or, to speak in terms of the dream, the boundary cannot be crossed. If, despite that, the dreamer makes ready to cross the border-line, the unconscious becomes activated, seizes her, and holds her fast. The dream and its material characterize the collective unconscious partly as a lower animal that lives hidden in the depths of the water, and partly as a dangerous disease that can be cured only by a timely operation. To what extent this characterization is apt has already been seen. As we have said, the animal symbol points specifically to the extra-human, the transpersonal; for the contents of the collective unconscious are not only the residues of archaic, specifically human modes of functioning, but also the residues of functions from man's animal ancestry, whose duration in time was infinitely greater than the relatively brief epoch of specifically human existence. These residues, or "engrams," as Semon calls them,[7]

---

[7] In his philosophical dissertation on Leibniz's theory of the unconscious (*Das Unbewusste bei Leibniz in Beziehung zu modernen Theorien*), Ganz has used the engram theory of R. W. Semon to explain the collective unconscious. The concept of the collective unconscious advanced by me coincides only at certain points with Semon's concept of the phylogenetic *mneme*. Cf. Semon, *Die Mneme als erhaltendes Prinzip im Wechsel des organischen Geschehens* (1904); trans. by L. Simon as *The Mneme*.

are extremely liable, when activated, not only to retard the pace of development, but actually to force it into regression until the store of energy that activated the unconscious has been used up. But the energy becomes serviceable again by being brought into play through man's conscious attitude towards the collective unconscious. The religions have established this cycle of energy in a concrete way by means of ritual communion with the gods. This method, however, is too much at variance with our intellectual morality, and has moreover been too radically supplanted by Christianity, for us to accept it as an ideal, or even possible, solution of the problem. If on the other hand we take the figures of the unconscious as collective psychic phenomena or functions, this hypothesis in no way violates our intellectual conscience. It offers a rationally acceptable solution, and at the same time a possible method of effecting a settlement with the activated residues of our racial history. This settlement makes the crossing of previous boundaries altogether feasible and is therefore appropriately called the *transcendent function*. It is synonymous with progressive development towards a new attitude.

160   The parallel with the hero-myth is very striking. More often than not the typical struggle of the hero with the monster (the unconscious content) takes place beside the water, perhaps at a ford. This is the case particularly in the Redskin myths with which Longfellow's *Hiawatha* has made us familiar. In the decisive battle the hero is, like Jonah, invariably swallowed by the monster, as Frobenius has shown[8] with a wealth of detail. But, once inside the monster, the hero begins to settle accounts with the creature in his own way, while it swims eastwards with him towards the rising sun. He cuts off a portion of the viscera, the heart for instance, or some essential organ by virtue of which the monster lives (i.e., the valuable energy that activates the unconscious). Thus he kills the monster, which then drifts to land, where the hero, new-born through the transcendent function (the "night sea journey," as Frobenius calls it), steps forth, sometimes in the company of all those whom the monster has previously devoured. In this manner the normal state of things is restored, since the unconscious, robbed of its energy, no longer occupies the dominant position. Thus the myth graphi-

8 Frobenius, *Das Zeitalter des Sonnengottes.*

cally describes the problem which also engages our patient.[9]

161 I must now emphasize the not unimportant fact, which must also have struck the reader, that in the dream the collective unconscious appears under a very negative aspect, as something dangerous and harmful. This is because the patient has a richly developed, indeed positively luxuriant, fantasy life, possibly due to her literary gift. Her powers of fantasy are a symptom of illness in that she revels in them far too much and allows real life to slip by. Any more mythology would be exceedingly dangerous for her, because a great chunk of external life stands before her, still unlived. She has too little hold upon life to risk all at once a complete reversal of standpoint. The collective unconscious has fallen upon her and threatens to bear her away from a reality whose demands have not been adequately met. Accordingly, as the dream indicates, the collective unconscious had to be presented to her as something dangerous, otherwise she would have been only too ready to make it a refuge from the demands of life.

162 In judging a dream we must observe very carefully *how* the figures are introduced. For example, the crab that personifies the unconscious is negative in that it "walks backwards" and, in addition, holds back the dreamer at the critical moment. Misled by the so-called dream mechanisms of Freudian manufacture, such as displacement, inversion, etc., people have imagined they could make themselves independent of the "façade" of the dream by supposing that the true dream-thoughts lay hidden behind it. As against this I have long maintained that we have no right to accuse the dream of, so to speak, a deliberate manoeuvre calculated to deceive. Nature is often obscure or impenetrable, but she is not, like man, deceitful. We must therefore take it that the dream is just what it pretends to be, neither more nor less.[10] If it shows something in a negative light, there is no reason for assuming that it is meant positively. The archetypal "danger at the ford" is so patent that one is almost

---

[9] Those of my readers who have a deeper interest in the problem of opposites and its solution, as well as in the mythological activity of the unconscious, are referred to *Symbols of Transformation, Psychological Types,* and *The Archetypes and the Collective Unconscious.* [Cf. also *Mysterium Coniunctionis.*—EDITORS.]

[10] Cf. "General Aspects of Dream Psychology."

tempted to take the dream as a warning. But I must discountenance all such anthropomorphic interpretations. The dream itself wants nothing; it is a self-evident content, a plain natural fact like the sugar in the blood of a diabetic or the fever in a patient with typhus. It is only we who, if we are clever and can unriddle the signs of nature, turn it into a warning.

163   But—a warning of what? Of the obvious danger that the unconscious might overpower the dreamer at the moment of crossing. And what would being overpowered mean? An invasion by the unconscious may very easily occur at moments of critical change and decision. The bank from which she approaches the river is her situation as known to us so far. This situation has precipitated her into a neurotic deadlock, as though she had come up against an impassable obstacle. The obstacle is represented by the dream as a perfectly passable river. So things do not seem to be very serious. But in the river, most unexpectedly, the crab is hiding, and this represents the real danger on account of which the river is, or appears to be, impassable. For had she only known beforehand that the dangerous crab was lurking at this particular spot, she might perhaps have ventured to cross somewhere else, or have taken other precautions. In the dreamer's present situation it is eminently desirable that a crossing should be made. The crossing means in the first place a carrying over—a transference—of the earlier situation to the doctor. That is the new feature. Were it not for the unpredictable unconscious, this would not involve such a great risk. But we saw that through the transference the activity of archetypal figures is liable to be let loose, a fact we had not banked on. We have reckoned without our host, for we "forgot the gods."

164   Our dreamer is not a religious person, she is "modern." She has forgotten the religion she was once taught, she knows nothing of those moments when the gods intervene, or rather she does not know that there are age-old situations whose nature it is to stir us to the depths. One such situation is love, its passion and its danger. Love may summon forth unsuspected powers in the soul for which we had better be prepared. "Religio" in the sense of a "careful consideration" of unknown dangers and agencies—that is what is in question here. From a simple projection love may come upon her with all its fatal power, some dazzling illusion that might throw her life off its natural course.

Is it a good thing or a bad, God or devil, that will befall the dreamer? Without knowing which, she feels that she is already in its clutches. And who can say whether she will be able to cope with this complication! Until now she had managed to circumvent such an eventuality, but now it threatens to seize hold of her. That is a risk we should avoid, or, if we must take the plunge, we need a good deal of "trust in God" or "faith" in a successful issue. Thus, unsought and unexpected, the question creeps in of one's religious attitude to fate.

165   The dream as it stands leaves the dreamer no alternative at present but to withdraw her foot carefully; for to go on would be fatal. She cannot yet leave the neurotic situation, because the dream gives her no positive indication of any help from the unconscious. The unconscious powers are still inauspicious and obviously expect more work and a deeper insight from the dreamer before she can really venture across.

166   I certainly do not wish, by this negative example, to convey the impression that the unconscious plays a negative role in all cases. I will therefore add two further dreams, this time of a young man, which illuminate another and more favourable side of the unconscious. I do this the more readily since the solution of the problem of opposites can be reached only irrationally, by way of contributions from the unconscious, i.e., from dreams.

167   First I must acquaint the reader in some measure with the personality of the dreamer, for without this acquaintance he will hardly be able to transport himself into the peculiar atmosphere of the dreams. There are dreams that are pure poems and can therefore only be understood through the mood they convey as a whole. The dreamer is a youth of a little over twenty, still entirely boyish in appearance. There is even a touch of girlishness in his looks and manner of expression. The latter betrays a very good education and upbringing. He is intelligent, with pronounced intellectual and aesthetic interests. His aestheticism is very much in evidence: we are made instantly aware of his good taste and his fine appreciation of all forms of art. His feelings are tender and soft, given to the enthusiasms typical of puberty, but somewhat effeminate. There is no trace of adolescent callowness. Undoubtedly he is too young for his age, a clear case of retarded development. It is quite in keeping with this that he should have come to me on account of his homosexuality. The

night preceding his first visit he had the following dream: *"I am in a lofty cathedral filled with mysterious twilight. They tell me that it is the cathedral at Lourdes. In the centre there is a deep dark well, into which I have to descend."*

168   The dream is clearly a coherent expression of mood. The dreamer's comments are as follows: "Lourdes is the mystic fount of healing. Naturally I remembered yesterday that I was going to you for treatment and was in search of a cure. There is said to be a well like this at Lourdes. It would be rather unpleasant to go down into this water. The well in the church was ever so deep."

169   Now what does dream tell us? On the surface it seems clear enough, and we might be content to take it as a kind of poetic formulation of the mood of the day before. But we should never stop there, for experience shows that dreams are much deeper and more significant. One might almost suppose that the dreamer came to the doctor in a highly poetic mood and was entering upon the treatment as though it were a sacred religious act to be performed in the mystical half-light of some awe-inspiring sanctuary. But this does not fit the facts at all. The patient merely came to the doctor to be treated for that unpleasant matter, his homosexuality, which is anything but poetic. At any rate we cannot see from the mood of the preceding day why he should dream so poetically, if we were to accept so direct a causation for the origin of the dream. But we might conjecture, perhaps, that the dream was stimulated precisely by the dreamer's impressions of that highly unpoetical affair which impelled him to come to me for treatment. We might even suppose that he dreamed in such an intensely poetical manner just because of the unpoeticalness of his mood on the day before, much as a man who has fasted by day dreams of delicious meals at night. It cannot be denied that the thought of treatment, of the cure and its unpleasant procedure, recurs in the dream, but poetically transfigured, in a guise which meets most effectively the lively aesthetic and emotional needs of the dreamer. He will be drawn on irresistibly by this inviting picture, despite the fact that the well is dark, deep, and cold. Something of the dream-mood will persist after sleep and will even linger on into the morning of the day on which he has to submit to the unpleasant and unpoetical duty of visiting me. Perhaps the drab reality will be

touched by the bright, golden after-glow of the dream feeling.
170   Is this, perhaps, the purpose of the dream? That would not be impossible, for in my experience the vast majority of dreams are compensatory.[11] They always stress the other side in order to maintain the psychic equilibrium. But the compensation of mood is not the only purpose of the dream picture. The dream also provides a *mental corrective*. The patient had of course nothing like an adequate understanding of the treatment to which he was about to submit himself. But the dream gives him a picture which describes in poetic metaphors the nature of the treatment before him. This becomes immediately apparent if we follow up his associations and comments on the image of the cathedral: "Cathedral," he says, "makes me think of Cologne Cathedral. Even as a child I was fascinated by it. I remember my mother telling me of it for the first time, and I also remember how, whenever I saw a village church, I used to ask if that were Cologne Cathedral. I wanted to be a priest in a cathedral like that."

171   In these associations the patient is describing a very important experience of his childhood. As in nearly all cases of this kind, he had a particularly close tie with his mother. By this we are not to understand a particularly good or intense *conscious* relationship, but something in the nature of a secret, subterranean tie which expresses itself consciously, perhaps, only in the retarded development of character, i.e., in a relative infantilism. The developing personality naturally veers away from such an unconscious infantile bond; for nothing is more obstructive to development than persistence in an unconscious—we could also say, a psychically embryonic—state. For this reason instinct seizes on the first opportunity to replace the mother by another object. If it is to be a real mother-substitute, this object must be, in some sense, an analogy of her. This is entirely the case with our patient. The intensity with which his childish fantasy seized upon the symbol of Cologne Cathedral corresponds to the strength of his unconscious need to find a substitute for the mother. The unconscious need is heightened still further in a case where the infantile bond could become harmful. Hence the enthusiasm with which his childish imagination took up the idea

[11] The idea of compensation has already been extensively used by Alfred Adler.

of the Church; for the Church is, in the fullest sense, a mother. We speak not only of Mother Church, but even of the Church's womb. In the ceremony known as the *benedictio fontis*, the baptismal font is apostrophized as "immaculatus divini fontis uterus"—the immaculate womb of the divine font. We naturally think that a man must have known this meaning consciously before it could get to work in his fantasy, and that an unknowing child could not possibly be affected by these significations. Such analogies certainly do not work by way of the conscious mind, but in quite another manner.

172   The Church represents a higher spiritual substitute for the purely natural, or "carnal," tie to the parents. Consequently it frees the individual from an unconscious natural relationship which, strictly speaking, is not a relationship at all but simply a condition of inchoate, unconscious identity. This, just because it is unconscious, possesses a tremendous inertia and offers the utmost resistance to any kind of spiritual development. It would be hard to say what the essential difference is between this state and the soul of an animal. Now, it is by no means the special prerogative of the Christian Church to try to make it possible for the individual to detach himself from his original, animal-like condition; the Church is simply the latest, and specifically Western, form of an instinctive striving that is probably as old as mankind itself. It is a striving that can be found in the most varied forms among all primitive peoples who are in any way developed and have not yet become degenerate: I mean the institution or rite of initiation into manhood. When he has reached puberty the young man is conducted to the "men's house," or some other place of consecration, where he is systematically alienated from his family. At the same time he is initiated into the religious mysteries, and in this way is ushered not only into a wholly new set of relationships, but, as a renewed and changed personality, into a new world, like one reborn (*quasimodo genitus*). The initiation is often attended by all kinds of tortures, sometimes including such things as circumcision and the like. These practices are undoubtedly very old. They have almost become instinctive mechanisms, with the result that they continue to repeat themselves without external compulsion, as in the "baptisms" of German students or the

even more wildly extravagant initiations in American students' fraternities. They are engraved on the unconscious as a primordial image.

173   When his mother told him as a little boy about Cologne Cathedral, this primordial image was stirred and awakened to life. But there was no priestly instructor to develop it further, so the child remained in his mother's hands. Yet the longing for a man's leadership continued to grow in the boy, taking the form of homosexual leanings—a faulty development that might never have come about had a man been there to educate his childish fantasies. The deviation towards homosexuality has, to be sure, numerous historical precedents. In ancient Greece, as also in certain primitive communities, homosexuality and education were practically synonymous. Viewed in this light, the homosexuality of adolescence is only a misunderstanding of the otherwise very appropriate need for masculine guidance. One might also say that the fear of incest which is based on the mother-complex extends to women in general; but in my opinion an immature man is quite right to be afraid of women, because his relations with women are generally disastrous.

174   According to the dream, then, what the initiation of the treatment signifies for the patient is the fulfilment of the true meaning of his homosexuality, i.e., his entry into the world of the adult man. All that we have been forced to discuss here in such tedious and long-winded detail, in order to understand it properly, the dream has condensed into a few vivid metaphors, thus creating a picture which works far more effectively on the imagination, feeling, and understanding of the dreamer than any learned discourse. Consequently the patient was better and more intelligently prepared for the treatment than if he had been overwhelmed with medical and pedagogical maxims. (For this reason I regard dreams not only as a valuable source of information but as an extraordinarily effective instrument of education.)

175   We come now to the second dream. I must explain in advance that in the first consultation I did not refer in any way to the dream we have just been discussing. It was not even mentioned. Nor was there a word said that was even remotely connected with the foregoing. This is the second dream: *"I am in a great Gothic cathedral. At the altar stands a priest. I stand be-*

fore him with my friend, holding in my hand a little Japanese ivory figure, with the feeling that it is going to be baptized. Suddenly an elderly woman appears, takes the fraternity ring from my friend's finger, and puts it on her own. My friend is afraid that this may bind him in some way. But at the same moment there is a sound of wonderful organ music."

176   Here I will only bring out briefly those points which continue and supplement the dream of the preceding day. The second dream is unmistakably connected with the first: once more the dreamer is in church, that is, in the state of initiation into manhood. But a new figure has been added: the priest, whose absence in the previous situation we have already noted. The dream therefore confirms that the unconscious meaning of his homosexuality has been fulfilled and that a further development can be started. The actual initiation ceremony, namely the baptism, may now begin. The dream symbolism corroborates what I said before, namely that it is not the prerogative of the Christian Church to bring about such transitions and psychic transformations, but that behind the Church there is a living primordial image which in certain conditions is capable of enforcing them.

177   What, according to the dream, is to be baptized is a little Japanese ivory figure. The patient says of this: "It was a tiny, grotesque little manikin that reminded me of the male organ. It was certainly odd that this member was to be baptized. But after all, with the Jews circumcision is a sort of baptism. That must be a reference to my homosexuality, because the friend standing with me before the altar is the one with whom I have sexual relations. We belong to the same fraternity. The fraternity ring obviously stands for our relationship."

178   We know that in common usage the ring is the token of a bond or relationship, as for example the wedding ring. We can therefore safely take the fraternity ring in this case as symbolizing the homosexual relationship, and the fact that the dreamer appears together with his friend points in the same direction.

179   The complaint to be remedied is homosexuality. The dreamer is to be led out of this relatively childish condition and initiated into the adult state by means of a kind of circumcision ceremony under the supervision of a priest. These ideas correspond exactly to my analysis of the previous dream. Thus far the development has proceeded logically and consistently with the

aid of archetypal images. But now a disturbing factor comes on the scene. An elderly woman suddenly takes possession of the fraternity ring; in other words, she draws to herself what has hitherto been a homosexual relationship, thus causing the dreamer to fear that he is getting involved in a new relationship with obligations of its own. Since the ring is now on the hand of a woman, a marriage of sorts has been contracted, i.e., the homosexual relationship seems to have passed over into a heterosexual one, but a heterosexual relationship of a peculiar kind since it concerns an elderly woman. "She is a friend of my mother's," says the patient. "I am very fond of her, in fact she is like a mother to me."

180　　From this remark we can see what has happened in the dream: as a result of the initiation the homosexual tie has been cut and a heterosexual relationship substituted for it, a platonic friendship with a motherly type of woman. In spite of her resemblance to his mother, this woman is not his mother any longer, so the relationship with her signifies a step beyond the mother towards masculinity, and hence a partial conquest of his adolescent homosexuality.

181　　The fear of the new tie can easily be understood, firstly as fear which the woman's resemblance to his mother might naturally arouse—it might be that the dissolution of the homosexual tie has led to a complete regression to the mother—and secondly as fear of the new and unknown factors in the adult heterosexual state with its possible obligations, such as marriage, etc. That we are in fact concerned here not with a regression but with a progression seems to be confirmed by the music that now peals forth. The patient is musical and especially susceptible to solemn organ music. Therefore music signifies for him a very positive feeling, so in this case it forms a harmonious conclusion to the dream, which in its turn is well qualified to leave behind a beautiful, holy feeling for the following morning.

182　　If you consider the fact that up to now the patient had seen me for only one consultation, in which little more was discussed than a general anamnesis, you will doubtless agree with me when I say that both dreams make astonishing anticipations. They show the patient's situation in a highly remarkable light, and one that is very strange to the conscious mind, while at the same time lending to the banal medical situation an aspect that is uniquely attuned to the mental peculiarities of the dreamer, and thus capable of stringing his aesthetic, intellectual, and religious interests to concert pitch. No better conditions for treatment could possibly be imagined. One is almost persuaded, from the meaning of these dreams, that the patient entered upon the treatment with the utmost readiness and hopefulness, quite prepared to cast aside his boyishness and become a man. In reality, however, this was not the case at all. Consciously he was full of hesitation and resistance; moreover, as the treatment progressed, he constantly showed himself antagonistic and difficult, ever ready to slip back into his previous infantilism. Consequently the dreams stand in strict contrast to his conscious behaviour. They move along a progressive line and take the part of the educator. They clearly reveal their special function. This function I have called compensation. The unconscious progressiveness and the conscious regressiveness together form a pair of opposites which, as it were, keeps the scales balanced. The influence of the educator tilts the balance in favour of progression.

183   In the case of this young man the images of the collective unconscious play an entirely positive role, which comes from the fact that he has no really dangerous tendency to fall back on a fantasy-substitute for reality and to entrench himself behind it against life. The effect of these unconscious images has something fateful about it. Perhaps—who knows?—these eternal images are what men mean by fate.

184   The archetypes are of course always at work everywhere. But practical treatment, especially in the case of young people, does not always require the patient to come to close quarters with them. At the climacteric, on the other hand, it is necessary to give special attention to the images of the collective unconscious, because they are the source from which hints may be drawn for the solution of the problem of opposites. From the conscious elaboration of this material the transcendent function reveals itself as a mode of apprehension mediated by the archetypes and capable of uniting the opposites. By "apprehension" I do not mean simply intellectual understanding, but understanding through experience. An archetype, as we have said, is a dynamic image, a fragment of the objective psyche, which can be truly understood only if experienced as an autonomous entity.

185   A general account of this process, which may extend over a

long period of time, would be pointless—even if such a description were possible—because it takes the greatest imaginable variety of forms in different individuals. The only common factor is the emergence of certain definite archetypes. I would mention in particular the shadow, the animal, the wise old man, the anima, the animus, the mother, the child, besides an indefinite number of archetypes representative of situations. A special position must be accorded to those archetypes which stand for the goal of the developmental process. The reader will find the necessary information on this point in my *Psychology and Alchemy*, as well as in "Psychology and Religion" and the volume written in collaboration with Richard Wilhelm, *The Secret of the Golden Flower*.

186   The transcendent function does not proceed without aim and purpose, but leads to the revelation of the essential man. It is in the first place a purely natural process, which may in some cases pursue its course without the knowledge or assistance of the individual, and can sometimes forcibly accomplish itself in the face of opposition. The meaning and purpose of the process is the realization, in all its aspects, of the personality originally hidden away in the embryonic germ-plasm; the production and unfolding of the original, potential wholeness. The symbols used by the unconscious to this end are the same as those which mankind has always used to express wholeness, completeness, and perfection: symbols, as a rule, of the quaternity and the circle. For these reasons I have termed this the *individuation process*.

187   This natural process of individuation served me both as a model and guiding principle for my method of treatment. The unconscious compensation of a neurotic conscious attitude contains all the elements that could effectively and healthily correct the one-sidedness of the conscious mind if these elements were made conscious, i.e., were understood and integrated into it as realities. It is only very seldom that a dream achieves such intensity that the shock is enough to throw the conscious mind out of the saddle. As a rule dreams are too feeble and too unintelligible to exercise a radical influence on consciousness. In consequence, the compensation runs underground in the unconscious and has no immediate effect. But it has some effect all the same; only, it is indirect in so far as the unconscious opposition will,

if consistently ignored, arrange symptoms and situations which irresistibly thwart our conscious intentions. The aim of the treatment is therefore to understand and to appreciate, so far as practicable, dreams and all other manifestations of the unconscious, firstly in order to prevent the formation of an unconscious opposition which becomes more dangerous as time goes on, and secondly in order to make the fullest possible use of the healing factor of compensation.

88   These proceedings naturally rest on the assumption that a man is capable of attaining wholeness, in other words, that he has it in him to be healthy. I mention this assumption because there are without doubt individuals who are not at bottom altogether viable and who rapidly perish if, for any reason, they come face to face with their wholeness. Even if this does not happen, they merely lead a miserable existence for the rest of their days as fragments or partial personalities, shored up by social or psychic parasitism. Such people are, very much to the misfortune of others, more often than not inveterate humbugs who cover up their deadly emptiness under a fine outward show. It would be a hopeless undertaking to try to treat them with the method here discussed. The only thing that "helps" here is to keep up the show, for the truth would be unendurable or useless.

89   When a case is treated in the manner indicated, the initiative lies with the unconscious, but all criticism, choice, and decision lie with the conscious mind. If the decision is right, it will be confirmed by dreams indicative of progress; in the other event correction will follow from the side of the unconscious. The course of treatment is thus rather like a running conversation with the unconscious. That the correct interpretation of dreams is of paramount importance should be sufficiently clear from what has been said. But when, you may rightly ask, is one sure of the interpretation? Is there anything approaching a reliable criterion for the correctness of an interpretation? This question, happily, can be answered in the affirmative. If we have made a wrong interpretation, or if it is somehow incomplete, we may be able to see it from the next dream. Thus, for example, the earlier motif will be repeated in clearer form, or our interpretation may be deflated by some ironic paraphrase, or it may meet with straightforward violent opposition. Now supposing

that these interpretations also go astray, the general inconclusiveness and futility of our procedure will make itself felt soon enough in the bleakness, sterility, and pointlessness of the undertaking, so that doctor and patient alike will be suffocated either by boredom or by doubt. Just as the reward of a correct interpretation is an uprush of life, so an incorrect one dooms them to deadlock, resistance, doubt, and mutual desiccation. Stoppages can of course also arise from the resistance of the patient, as for instance from an obstinate clinging to outworn illusions or to infantile demands. Sometimes, too, the doctor lacks the necessary understanding, as once happened to me in the case of a very intelligent patient, a woman who, for various reasons, looked to me rather a rum customer. After a satisfactory beginning I had the feeling more and more that somehow my interpretation of her dreams was not quite hitting the mark. As I was unable to lay my finger on the source of error, I tried to talk myself out of my doubts. But during the consulting hours I became aware of the growing dullness of our conversation, with a steadily mounting sense of excruciating futility. Finally I resolved to speak about it at the next opportunity to my patient, who, it seemed to me, had not failed to notice this fact. The next night I had the following dream: *I was walking along a country road through a valley lit by the evening sun. To my right, standing on a steep hill, was a castle, and on the topmost tower, on a kind of balustrade, sat a woman. In order to see her properly I had to bend my head back so far that I got a crick in the neck. Even in my dream I recognized the woman as my patient.*[12]

190   From this I concluded that if I had to look up so much in the dream, I must obviously have looked down on my patient in reality. When I told her the dream together with the interpretation, a complete change came over the situation at once and the treatment shot ahead beyond all expectation. Experiences of this kind, although paid for very dearly, lead to an unshakable confidence in the reliability of dream compensations.

191   To the manifold problems involved in this method of treatment all my labours and researches have been devoted for the last ten years. But since, in this present account of analytical psychology, I am concerned only to provide a general survey, a

12 [Further details in "The Realities of Practical Psychotherapy," in the 2nd edn. of *The Practice of Psychotherapy*, pars. 540ff. Cf. infra, par. 281.—EDITORS.]

more detailed exposition of the widely ramified scientific, philosophical, and religious implications must remain in abeyance. For this I shall have to refer my reader to the literature I have mentioned.

VIII

GENERAL REMARKS ON THE THERAPEUTIC
APPROACH TO THE UNCONSCIOUS

¹⁹²   We are greatly mistaken if we think that the unconscious is something harmless that could be made into an object of entertainment, a parlour game. Certainly the unconscious is not always and in all circumstances dangerous, but as soon as a neurosis is present it is a sign of a special heaping up of energy in the unconscious, like a charge that may explode. Here caution is indicated. One never knows what one may be releasing when one begins to analyse dreams. Something deeply buried and invisible may thereby be set in motion, very probably something that would have come to light sooner or later anyway—but again, it might not. It is as if one were digging an artesian well and ran the risk of stumbling on a volcano. When neurotic symptoms are present one must proceed very carefully. But the neurotic cases are not by a long way the most dangerous. There are cases of people, apparently quite normal, showing no especial neurotic symptoms—they may themselves be doctors and educators—priding themselves on their normality, models of good upbringing, with exceptionally normal views and habits of life, yet whose normality is an artificial compensation for a latent psychosis. They themselves suspect nothing of their condition. Their suspicions may perhaps find only an indirect expression in the fact that they are particularly interested in psychology and psychiatry, and are attracted to these things as a moth to the light. But since the analytical technique activates the unconscious and brings it to the fore, in these cases the healthful compensation is destroyed, the unconscious breaks forth in the form of uncontrollable fantasies and overwrought states which may, in certain circumstances, lead to mental disorder and possibly even to suicide. Unfortunately these latent psychoses are not so very uncommon.

93   The danger of stumbling on cases like these threatens everybody who concerns himself with the analysis of the unconscious, even if he be equipped with a large measure of experience and skill. Through clumsiness, mistaken ideas, arbitrary interpretations, and so forth, he may even wreck cases that need not necessarily have turned out badly. This is by no means peculiar to the analysis of the unconscious, but is the penalty of all medical intervention that miscarries. The assertion that analysis drives people mad is obviously just as stupid as the vulgar notion that the psychiatrist is bound to go mad because he deals with lunatics.

94   Apart from the risks of treatment, the unconscious may also turn dangerous on its own account. One of the commonest forms of danger is the instigating of accidents. A very large number of accidents of every description, more than people would ever guess, are of psychic causation, ranging from trivial mishaps like stumbling, banging oneself, burning one's fingers, etc., to car smashes and catastrophes in the mountains: all these may be psychically caused and may sometimes have been preparing for weeks or even months. I have examined many cases of this kind, and often I could point to dreams which showed signs of a tendency to self-injury weeks beforehand. All those accidents that happen from so-called carelessness should be examined for such determinants. We know of course that when for one reason or another we feel out of sorts, we are liable to commit not only the minor follies, but something really dangerous which, given the right psychological moment, may well put an end to our lives. The popular saying, "Old so-and-so chose the right time to die," comes from a sure sense of the secret psychological cause in question. In the same way, bodily ills can be brought into being or protracted. A wrong functioning of the psyche can do much to injure the body, just as conversely a bodily illness can affect the psyche; for psyche and body are not separate entities but one and the same life. Thus there is seldom a bodily ailment that does not show psychic complications, even if it is not psychically caused.

195   It would be wrong, however, to dwell only on the unfavourable side of the unconscious. In all ordinary cases the unconscious is unfavourable or dangerous only because we are not at one with it and therefore in opposition to it. A negative attitude

115

to the unconscious, or its splitting off, is detrimental in so far as the dynamics of the unconscious are identical with instinctual energy.[1] Disalliance with the unconscious is synonymous with loss of instinct and rootlessness.

196   If we can successfully develop that function which I have called transcendent, the disharmony ceases and we can then enjoy the favourable side of the unconscious. The unconscious then gives us all the encouragement and help that a bountiful nature can shower upon man. It holds possibilities which are locked away from the conscious mind, for it has at its disposal all subliminal psychic contents, all those things which have been forgotten or overlooked, as well as the wisdom and experience of uncounted centuries which are laid down in its archetypal organs.

197   The unconscious is continually active, combining its material in ways which serve the future. It produces, no less than the conscious mind, subliminal combinations that are prospective; only, they are markedly superior to the conscious combinations both in refinement and in scope. For these reasons the unconscious could serve man as a unique guide, provided that he can resist the lure of being misguided.

198   In practice the treatment is adjusted according to the therapeutic results obtained. Results may appear at almost any stage of the treatment, quite irrespective of the severity or duration of the illness. And conversely, the treatment of a severe case may last a very long time without reaching, or needing to reach, the higher stages of development. There are a fair number who, even after therapeutic results have been obtained, go through further stages of transformation for the sake of their own development. So it is not true that one must be a serious case in order to go through the whole process. At all events only those individuals can attain to a higher degree of consciousness who are destined to it and called to it from the beginning, i.e., who have a capacity and an urge for higher differentiation. In this matter men differ extremely, as also do the animal species, among whom there are conservatives and progressives. Nature is aristocratic, but not in the sense of having reserved the possibility of differentiation exclusively for species high in the scale. So too with the possiblity of psychic development: it is not reserved for

1 Cf. "Instinct and the Unconscious."

specially gifted individuals. In other words, in order to undergo a far-reaching psychological development, neither outstanding intelligence nor any other talent is necessary, since in this development moral qualities can make up for intellectual shortcomings. It must not on any account be imagined that the treatment consists in grafting upon people's minds general formulas and complicated doctrines. There is no question of that. Each can take what he needs, in his own way and in his own language. What I have presented here is an intellectual formulation; it is not the sort of thing discussed in the general run of practical work. The little snippets of case histories I have woven into my theme give a rough idea of what happens in practice.

199 If, after all that has been related in the foregoing chapters, the reader should still not feel capable of forming a clear picture of the theory and practice of modern medical psychology, that would not surprise me so very much. I would, on the contrary, be inclined to blame my faulty gift of exposition, since I can hardly hope to give a concrete picture of that wide field of thought and experience which is the domain of medical psychology. On paper the interpretation of a dream may look arbitrary, muddled, and spurious; but the same thing in reality can be a little drama of unsurpassed realism. To *experience* a dream and its interpretation is very different from having a tepid rehash set before you on paper. Everything about this psychology is, in the deepest sense, experience; the entire theory, even where it puts on the most abstract airs, is the direct outcome of something experienced. If I accuse the Freudian sexual theory of one-sidedness, that does not mean that it rests on rootless speculation; it too is a faithful picture of real facts which force themselves upon our practical observation. And if the inferences made from them proliferate into a one-sided theory, that only goes to show with what powers of persuasion, both objective and subjective, the facts in question themselves bring to bear. The individual investigator can hardly be asked to rise superior to his own deepest impressions and their abstract formulation; for the acquisition of such impressions as well as their conceptual mastery is in itself the labour of a lifetime. For my part, I had the great advantage over both Freud and Adler of not having grown up within the narrow confines of a psychology of the neuroses; rather, I approach them from the side of psychiatry, prepared

for modern psychology by Nietzsche, and apart from Freud's views I also had before my eyes the growth of the views of Adler. In this way I found myself in the thick of the conflict from the very beginning, and was forced to regard not only the existing opinions, but my own as well, as relative, or rather as expressions of a certain psychological type. Just as the Breuer case we have discussed was decisive for Freud, so a decisive experience underlies my own views. Towards the end of my medical training I observed for a long period a case of somnambulism in a young girl. It became the theme of my doctor's dissertation.[2] For one acquainted with my scientific writings it may not be without interest to compare this forty-year-old study with my later ideas.

200   Work in this field is pioneer work. I have often made mistakes and had many times to forget what I had learned. But I know and am content to know that as surely as light comes out of darkness, truth is born of error. I have let Guglielmo Ferrero's *mot* about the "misérable vanité du savant" [3] serve me for a warning, and have therefore neither feared my mistakes nor seriously regretted them. For me, scientific research work was never a milch-cow or a means of prestige, but a struggle, often a bitter one, forced upon me by daily psychological experience of the sick. Hence not everything I bring forth is written out of my head, but much of it comes from the heart also, a fact I would beg the gracious reader not to overlook if, following up the intellectual line of thought, he comes upon certain lacunae that have not been properly filled in. A harmonious flow of exposition can be expected only when one is writing about things which one already knows. But when, urged on by the need to help and to heal, one acts as a path-finder, one must speak also of realities as yet unknown.

2 "On the Psychology and Pathology of So-called Occult Phenomena."
3 "C'est donc un devoir moral de l'homme de science de s'exposer à commettre des erreurs et à subir des critiques, pour que la science avance toujours. . . . Ceux qui sont doués d'un esprit assez sérieux et froid pour ne pas croire que tout ce qu'ils écrivent est l'expression de la vérité absolue et éternelle, approuvent cette théorie qui place les raisons de la science au-dessus de la misérable vanité et du mesquin amour propre du savant."—*Les Lois psychologiques du symbolisme*, p. viii; trans. of *I simboli in rapporto alla storia e filosofia del diritto alla psicologia e alla sociologia* (1893).

CONCLUSION

201   In conclusion I must ask the reader to forgive me for having ventured to say in these few pages so much that is new and perhaps hard to understand. I expose myself to his critical judgment because I feel it is the duty of one who goes his own way to inform society of what he finds on his voyage of discovery, be it cooling water for the thirsty or the sandy wastes of unfruitful error. The one helps, the other warns. Not the criticism of individual contemporaries will decide the truth or falsity of his discoveries, but future generations. There are things that are not yet true today, perhaps we dare not find them true, but tomorrow they may be. So every man whose fate it is to go his individual way must proceed with hopefulness and watchfulness, ever conscious of his loneliness and its dangers. The peculiarity of the way here described is largely due to the fact that in psychology, which springs from and acts upon real life, we can no longer appeal to the narrowly intellectual, scientific standpoint, but are driven to take account of the standpoint of feeling, and consequently of everything that the psyche actually contains. In practical psychology we are dealing not with any generalized human psyche, but with individual human beings and the multitudinous problems that oppress them. A psychology that satisfies the intellect alone can never be practical, for the totality of the psyche can never be grasped by intellect alone. Whether we will or no, philosophy keeps breaking through, because the psyche seeks an expression that will embrace its total nature.

II

THE RELATIONS BETWEEN THE
EGO AND THE UNCONSCIOUS

PREFACE TO THE SECOND EDITION (1935)

This little book is the outcome of a lecture which was originally published in 1916 under the title "La Structure de l'inconscient."[1] This same lecture later appeared in English under the title "The Conception of the Unconscious" in my *Collected Papers on Analytical Psychology*.[2] I mention these facts because I wish to place it on record that the present essay is not making its first appearance, but is rather the expression of a long-standing endeavour to grasp and—at least in its essential features—to depict the strange character and course of that *drame intérieur*, the transformation process of the unconscious psyche. This idea of the independence of the unconscious, which distinguishes my views so radically from those of Freud, came to me as far back as 1902, when I was engaged in studying the psychic history of a young girl somnambulist.[3] In a lecture given in Zurich [1908] on "The Content of the Psychoses," I approached this idea from another side. In 1912, I illustrated some of the main points of the process in an individual case and at the same time I indicated the historical and ethnological parallels to these seemingly universal psychic events.[4] In the above-mentioned essay, "La Structure de l'inconscient," I attempted for the first time to give a comprehensive account of the whole process. It was a mere attempt, of whose inadequacy I was painfully aware. The difficulties presented by the material were so great that I could not hope to do them anything like justice in a single essay. I therefore let it rest at the stage of an "interim report," with the firm intention of returning to this theme at a later opportunity. Twelve years of further experience enabled me, in 1928, to undertake a thorough revision of my formulations of 1916, and the result of these labours was the little book *Die Beziehungen*

[1] Cf. below, pars. 442ff.: "The Structure of the Unconscious."
[2] 2nd edn., London, 1917; New York, 1920.
[3] "On the Psychology and Pathology of So-called Occult Phenomena."
[4] *Wandlungen und Symbole der Libido* (Leipzig and Vienna, 1912); trans. by Beatrice M. Hinkle as *Psychology of the Unconscious* (New York, 1916; London, 1917). [Rewritten as *Symbole der Wandlung* (Zurich, 1952), trans. in *Coll. Works*, Vol. 5: *Symbols of Transformation.*—EDITORS.]

zwischen dem Ich und dem Unbewussten. [5] This time I tried to describe chiefly the relation of the ego-consciousness to the unconscious process. Following this intention, I concerned myself more particularly with those phenomena which are to be regarded as the reactive symptoms of the conscious personality to the influences of the unconscious. In this way I tried to effect an indirect approach to the unconscious process itself. These investigations have not yet come to a satisfactory conclusion, for the answer to the crucial problem of the nature and essence of the unconscious process has still to be found. I would not venture upon this exceedingly difficult task without the fullest possible experience. Its solution is reserved for the future.

I trust the reader of this book will bear with me if I beg him to regard it—should he persevere—as an earnest attempt on my part to form an intellectual conception of a new and hitherto unexplored field of experience. It is not concerned with a clever system of thought, but with the formulation of complex psychic experiences which have never yet been the subject of scientific study. Since the psyche is an irrational datum and cannot, in accordance with the old picture, be equated with a more or less divine Reason, it should not surprise us if in the course of psychological experience we come across, with extreme frequency, processes and happenings which run counter to our rational expectations and are therefore rejected by the rationalistic attitude of our conscious mind. Such an attitude is naturally not very skilled at psychological observation because it is in the highest degree unscientific. We must not attempt to tell nature what to do if we want to observe her operations undisturbed.

It is twenty-eight years of psychological and psychiatric experience that I am trying to sum up here, so perhaps my little book may lay some claim to serious consideration. Naturally I could not say everything in this single exposition. The reader will find a development of the last chapter, [with reference to the concept of the self], in my commentary to *The Secret of the Golden Flower,* the book I brought out in collaboration with my friend Richard Wilhelm. I did not wish to omit reference to this publication, because Oriental philosophy has been con-

5 [Trans. by H. G. and C. F. Baynes as "The Relations Between the Ego and the Unconscious" in *Two Essays on Analytical Psychology* (London and New York, 1928).]

cerned with these interior psychic processes for many hundreds of years and is therefore, in view of the great need for comparative material, of inestimable value in psychological research.

October 1934   C. G. JUNG

PREFACE TO THE THIRD EDITION (1938)

The new edition is published without changes. Since this work first appeared no new points of view have emerged which might have made revisions desirable. I would like to preserve the character of this little book—an unpretentious introduction to the psychological problems of the process of individuation—and not burden it with copious details that might limit its readability.

April 1938   C. G. JUNG

PART ONE

THE EFFECTS OF THE UNCONSCIOUS
UPON CONSCIOUSNESS

I

THE PERSONAL AND THE COLLECTIVE
UNCONSCIOUS

202   In Freud's view, as most people know, the contents of the
unconscious are reducible to infantile tendencies which are repressed because of their incompatible character. Repression is a
process that begins in early childhood under the moral influence
of the environment and continues throughout life. By means of
analysis the repressions are removed and the repressed wishes
made conscious.

203   According to this theory, the unconscious contains only
those parts of the personality which could just as well be conscious, and have been suppressed only through the process of
education. Although from one point of view the infantile tendencies of the unconscious are the most conspicuous, it would
nonetheless be a mistake to define or evaluate the unconscious
entirely in these terms. The unconscious has still another side to
it: it includes not only repressed contents, but all psychic material that lies below the threshold of consciousness. It is impossible to explain the subliminal nature of all this material on the
principle of repression, for in that case the removal of repression
ought to endow a person with a prodigious memory which would
thenceforth forget nothing.

204   We therefore emphatically affirm that in addition to the repressed material the unconscious contains all those psychic components that have fallen below the threshold, as well as sub-

127

liminal sense-perceptions. Moreover we know, from abundant experience as well as for theoretical reasons, that the unconscious also contains all the material that has *not yet* reached the threshold of consciousness. These are the seeds of future conscious contents. Equally we have reason to suppose that the unconscious is never quiescent in the sense of being inactive, but is ceaselessly engaged in grouping and regrouping its contents. This activity should be thought of as completely autonomous only in pathological cases; normally it is co-ordinated with the conscious mind in a compensatory relationship.

205   It is to be assumed that all these contents are of a personal nature in so far as they are acquired during the individual's life. Since this life is limited, the number of acquired contents in the unconscious must also be limited. This being so, it might be thought possible to empty the unconscious either by analysis or by making a complete inventory of the unconscious contents, on the ground that the unconscious cannot produce anything more than what is already known and assimilated into consciousness. We should also have to suppose, as already said, that if one could arrest the descent of conscious contents into the unconscious by doing away with repression, unconscious productivity would be paralysed. This is possible only to a very limited extent, as we know from experience. We urge our patients to hold fast to repressed contents that have been re-associated with consciousness, and to assimilate them into their plan of life. But this procedure, as we may daily convince ourselves, makes no impression on the unconscious, since it calmly goes on producing dreams and fantasies which, according to Freud's original theory, must arise from personal repressions. If in such cases we pursue our observations systematically and without prejudice, we shall find material which, although similar in form to the previous personal contents, yet seems to contain allusions that go far beyond the personal sphere.

206   Casting about in my mind for an example to illustrate what I have just said, I have a particularly vivid memory of a woman patient with a mild hysterical neurosis which, as we expressed it in those days [about 1910], had its principal cause in a "father-complex." By this we wanted to denote the fact that the patient's peculiar relationship to her father stood in her way. She had been on very good terms with her father, who had since

died. It was a relationship chiefly of feeling. In such cases it is usually the intellectual function that is developed, and this later becomes the bridge to the world. Accordingly our patient became a student of philosophy. Her energetic pursuit of knowledge was motivated by her need to extricate herself from the emotional entanglement with her father. This operation may succeed if her feelings can find an outlet on the new intellectual level, perhaps in the formation of an emotional tie with a suitable man, equivalent to the former tie. In this particular case, however, the transition refused to take place, because the patient's feelings remained suspended, oscillating between her father and a man who was not altogether suitable. The progress of her life was thus held up, and that inner disunity so characteristic of a neurosis promptly made its appearance. The so-called normal person would probably be able to break the emotional bond in one or the other direction by a powerful act of will, or else—and this is perhaps the more usual thing—he would come through the difficulty unconsciously, on the smooth path of instinct, without ever being aware of the sort of conflict that lay behind his headaches or other physical discomforts. But any weakness of instinct (which may have many causes) is enough to hinder a smooth unconscious transition. Then all progress is delayed by conflict, and the resulting stasis of life is equivalent to a neurosis. In consequence of the standstill, psychic energy flows off in every conceivable direction, apparently quite uselessly. For instance, there are excessive innervations of the sympathetic system, which lead to nervous disorders of the stomach and intestines; or the vagus (and consequently the heart) is stimulated; or fantasies and memories, uninteresting enough in themselves, become overvalued and prey on the conscious mind (mountains out of molehills). In this state a new motive is needed to put an end to the morbid suspension. Nature herself paves the way for this, unconsciously and indirectly, through the phenomenon of the transference (Freud). In the course of treatment the patient transfers the father-imago to the doctor, thus making him, in a sense, the father, and in the sense that he is *not* the father, also making him a substitute for the man she cannot reach. The doctor therefore becomes both a father and a kind of lover—in other words, an object of conflict. In him the opposites are united, and for this reason he stands for a quasi-ideal solution of the conflict. Without in the least wishing it, he draws upon himself an over-valuation that is almost incredible to the outsider, for to the patient he seems like a saviour or a god. This way of speaking is not altogether so laughable as it sounds. It is indeed a bit much to be a father and lover at once. Nobody could possibly stand up to it in the long run, precisely because it is too much of a good thing. One would have to be a demigod at least to sustain such a role without a break, for all the time one would have to be the giver. To the patient in the state of transference, this provisional solution naturally seems ideal, but only at first; in the end she comes to a standstill that is just as bad as the neurotic conflict was. Fundamentally, nothing has yet happened that might lead to a real solution. The conflict has merely been transferred. Nevertheless a successful transference can—at least temporarily—cause the whole neurosis to disappear, and for this reason it has been very rightly recognized by Freud as a healing factor of first-rate importance, but, at the same time, as a provisional state only, for although it holds out the possibility of a cure, it is far from being the cure itself.

207   This somewhat lengthy discussion seemed to me essential if my example was to be understood, for my patient had arrived at the state of transference and had already reached the upper limit where the standstill begins to make itself disagreeable. The question now arose: what next? I had of course become the complete saviour, and the thought of having to give me up was not only exceedingly distasteful to the patient, but positively terrifying. In such a situation "sound common sense" generally comes out with a whole repertory of admonitions: "you simply must," "you really ought," "you just cannot," etc. So far as sound common sense is, happily, not too rare and not entirely without effect (pessimists, I know, exist), a rational motive can, in the exuberant feeling of buoyancy you get from the transference, release so much enthusiasm that a painful sacrifice can be risked with a mighty effort of will. If successful—and these things sometimes are—the sacrifice bears blessed fruit, and the erstwhile patient leaps at one bound into the state of being practically cured. The doctor is generally so delighted that he fails to tackle the theoretical difficulties connected with this little miracle.

208   If the leap does not succeed—and it did not succeed with my patient—one is then faced with the problem of resolving the

transference. Here "psychoanalytic" theory shrouds itself in a thick darkness. Apparently we are to fall back on some nebulous trust in fate: somehow or other the matter will settle itself. "The transference stops automatically when the patient runs out of money," as a slightly cynical colleague once remarked to me. Or the ineluctable demands of life make it impossible for the patient to linger on in the transference—demands which compel the involuntary sacrifice, sometimes with a more or less complete relapse as a result. (One may look in vain for accounts of such cases in the books that sing the praises of psychoanalysis!)

209 To be sure, there are hopeless cases where nothing helps; but there are also cases that do not get stuck and do not inevitably leave the transference situation with bitter hearts and sore heads. I told myself, at this juncture with my patient, that there must be a clear and respectable way out of the impasse. My patient had long since run out of money—if indeed she ever possessed any—but I was curious to know what means nature would devise for a satisfactory way out of the transference deadlock. Since I never imagined that I was blessed with that "sound common sense" which always knows exactly what to do in every quandary, and since my patient knew as little as I, I suggested to her that we could at least keep an eye open for any movements coming from a sphere of the psyche uncontaminated by our superior wisdom and our conscious plannings. That meant first and foremost her dreams.

210 Dreams contain images and thought-associations which we do not create with conscious intent. They arise spontaneously without our assistance and are representatives of a psychic activity withdrawn from our arbitrary will. Therefore the dream is, properly speaking, a highly objective, natural product of the psyche, from which we might expect indications, or at least hints, about certain basic trends in the psychic process. Now, since the psychic process, like any other life-process, is not just a causal sequence, but is also a process with a teleological orientation, we might expect dreams to give us certain *indicia* about the objective causality as well as about the objective tendencies, precisely because dreams are nothing less than self-representations of the psychic life-process.

211 On the basis of these reflections, then, we subjected the dreams to a careful examination. It would lead too far to quote

word for word all the dreams that now followed. Let it suffice to sketch their main character: the majority referred to the person of the doctor, that is to say, the actors were unmistakably the dreamer herself and her doctor. The latter, however, seldom appeared in his natural shape, but was generally distorted in a remarkable way. Sometimes his figure was of supernatural size, sometimes he seemed to be extremely aged, then again he resembled her father, but was at the same time curiously woven into nature, as in the following dream: *Her father (who in reality was of small stature) was standing with her on a hill that was covered with wheat-fields. She was quite tiny beside him, and he seemed to her like a giant. He lifted her up from the ground and held her in his arms like a little child. The wind swept over the wheat-fields, and as the wheat swayed in the wind, he rocked her in his arms.*

212   From this dream and from others like it I could discern various things. Above all I got the impression that her unconscious was holding unshakably to the idea of my being the father-lover, so that the fatal tie we were trying to undo appeared to be doubly strengthened. Moreover one could hardly avoid seeing that the unconscious placed a special emphasis on the supernatural, almost "divine" nature of the father-lover, thus accentuating still further the over-valuation occasioned by the transference. I therefore asked myself whether the patient had still not understood the wholly fantastic character of her transference, or whether perhaps the unconscious could never be reached by understanding at all, but must blindly and idiotically pursue some nonsensical chimera. Freud's idea that the unconscious can "do nothing but wish," Schopenhauer's blind and aimless Will, the gnostic demiurge who in his vanity deems himself perfect and then in the blindness of his limitation creates something lamentably imperfect—all these pessimistic suspicions of an essentially negative background to the world and the soul came threateningly near. And there would indeed be nothing to set against this except a well-meaning "you ought," reinforced by a stroke of the axe that would cut down the whole phantasmagoria for good and all.

213   But, as I turned the dreams over and over in my mind, there dawned on me another possibility. I said to myself: it cannot be denied that the dreams continue to speak in the same old meta-

phors with which our conversations have made the patient as well as myself sickeningly familiar. But the patient has an undoubted understanding of her transference fantasy. She knows that I appear to her as a semi-divine father-lover, and she can, at least intellectually, distinguish this from my factual reality. Therefore the dreams are obviously reiterating the conscious standpoint minus the conscious criticism, which they completely ignore. They reiterate the conscious contents, not *in toto,* but insist on the fantastic standpoint as opposed to "sound common sense."

214   I naturally asked myself what was the source of this obstinacy and what was its purpose? That it must have some purposive meaning I was convinced, for there is no truly living thing that does not have a final meaning, that can in other words be explained as a mere left-over from antecedent facts. But the energy of the transference is so strong that it gives one the impression of a vital instinct. That being so, what is the purpose of such fantasies? A careful examination and analysis of the dreams, especially of the one just quoted, revealed a very marked tendency—in contrast to conscious criticism, which always seeks to reduce things to human proportions—to endow the person of the doctor with superhuman attributes. He had to be gigantic, primordial, huger than the father, like the wind that sweeps over the earth—was he then to be made into a god? Or, I said to myself, was it rather the case that the unconscious was trying to *create* a god out of the person of the doctor, as it were to free a vision of God from the veils of the personal, so that the transference to the person of the doctor was no more than a misunderstanding on the part of the conscious mind, a stupid trick played by "sound common sense"? Was the urge of the unconscious perhaps only apparently reaching out towards the person, but in a deeper sense towards a god? Could the longing for a god be a *passion* welling up from our darkest, instinctual nature, a passion unswayed by any outside influences, deeper and stronger perhaps than the love for a human person? Or was it perhaps the highest and truest meaning of that inappropriate love we call "transference," a little bit of real *Gottesminne,* that has been lost to consciousness ever since the fifteenth century?

215   No one will doubt the reality of a passionate longing for a human person; but that a fragment of religious psychology, an

historical anachronism, indeed something of a medieval curiosity—we are reminded of Mechtild of Magdeburg—should come to light as an immediate living reality in the middle of the consulting-room, and be expressed in the prosaic figure of the doctor, seems almost too fantastic to be taken seriously.

216   A genuinely scientific attitude must be unprejudiced. The sole criterion for the validity of an hypothesis is whether or not it possesses an heuristic—i.e., explanatory—value. The question now is, can we regard the possibilities set forth above as a valid hypothesis? There is no *a priori* reason why it should not be just as possible that the unconscious tendencies have a goal beyond the human person, as that the unconscious can "do nothing but wish." Experience alone can decide which is the more suitable hypothesis. This new hypothesis was not entirely plausible to my very critical patient. The earlier view that I was the father-lover, and as such presented an ideal solution of the conflict, was incomparably more attractive to her way of feeling. Nevertheless her intellect was sufficiently keen to appreciate the theoretical possibility of the new hypothesis. Meanwhile the dreams continued to disintegrate the person of the doctor and swell him to ever vaster proportions. Concurrently with this there now occurred something which at first I alone perceived, and with the utmost astonishment, namely a kind of subterranean undermining of the transference. Her relations with a certain friend deepened perceptibly, notwithstanding the fact that consciously she still clung to the transference. So that when the time came for leaving me, it was no catastrophe, but a perfectly reasonable parting. I had the privilege of being the only witness during the process of severance. I saw how the transpersonal control-point developed—I cannot call it anything else—a *guiding function* and step by step gathered to itself all the former personal over-valuations; how, with this afflux of energy, it gained influence over the resisting conscious mind without the patient's consciously noticing what was happening. From this I realized that the dreams were not just fantasies, but self-representations of unconscious developments which allowed the psyche of the patient gradually to grow out of the pointless personal tie.[1]

217   This change took place, as I showed, through the unconscious development of a transpersonal control-point; a virtual

[1] Cf. the "transcendent function" in *Psychological Types*, Def. 51, "Symbol."

goal, as it were, that expressed itself symbolically in a form which can only be described as a vision of God. The dreams swelled the human person of the doctor to superhuman proportions, making him a gigantic primordial father who is at the same time the wind, and in whose protecting arms the dreamer rests like an infant. If we try to make the patient's conscious, and traditionally Christian, idea of God responsible for the divine image in the dreams, we would still have to lay stress on the distortion. In religious matters the patient had a critical and agnostic attitude, and her idea of a possible deity had long since passed into the realm of the inconceivable, i.e., had dwindled into a complete abstraction. In contrast to this, the god-image of the dreams corresponded to the archaic conception of a nature-daemon, something like Wotan. Θεὸς τὸ πνεῦμα, 'God is spirit,' is here translated back into its original form where πνεῦμα means 'wind': God is the wind, stronger and mightier than man, an invisible breath-spirit. As in Hebrew *ruah,* so in Arabic *ruh* means breath and spirit.[2] Out of the purely personal form the dreams develop an archaic god-image that is infinitely far from the conscious idea of God. It might be objected that this is simply an infantile image, a childhood memory. I would have no quarrel with this assumption if we were dealing with an old man sitting on a golden throne in heaven. But there is no trace of any sentimentality of that kind; instead, we have a primordial idea that can correspond only to an archaic mentality.

218   These primordial ideas, of which I have given a great many examples in my *Symbols of Transformation,* oblige one to make, in regard to unconscious material, a distinction of quite a different character from that between "preconscious" and "unconscious" or "subconscious" and "unconscious." The justification for these distinctions need not be discussed here. They have their specific value and are worth elaborating further as points of view. The fundamental distinction which experience has forced upon me claims to be no more than that. It should be evident from the foregoing that we have to distinguish in the unconscious a layer which we may call the *personal unconscious.* The materials contained in this layer are of a personal nature in so far as they have the character partly of acquisitions derived

[2] For a fuller elaboration of this theme see *Symbols of Transformation,* index, s.v. "wind."

from the individual's life and partly of psychological factors which could just as well be conscious. It can readily be understood that incompatible psychological elements are liable to repression and therefore become unconscious. But on the other hand this implies the possibility of making and keeping the repressed contents conscious once they have been recognized. We recognize them as personal contents because their effects, or their partial manifestation, or their source can be discovered in our personal past. They are the integral components of the personality, they belong to its inventory, and their loss to consciousness produces an inferiority in one respect or another—an inferiority, moreover, that has the psychological character not so much of an organic lesion or an inborn defect as of a lack which gives rise to a feeling of moral resentment. The sense of moral inferiority always indicates that the missing element is something which, to judge by this feeling about it, really ought not be missing, or which could be made conscious if only one took sufficient trouble. The moral inferiority does not come from a collision with the generally accepted and, in a sense, arbitrary moral law, but from the conflict with one's own self which, for reasons of psychic equilibrium, demands that the deficit be redressed. Whenever a sense of moral inferiority appears, it indicates not only a need to assimilate an unconscious component, but also the possibility of such assimilation. In the last resort it is a man's moral qualities which force him, either through direct recognition of the need or indirectly through a painful neurosis, to assimilate his unconscious self and to keep himself fully conscious. Whoever progresses along this road of self-realization must inevitably bring into consciousness the contents of the personal unconscious, thus enlarging the scope of his personality. I should add at once that this enlargement has to do primarily with one's moral consciousness, one's knowledge of oneself, for the unconscious contents that are released and brought into consciousness by analysis are usually unpleasant—which is precisely why these wishes, memories, tendencies, plans, etc. were repressed. These are the contents that are brought to light in much the same way by a thorough confession, though to a much more limited extent. The rest comes out as a rule in dream analysis. It is often very interesting to watch how the dreams fetch up the essential points, bit by bit and with the nicest choice.

The total material that is added to consciousness causes a considerable widening of the horizon, a deepened self-knowledge which, more than anything else, one would think, is calculated to humanize a man and make him modest. But even self-knowledge, assumed by all wise men to be the best and most efficacious, has different effects on different characters. We make very remarkable discoveries in this respect in practical analysis, but I shall deal with this question in the next chapter.

219   As my example of the archaic idea of God shows, the unconscious seems to contain other things besides personal acquisitions and belongings. My patient was quite unconscious of the derivation of "spirit" from "wind," or of the parallelism between the two. This content was not the product of her thinking, nor had she ever been taught it. The critical passage in the New Testament was inaccessible to her—τὸ πνεῦμα πνεῖ ὅπου θέλει —since she knew no Greek. If we must take it as a wholly personal acquisition, it might be a case of so-called cryptomnesia,[3] the unconscious recollection of a thought which the dreamer had once read somewhere. I have nothing against such a possibility in this particular case; but I have seen a sufficient number of other cases—many of them are to be found in the book mentioned above—where cryptomnesia can be excluded with certainty. Even if it were a case of cryptomnesia, which seems to me very improbable, we should still have to explain what the predisposition was that caused just this image to be retained and later, as Semon puts it, "ecphorated" (ἐκφορεῖν, Latin efferre, 'to produce'). In any case, cryptomnesia or no cryptomnesia, we are dealing with a genuine and thoroughly primitive god-image that grew up in the unconscious of a civilized person and produced a living effect—an effect which might well give the psychologist of religion food for reflection. There is nothing about this image that could be called personal: it is a wholly collective image, the ethnic origin of which has long been known to us. Here is an historical image of world-wide distribution that has come into existence again through a natural psychic function. This is not so very surprising, since my patient was born into the

---

3 Cf. Flournoy, Des Indes à la planète Mars: Étude sur un cas de somnambulisme avec glossolalie (trans. by D. B. Vermilye as From India to the Planet Mars), and Jung, "Psychology and Pathology of So-called Occult Phenomena," pars. 138ff.

world with a human brain which presumably still functions to-day much as it did of old. We are dealing with a reactivated *archetype,* as I have elsewhere called these primordial images.[4] These ancient images are restored to life by the primitive, ana-logical mode of thinking peculiar to dreams. It is not a question of inherited ideas, but of inherited thought-patterns.[5]

220   In view of these facts we must assume that the unconscious contains not only personal, but also impersonal collective com-ponents in the form of inherited categories[6] or archetypes. I have therefore advanced the hypothesis that at its deeper levels the unconscious possesses collective contents in a relatively ac-tive state. That is why I speak of a collective unconscious.

[4] Cf. *Psychological Types,* Def. 26.

[5] Consequently, the accusation of "fanciful mysticism" levelled at my ideas is lacking in foundation.

[6] Hubert and Mauss, *Mélanges d'histoire des religions,* p. xxix.

II

PHENOMENA RESULTING FROM
THE ASSIMILATION OF
THE UNCONSCIOUS

221   The process of assimilating the unconscious leads to some
very remarkable phenomena. It produces in some patients an
unmistakable and often unpleasant increase of self-confidence
and conceit: they are full of themselves, they know everything,
they imagine themselves to be fully informed of everything concerning their unconscious, and are persuaded that they understand perfectly everything that comes out of it. At every
interview with the doctor they get more and more above themselves. Others on the contrary feel themselves more and more
crushed under the contents of the unconscious, they lose their
self-confidence and abandon themselves with dull resignation to
all the extraordinary things that the unconscious produces. The
former, overflowing with feelings of their own importance, assume a responsibility for the unconscious that goes much too far,
beyond all reasonable bounds; the others finally give up all sense
of responsibility, overcome by a sense of the powerlessness of the
ego against the fate working through the unconscious.

222   If we analyse these two modes of reaction more deeply, we
find that the optimistic self-confidence of the first conceals a profound sense of impotence, for which their conscious optimism
acts as an unsuccessful compensation; while the pessimistic resignation of the others masks a defiant will to power, far surpassing in cocksureness the conscious optimism of the first type.

223   With these two modes of reaction I have sketched only two
crude extremes. A finer shading would have been truer to reality. As I have said elsewhere, every analysand starts by unconsciously misusing his newly won knowledge in the interests of
his abnormal, neurotic attitude, unless he is sufficiently freed
from his symptoms in the early stages to be able to dispense with
further treatment altogether. A very important contributory

factor is that in the early stages everything is still understood on the objective level, i.e., without distinction between imago and object, so that everything is referred directly to the object. Hence the man for whom "other people" are the objects of prime importance will conclude from any self-knowledge he may have imbibed at this stage of the analysis: "Aha! so that is what other people are like!" He will therefore feel it his duty, according to his nature, tolerant or otherwise, to enlighten the world. But the other man, who feels himself to be more the object of his fellows than their subject, will be weighed down by this self-knowledge and become correspondingly depressed. (I am naturally leaving out of account those numerous and more superficial natures who experience these problems only by the way.) In both cases the relation to the object is reinforced—in the first case in an active, in the second case in a reactive sense. The collective element is markedly accentuated. The one extends the sphere of his action, the other the sphere of his suffering.

224   Adler has employed the term "godlikeness" to characterize certain basic features of neurotic power psychology. If I likewise borrow the same term from *Faust*, I use it here more in the sense of that well-known passage where Mephisto writes "Eritis sicut Deus, scientes bonum et malum" in the student's album, and makes the following aside:

> Just follow the old advice
> And my cousin the snake.
> There'll come a time when your godlikeness
> Will make you quiver and quake.[1]

The godlikeness evidently refers to knowledge, the knowledge of good and evil. The analysis and conscious realization of unconscious contents engender a certain superior tolerance, thanks to which even relatively indigestible portions of one's unconscious characterology can be accepted. This tolerance may look very wise and superior, but often it is no more than a grand gesture that brings all sorts of consequences in its train. Two spheres have been brought together which before were kept anxiously apart. After considerable resistances have been overcome, the union of opposites is successfully achieved, at least to

[1] *Faust,* Part I, 3rd scene in Faust's study.

all appearances. The deeper understanding thus gained, the juxtaposition of what was before separated, and hence the apparent overcoming of the moral conflict, give rise to a feeling of superiority that may well be expressed by the term "godlikeness." But this same juxtaposition of good and evil can have a very different effect on a different kind of temperament. Not everyone will feel himself a superman, holding in his hands the scales of good and evil. It may also seem as though he were a helpless object caught between hammer and anvil; not in the least a Hercules at the parting of the ways, but rather a rudderless ship buffeted between Scylla and Charybdis. For without knowing it, he is caught up in perhaps the greatest and most ancient of human conflicts, experiencing the throes of eternal principles in collision. Well might he feel himself like a Prometheus chained to the Caucasus, or as one crucified. This would be a "godlikeness" in suffering. Godlikeness is certainly not a scientific concept, although it aptly characterizes the psychological state in question. Nor do I imagine that every reader will immediately grasp the peculiar state of mind implied by "godlikeness." The term belongs too exclusively to the sphere of *belles-lettres*. So I should probably be better advised to give a more circumspect description of this state. The insight and understanding, then, gained by the analysand usually reveal much to him that was before unconscious. He naturally applies this knowledge to his environment; in consequence he sees, or thinks he sees, many things that before were invisible. Since his knowledge was helpful to him, he readily assumes that it would be useful also to others. In this way he is liable to become arrogant; it may be well meant, but it is nonetheless annoying to other people. He feels as though he possesses a key that opens many, perhaps even all, doors. Psychoanalysis itself has this same bland unconsciousness of its limitations, as can clearly be seen from the way it meddles with works of art.

225   Since human nature is not compounded wholly of light, but also abounds in shadows, the insight gained in practical analysis is often somewhat painful, the more so if, as is generally the case, one has previously neglected the other side. Hence there are people who take their newly won insight very much to heart, far too much in fact, quite forgetting that they are not unique in having a shadow-side. They allow themselves to get unduly de-

pressed and are then inclined to doubt everything, finding nothing right anywhere. That is why many excellent analysts with very good ideas can never bring themselves to publish them, because the psychic problem, as they see it, is so overwhelmingly vast that it seems to them almost impossible to tackle it scientifically. One man's optimism makes him overweening, while another's pessimism makes him over-anxious and despondent. Such are the forms which the great conflict takes when reduced to a smaller scale. But even in these lesser proportions the essence of the conflict is easily recognized: the arrogance of the one and the despondency of the other share a common uncertainty as to their boundaries. The one is excessively expanded, the other excessively contracted. Their individual boundaries are in some way obliterated. If we now consider the fact that, as a result of psychic compensation, great humility stands very close to pride, and that "pride goeth before a fall," we can easily discover behind the haughtiness certain traits of an anxious sense of inferiority. In fact we shall see clearly how his uncertainty forces the enthusiast to puff up his truths, of which he feels none too sure, and to win proselytes to his side in order that his followers may prove to himself the value and trustworthiness of his own convictions. Nor is he altogether so happy in his fund of knowledge as to be able to hold out alone; at bottom he feels isolated by it, and the secret fear of being left alone with it induces him to trot out his opinions and interpretations in and out of season, because only when convincing someone else does he feel safe from gnawing doubts.

226   It is just the reverse with our despondent friend. The more he withdraws and hides himself, the greater becomes his secret need to be understood and recognized. Although he speaks of his inferiority he does not really believe it. There arises within him a defiant conviction of his unrecognized merits, and in consequence he is sensitive to the slightest disapprobation, always wearing the stricken air of one who is misunderstood and deprived of his rightful due. In this way he nurses a morbid pride and an insolent discontent—which is the very last thing he wants and for which his environment has to pay all the more dearly.

227   Both are at once too small and too big; their individual mean, never very secure, now becomes shakier than ever. It

sounds almost grotesque to describe such a state as "godlike." But since each in his way steps beyond his human proportions, both of them are a little "superhuman" and therefore, figuratively speaking, godlike. If we wish to avoid the use of this metaphor, I would suggest that we speak instead of "psychic inflation." The term seems to me appropriate in so far as the state we are discussing involves an extension of the personality beyond individual limits, in other words, a state of being puffed up. In such a state a man fills a space which normally he cannot fill. He can only fill it by appropriating to himself contents and qualities which properly exist for themselves alone and should therefore remain outside our bounds. What lies outside ourselves belongs either to someone else, or to everyone, or to no one. Since psychic inflation is by no means a phenomenon induced exclusively by analysis, but occurs just as often in ordinary life, we can investigate it equally well in other cases. A very common instance is the humourless way in which many men identify themselves with their business or their titles. The office I hold is certainly my special activity; but it is also a collective factor that has come into existence historically through the cooperation of many people and whose dignity rests solely on collective approval. When, therefore, I identify myself with my office or title, I behave as though I myself were the whole complex of social factors of which that office consists, or as though I were not only the bearer of the office, but also and at the same time the approval of society. I have made an extraordinary extension of myself and have usurped qualities which are not in me but outside me. *L'état c'est moi* is the motto for such people.

228   In the case of inflation through knowledge we are dealing with something similar in principle, though psychologically more subtle. Here it is not the dignity of an office that causes the inflation, but very significant fantasies. I will explain what I mean by a practical example, choosing a mental case whom I happened to know personally and who is also mentioned in a publication by Maeder.[2] The case is characterized by a high degree of inflation. (In mental cases we can observe all the phenomena that are present only fleetingly in normal people, in a

2 Maeder, "Psychologische Untersuchungen an Dementia-Praecox-Kranken" (1910), pp. 209ff.

cruder and enlarged form.) [3] The patient suffered from paranoid dementia with megalomania. He was in telephonic communication with the Mother of God and other great ones. In human reality he was a wretched locksmith's apprentice who at the age of nineteen had become incurably insane. He had never been blessed with intelligence, but he had, among other things, hit upon the magnificent idea that the world was his picture-book, the pages of which he could turn at will. The proof was quite simple: he had only to turn round, and there was a new page for him to see.

229   This is Schopenhauer's "world as will and idea" in unadorned, primitive concreteness of vision. A shattering idea indeed, born of extreme alienation and seclusion from the world, but so naïvely and simply expressed that at first one can only smile at the grotesqueness of it. And yet this primitive way of looking lies at the very heart of Schopenhauer's brilliant vision of the world. Only a genius or a madman could so disentangle himself from the bonds of reality as to see the world as his picture-book. Did the patient actually work out or build up such a vision, or did it just befall him? Or did he perhaps fall into it? His pathological disintegration and inflation point rather to the latter. It is no longer *he* that thinks and speaks, but *it* thinks and speaks within him: he hears voices. So the difference between him and Schopenhauer is that, in him, the vision remained at the stage of a mere spontaneous growth, while Schopenhauer abstracted it and expressed it in language of universal validity. In so doing he raised it out of its subterranean beginnings into the clear light of collective consciousness. But it would be quite wrong to suppose that the patient's vision had a purely personal character or value, as though it were something that belonged to him. If that were so, he would be a philosopher. A man is a philosopher of genius only when he succeeds in transmuting the primitive and merely natural vision into an abstract idea be-

[3] When I was still a doctor at the psychiatric clinic in Zurich, I once took an intelligent layman through the sick-wards. He had never seen a lunatic asylum from the inside before. When we had finished our round, he exclaimed, "I tell you, it's just like Zurich in miniature! A quintessence of the population. It is as though all the types one meets every day on the streets had been assembled here in their classical purity. Nothing but oddities and picked specimens from top to bottom of society!" I had never looked at it from this angle before, but my friend was not far wrong.

longing to the common stock of consciousness. This achievement, and this alone, constitutes his personal value, for which he may take credit without necessarily succumbing to inflation. But the sick man's vision is an impersonal value, a natural growth against which he is powerless to defend himself, by which he is actually swallowed up and "wafted" clean out of the world. Far from *his* mastering the idea and expanding *it* into a philosophical view of the world, it is truer to say that the undoubted grandeur of his vision blew *him* up to pathological proportions. The personal value lies entirely in the philosophical achievement, not in the primary vision. To the philosopher as well this vision comes as so much increment, and is simply a part of the common property of mankind, in which, in principle, everyone has a share. The golden apples drop from the same tree, whether they be gathered by an imbecile locksmith's apprentice or by a Schopenhauer.

230   There is, however, yet another thing to be learnt from this example, namely that these transpersonal contents are not just inert or dead matter that can be annexed at will. Rather they are living entities which exert an attractive force upon the conscious mind. Identification with one's office or one's title is very attractive indeed, which is precisely why so many men are nothing more than the decorum accorded to them by society. In vain would one look for a personality behind the husk. Underneath all the padding one would find a very pitiable little creature. That is why the office—or whatever this outer husk may be—is so attractive: it offers easy compensation for personal deficiencies.

231   Outer attractions, such as offices, titles, and other social regalia are not the only things that cause inflation. These are simply impersonal quantities that lie outside in society, in the collective consciousness. But just as there is a society outside the individual, so there is a collective psyche outside the personal psyche, namely the collective unconscious, concealing, as the above example shows, elements that are no whit less attractive. And just as a man may suddenly step into the world on his professional dignity ("Messieurs, à présent je suis Roy"), so another may disappear out of it equally suddenly when it is his lot to behold one of those mighty images that put a new face upon the world. These are the magical *représentations collectives* which underlie the slogan, the catchword, and, on a higher level, the lan-

guage of the poet and mystic. I am reminded of another mental case who was neither a poet nor anything very outstanding, just a naturally quiet and rather sentimental youth. He had fallen in love with a girl and, as so often happens, had failed to ascertain whether his love was requited. His primitive *participation mystique* took it for granted that his agitations were plainly the agitations of the other, which on the lower levels of human psychology is naturally very often the case. Thus he built up a sentimental love-fantasy which precipitately collapsed when he discovered that the girl would have none of him. He was so desperate that he went straight to the river to drown himself. It was late at night, and the stars gleamed up at him from the dark water. It seemed to him that the stars were swimming two by two down the river, and a wonderful feeling came over him. He forgot his suicidal intentions and gazed fascinated at the strange, sweet drama. And gradually he became aware that every star was a face, and that all these pairs were lovers, who were carried along locked in a dreaming embrace. An entirely new understanding came to him: all had changed—his fate, his disappointment, even his love, receded and fell away. The memory of the girl grew distant, blurred; but instead, he felt with complete certainty that untold riches were promised him. He knew that an immense treasure lay hidden for him in the neighbouring observatory. The result was that he was arrested by the police at four o'clock in the morning, attempting to break into the observatory.

232   What had happened? His poor head had glimpsed a Dantesque vision, whose loveliness he could never have grasped had he read it in a poem. But he saw it, and it transformed him. What had hurt him most was now far away; a new and undreamed-of world of stars, tracing their silent courses far beyond this grievous earth, had opened out to him the moment he crossed "Proserpine's threshold." The intuition of untold wealth—and could any fail to be touched by this thought?—came to him like a revelation. For his poor turnip-head it was too much. He did not drown in the river, but in an eternal image, and its beauty perished with him.

233   Just as one man may disappear in his social role, so another may be engulfed in an inner vision and be lost to his surroundings. Many fathomless transformations of personality, like sud-

den conversions and other far-reaching changes of mind, originate in the attractive power of a collective image,[4] which, as the present example shows, can cause such a high degree of inflation that the entire personality is disintegrated. This disintegration is a mental disease, of a transitory or a permanent nature, a "splitting of the mind" or "schizophrenia," in Bleuler's term.[5] The pathological inflation naturally depends on some innate weakness of the personality against the autonomy of collective unconscious contents.

234 We shall probably get nearest to the truth if we think of the conscious and personal psyche as resting upon the broad basis of an inherited and universal psychic disposition which is as such unconscious, and that our personal psyche bears the same relation to the collective psyche as the individual to society.

235 But equally, just as the individual is not merely a unique and separate being, but is also a social being, so the human psyche is not a self-contained and wholly individual phenomenon, but also a collective one. And just as certain social functions or instincts are opposed to the interests of single individuals, so the human psyche exhibits certain functions or tendencies which, on account of their collective nature, are opposed to individual needs. The reason for this is that every man is born with a highly differentiated brain and is thus assured of a wide range of mental functioning which is neither developed ontogenetically nor acquired. But, to the degree that human brains are uniformly differentiated, the mental functioning thereby made possible is also collective and universal. This explains, for example, the interesting fact that the unconscious processes of the most widely separated peoples and races show a quite remarkable correspondence, which displays itself, among other things, in the extraordinary but well-authenticated analogies between the forms and motifs of autochthonous myths. The universal similarity of human brains leads to the universal possibility of a uniform mental functioning. This functioning is the *collective psyche*. Inasmuch as there are differentiations corresponding to race, tribe, and even family, there is also a collective psyche lim-

---

4 Cf. *Psychological Types*, Def. 26, "Image." Léon Daudet, in *L'Hérédo*, calls this process "autofécondation intérieure," by which he means the reawakening of an ancestral soul.

5 Bleuler, *Dementia Praecox or the Group of Schizophrenias* (orig. 1911).

ited to race, tribe, and family over and above the "universal" collective psyche. To borrow an expression from Pierre Janet,[6] the collective psyche comprises the *parties inférieures* of the psychic functions, that is to say those deep-rooted, well-nigh automatic portions of the individual psyche which are inherited and are to be found everywhere, and are thus impersonal or suprapersonal. Consciousness plus the personal unconscious constitutes the *parties supérieures* of the psychic functions, those portions, therefore, that are developed ontogenetically and acquired. Consequently, the individual who annexes the unconscious heritage of the collective psyche to what has accrued to him in the course of his ontogenetic development, as though it were part of the latter, enlarges the scope of his personality in an illegitimate way and suffers the consequences. In so far as the collective psyche comprises the *parties inférieures* of the psychic functions and thus forms the basis of every personality, it has the effect of crushing and devaluing the personality. This shows itself either in the aforementioned stifling of self-confidence or else in an unconscious heightening of the ego's importance to the point of a pathological will to power.

236   By raising the personal unconscious to consciousness, the analysis makes the subject aware of things which he is generally aware of in others, but never in himself. This discovery makes him therefore less individually unique, and more collective. His collectivization is not always a step to the bad; it may sometimes be a step to the good. There are people who repress their good qualities and consciously give free rein to their infantile desires. The lifting of personal repressions at first brings purely personal contents into consciousness; but attached to them are the collective elements of the unconscious, the ever-present instincts, qualities, and ideas (images) as well as all those "statistical" quotas of average virtue and average vice which we recognize when we say, "Everyone has in him something of the criminal, the genius, and the saint." Thus a living picture emerges, containing pretty well everything that moves upon the checkerboard of the world, the good and the bad, the fair and the foul. A sense of solidarity with the world is gradually built up, which is felt by many natures as something very positive and in certain cases actually is the deciding factor in the treatment of neurosis.

6 *Les Névroses* (1898).

I have myself seen cases who, in this condition, managed for the first time in their lives to arouse love, and even to experience it themselves; or, by daring to leap into the unknown, they get involved in the very fate for which they were suited. I have seen not a few who, taking this condition as final, remained for years in a state of enterprising euphoria. I have often heard such cases referred to as shining examples of analytical therapy. But I must point out that cases of this euphoric and enterprising type are so utterly lacking in differentiation from the world that nobody could pass them as fundamentally cured. To my way of thinking they are as much cured as not cured. I have had occasion to follow up the lives of such patients, and it must be owned that many of them showed symptoms of maladjustment, which, if persisted in, gradually leads to the sterility and monotony so characteristic of those who have divested themselves of their egos. Here too I am speaking of the border-line cases, and not of the less valuable, normal, average folk for whom the question of adaptation is more technical than problematical. If I were more of a therapist than an investigator, I would naturally be unable to check a certain optimism of judgment, because my eyes would then be glued to the number of cures. But my conscience as an investigator is concerned not with quantity but with quality. Nature is aristocratic, and one person of value outweighs ten lesser ones. My eye followed the valuable people, and from them I learned the dubiousness of the results of a purely personal analysis, and also to understand the reasons for this dubiousness.

237   If, through assimilation of the unconscious, we make the mistake of including the collective psyche in the inventory of personal psychic functions, a dissolution of the personality into its paired opposites inevitably follows. Besides the pair of opposites already discussed, megalomania and the sense of inferiority, which are so painfully evident in neurosis, there are many others, from which I will single out only the specifically moral pair of opposites, namely good and evil. The specific virtues and vices of humanity are contained in the collective psyche like everything else. One man arrogates collective virtue to himself as his personal merit, another takes collective vice as his personal guilt. Both are as illusory as the megalomania and the inferiority, because the imaginary virtues and the imaginary wickednesses are simply the moral pair of opposites contained in the

149

collective psyche, which have become perceptible or have been rendered conscious artificially. How much these paired opposites are contained in the collective psyche is exemplified by primitives: one observer will extol the greatest virtues in them, while another will record the very worst impressions of the self-same tribe. For the primitive, whose personal differentiation is, as we know, only just beginning, both judgments are true, because his psyche is essentially collective and therefore for the most part unconscious. He is still more or less identical with the collective psyche, and for that reason shares equally in the collective virtues and vices, without any personal attribution and without inner contradiction. The contradiction arises only when the personal development of the psyche begins, and when reason discovers the irreconcilable nature of the opposites. The consequence of this discovery is the conflict of repression. We want to be good, and therefore must repress evil; and with that the paradise of the collective psyche comes to an end. Repression of the collective psyche was absolutely necessary for the development of personality. In primitives, development of personality, or more accurately, development of the person, is a question of magical prestige. The figure of the medicine-man or chief leads the way: both make themselves conspicuous by the singularity of their ornaments and their mode of life, expressive of their social roles. The singularity of his outward tokens marks the individual off from the rest, and the segregation is still further enhanced by the possession of special ritual secrets. By these and similar means the primitive creates around him a shell, which might be called a persona (mask). Masks, as we know, are actually used among primitives in totem ceremonies—for instance, as a means of enhancing or changing the personality. In this way the outstanding individual is apparently removed from the sphere of the collective psyche, and to the degree that he succeeds in identifying himself with his persona, he actually is removed. This removal means magical prestige. One could easily assert that the impelling motive in this development is the will to power. But that would be to forget that the building up of prestige is always a product of collective compromise: not only must there be one who wants prestige, there must also be a public seeking somebody on whom to confer prestige. That being so, it would be incorrect to say that a man creates prestige for himself out of his individual will to power; it is on the contrary an entirely collective affair. Since society as a whole needs the magically effective figure, it uses this need of the will to power in the individual, and the will to submit in the mass, as a vehicle, and thus brings about the creation of personal prestige. The latter is a phenomenon which, as the history of political institutions shows, is of the utmost importance for the comity of nations.

238   The importance of personal prestige can hardly be overestimated, because the possibility of regressive dissolution in the collective psyche is a very real danger, not only for the outstanding individual but also for his followers. This possibility is most likely to occur when the goal of prestige—universal recognition —has been reached. The person then becomes a collective truth, and that is always the beginning of the end. To gain prestige is a positive achievement not only for the outstanding individual but also for the clan. The individual distinguishes himself by his deeds, the many by their renunciation of power. So long as this attitude needs to be fought for and defended against hostile influences, the achievement remains positive; but as soon as there are no more obstacles and universal recognition has been attained, prestige loses its positive value and usually becomes a dead letter. A schismatic movement then sets in, and the whole process begins again from the beginning.

239   Because personality is of such paramount importance for the life of the community, everything likely to disturb its development is sensed as a danger. But the greatest danger of all is the premature dissolution of prestige by an invasion of the collective psyche. Absolute secrecy is one of the best known primitive means of exorcising this danger. Collective thinking and feeling and collective effort are far less of a strain than individual functioning and effort; hence there is always a great temptation to allow collective functioning to take the place of individual differentiation of the personality. Once the personality has been differentiated and safeguarded by magical prestige, its levelling down and eventual dissolution in the collective psyche (e.g., Peter's denial) occasion a "loss of soul" in the individual, because an important personal achievement has been either neglected or allowed to slip into regression. For this reason taboo infringements are followed by Draconian punishments altogether in keeping with the seriousness of the situation. So long as we re-

151

gard these things from the causal point of view, as mere histori-cal survivals and metastases of the incest taboo,[7] it is impossible to understand what all these measures are for. If, however, we approach the problem from the teleological point of view, much that was quite inexplicable becomes clear.

240   For the development of personality, then, strict differentia-tion from the collective psyche is absolutely necessary, since par-tial or blurred differentiation leads to an immediate melting away of the individual in the collective. There is now a danger that in the analysis of the unconscious the collective and the per-sonal psyche may be fused together, with, as I have intimated, highly unfortunate results. These results are injurious both to the patient's life-feeling and to his fellow men, if he has any in-fluence at all on his environment. Through his identification with the collective psyche he will infallibly try to force the de-mands of his unconscious upon others, for identity with the col-lective psyche always brings with it a feeling of universal valid-ity—"godlikeness"—which completely ignores all differences in the personal psyche of his fellows. (The feeling of universal va-lidity comes, of course, from the universality of the collective psyche.) A collective attitude naturally presupposes this same collective psyche in others. But that means a ruthless disregard not only of individual differences but also of differences of a more general kind within the collective psyche itself, as for ex-ample differences of race.[8] This disregard for individuality ob-viously means the suffocation of the single individual, as a conse-quence of which the element of differentiation is obliterated from the community. The element of differentiation is the indi-vidual. All the highest achievements of virtue, as well as the

[7] Freud, *Totem and Taboo*.

[8] Thus it is a quite unpardonable mistake to accept the conclusions of a Jewish psychology as generally valid. Nobody would dream of taking Chinese or Indian psychology as binding upon ourselves. The cheap accusation of anti-Semitism that has been levelled at me on the ground of this criticism is about as intelligent as accusing me of an anti-Chinese prejudice. No doubt, on an earlier and deeper level of psychic development, where it is still impossible to distinguish between an Aryan, Semitic, Hamitic, or Mongolian mentality, all human races have a common collective psyche. But with the beginning of racial differentiation essential differences are developed in the collective psyche as well. For this reason we cannot transplant the spirit of a foreign race *in globo* into our own mentality without sensible injury to the latter, a fact which does not, however, deter sun-dry natures of feeble instinct from affecting Indian philosophy and the like.

blackest villainies, are individual. The larger a community is, and the more the sum total of collective factors peculiar to every large community rests on conservative prejudices detrimental to individuality, the more will the individual be morally and spiritually crushed, and, as a result, the one source of moral and spiritual progress for society is choked up. Naturally the only thing that can thrive in such an atmosphere is sociality and whatever is collective in the individual. Everything individual in him goes under, i.e., is doomed to repression. The individual elements lapse into the unconscious, where, by the law of necessity, they are transformed into something essentially baleful, destructive, and anarchical. Socially, this evil principle shows itself in the spectacular crimes—regicide and the like—perpetrated by certain prophetically-inclined individuals; but in the great mass of the community it remains in the background, and only manifests itself indirectly in the inexorable moral degeneration of society. It is a notorious fact that the morality of society as a whole is in inverse ratio to its size; for the greater the aggregation of individuals, the more the individual factors are blotted out, and with them morality, which rests entirely on the moral sense of the individual and the freedom necessary for this. Hence every man is, in a certain sense, unconsciously a worse man when he is in society than when acting alone; for he is carried by society and to that extent relieved of his individual responsibility. Any large company composed of wholly admirable persons has the morality and intelligence of an unwieldy, stupid, and violent animal. The bigger the organization, the more unavoidable is its immorality and blind stupidity (*Senatus bestia, senatores boni viri*). Society, by automatically stressing all the collective qualities in its individual representatives, puts a premium on mediocrity, on everything that settles down to vegetate in an easy, irresponsible way. Individuality will inevitably be driven to the wall. This process begins in school, continues at the university, and rules all departments in which the State has a hand. In a small social body, the individuality of its members is better safeguarded, and the greater is their relative freedom and the possibility of conscious responsibility. Without freedom there can be no morality. Our admiration for great organizations dwindles when once we become aware of the other side of the wonder: the tremendous piling up and accentuation of all that is primitive in man, and the unavoidable destruction of his individuality in the interests of the monstrosity that every great organization in fact is. The man of today, who resembles more or less the collective ideal, has made his heart into a den of murderers, as can easily be proved by the analysis of his unconscious, even though he himself is not in the least disturbed by it. And in so far as he is normally "adapted" [9] to his environment, it is true that the greatest infamy on the part of his group will not disturb him, so long as the majority of his fellows steadfastly believe in the exalted morality of their social organization. Now, all that I have said here about the influence of society upon the individual is identically true of the influence of the collective unconscious upon the individual psyche. But, as is apparent from my examples, the latter influence is as invisible as the former is visible. Hence it is not surprising that its inner effects are not understood, and that those to whom such things happen are called pathological freaks and treated as crazy. If one of them happened to be a real genius, the fact would not be noted until the next generation or the one after. So obvious does it seem to us that a man should drown in his own dignity, so utterly incomprehensible that he should seek anything other than what the mob wants, and that he should vanish permanently from view in this other. One could wish both of them a sense of humour, that —according to Schopenhauer—truly "divine" attribute of man which alone befits him to maintain his soul in freedom.

241   The collective instincts and fundamental forms of thinking and feeling whose activity is revealed by the analysis of the unconscious constitute, for the conscious personality, an acquisition which it cannot assimilate without considerable disturbance. It is therefore of the utmost importance in practical treatment to keep the integrity of the personality constantly in mind. For, if the collective psyche is taken to be the personal possession of the individual, it will result in a distortion or an overloading of the personality which is very difficult to deal with. Hence it is imperative to make a clear distinction between personal contents and those of the collective psyche. This distinction is far from easy, because the personal grows out of the collective psyche and is intimately bound up with it. So it is difficult to say exactly what contents are to be called personal and what collective.

9 Cf. "adjustment" and "adaptation" in *Psychological Types*, par. 564.

There is no doubt, for instance, that archaic symbolisms such as we frequently find in fantasies and dreams are collective factors. All basic instincts and basic forms of thinking and feeling are collective. Everything that all men agree in regarding as universal is collective, likewise everything that is universally understood, universally found, universally said and done. On closer examination one is always astonished to see how much of our so-called individual psychology is really collective. So much, indeed, that the individual traits are completely overshadowed by it. Since, however, individuation[10] is an ineluctable psychological necessity, we can see from the ascendancy of the collective what very special attention must be paid to this delicate plant "individuality" if it is not to be completely smothered.

242   Human beings have one faculty which, though it is of the greatest utility for collective purposes, is most pernicious for individuation, and that is the faculty of imitation. Collective psychology cannot dispense with imitation, for without it all mass organizations, the State and the social order, are impossible. Society is organized, indeed, less by law than by the propensity to imitation, implying equally suggestibility, suggestion, and mental contagion. But we see every day how people use, or rather abuse, the mechanism of imitation for the purpose of personal differentiation: they are content to ape some eminent personality, some striking characteristic or mode of behaviour, thereby achieving an outward distinction from the circle in which they move. We could almost say that as a punishment for this the uniformity of their minds with those of their neighbours, already real enough, is intensified into an unconscious, compulsive bondage to the environment. As a rule these specious attempts at individual differentiation stiffen into a pose, and the imitator remains at the same level as he always was, only several degrees more sterile than before. To find out what is truly individual in ourselves, profound reflection is needed; and suddenly we realize how uncommonly difficult the discovery of individuality is.

10 Ibid., Def. 29: "Individuation is a process of differentiation, having for its goal the development of the individual personality."—"As the individual is not just a single, separate being, but by his very existence presupposes a collective relationship, it follows that the process of individuation must lead to more intense and broader collective relationships and not to isolation."

III

THE PERSONA AS A SEGMENT OF
THE COLLECTIVE PSYCHE

243   In this chapter we come to a problem which, if overlooked, is liable to cause the greatest confusion. It will be remembered that in the analysis of the personal unconscious the first things to be added to consciousness are the personal contents, and I suggested that these contents, which have been repressed but are capable of becoming conscious, should be called the *personal unconscious*. I also showed that to annex the deeper layers of the unconscious, which I have called the *collective unconscious,* produces an enlargement of the personality leading to the state of inflation. This state is reached by simply continuing the analytical work, as in the case of the young woman discussed above. By continuing the analysis we add to the personal consciousness certain fundamental, general, and impersonal characteristics of humanity, thereby bringing about the inflation[1] I have just de-

---

[1] This phenomenon, which results from the extension of consciousness, is in no sense specific to analytical treatment. It occurs whenever people are overpowered by knowledge or by some new realization. "Knowledge puffeth up," Paul writes to the Corinthians, for the new knowledge had turned the heads of many, as indeed constantly happens. The inflation has nothing to do with the *kind* of knowledge, but simply and solely with the fact that any new knowledge can so seize hold of a weak head that he no longer sees and hears anything else. He is hypnotized by it, and instantly believes he has solved the riddle of the universe. But that is equivalent to almighty self-conceit. This process is such a general reaction that, in Genesis 2:17, eating of the tree of knowledge is represented as a deadly sin. It may not be immediately apparent why greater consciousness followed by self-conceit should be such a dangerous thing. Genesis represents the act of becoming conscious as a taboo infringement, as though knowledge meant that a sacrosanct barrier had been impiously overstepped. I think that Genesis is right in so far as every step towards greater consciousness is a kind of Promethean guilt: through knowledge, the gods are as it were robbed of their fire, that is, something that was the property of the unconscious powers is torn out of its natural context and subordinated to the whims of the conscious mind. The

156

scribed, which might be regarded as one of the unpleasant consequences of becoming fully conscious.

244   From this point of view the conscious personality is a more or less arbitrary segment of the collective psyche. It consists in a sum of psychic facts that are felt to be personal. The attribute "personal" means: pertaining exclusively to this particular person. A consciousness that is purely personal stresses its proprietary and original right to its contents with a certain anxiety, and in this way seeks to create a whole. But all those contents that refuse to fit into this whole are either overlooked and forgotten or repressed and denied. This is one way of educating oneself, but it is too arbitrary and too much of a violation. Far too much of our common humanity has to be sacrificed in the interests of an ideal image into which one tries to mould oneself. Hence these purely "personal" people are always very sensitive, for something may easily happen that will bring into consciousness an unwelcome portion of their real ("individual") character.

245   This arbitrary segment of collective psyche—often fashioned with considerable pains—I have called the *persona*. The term *persona* is really a very appropriate expression for this, for originally it meant the mask once worn by actors to indicate the role they played. If we endeavour to draw a precise distinction between what psychic material should be considered personal, and what impersonal, we soon find ourselves in the greatest dilemma, for by definition we have to say of the persona's contents what we have said of the impersonal unconscious, namely, that it is collective. It is only because the persona represents a more or less arbitrary and fortuitous segment of the collective psyche that we can make the mistake of regarding it *in toto* as something individual. It is, as its name implies, only a mask of the collective psyche, a mask that *feigns individuality,* making others and oneself believe that one is individual, whereas one is simply acting a role through which the collective psyche speaks.

man who has usurped the new knowledge suffers, however, a transformation or enlargement of consciousness, which no longer resembles that of his fellow men. He has raised himself above the human level of his age ("ye shall become like unto God"), but in so doing has alienated himself from humanity. The pain of this loneliness is the vengeance of the gods, for never again can he return to mankind. He is, as the myth says, chained to the lonely cliffs of the Caucasus, forsaken of God and man.

246   When we analyse the persona we strip off the mask, and discover that what seemed to be individual is at bottom collective; in other words, that the persona was only a mask of the collective psyche. Fundamentally the persona is nothing real: it is a compromise between individual and society as to what a man should appear to be. He takes a name, earns a title, exercises a function, he is this or that. In a certain sense all this is real, yet in relation to the essential individuality of the person concerned it is only a secondary reality, a compromise formation, in making which others often have a greater share than he. The persona is a semblance, a two-dimensional reality, to give it a nickname.

247   It would be wrong to leave the matter as it stands without at the same time recognizing that there is, after all, something individual in the peculiar choice and delineation of the persona, and that despite the exclusive identity of the ego-consciousness with the persona the unconscious self, one's real individuality, is always present and makes itself felt indirectly if not directly. Although the ego-consciousness is at first identical with the persona—that compromise role in which we parade before the community—yet the unconscious self can never be repressed to the point of extinction. Its influence is chiefly manifest in the special nature of the contrasting and compensating contents of the unconscious. The purely personal attitude of the conscious mind evokes reactions on the part of the unconscious, and these, together with personal repressions, contain the seeds of individual development in the guise of collective fantasies. Through the analysis of the personal unconscious, the conscious mind becomes suffused with collective material which brings with it the elements of individuality. I am well aware that this conclusion must be almost unintelligible to anyone not familiar with my views and technique, and particularly so to those who habitually regard the unconscious from the standpoint of Freudian theory. But if the reader will recall my example of the philosophy student, he can form a rough idea of what I mean. At the beginning of the treatment the patient was quite unconscious of the fact that her relation to her father was a fixation, and that she was therefore seeking a man like her father, whom she could then meet with her intellect. This in itself would not have been a mistake if her intellect had not had that peculiarly protesting

character such as is unfortunately often encountered in intellectual women. Such an intellect is always trying to point out
mistakes in others; it is pre-eminently critical, with a dis-
agreeably personal undertone, yet it always wants to be considered objective. This invariably makes a man bad-tempered, particularly if, as so often happens, the criticism touches on some
weak spot which, in the interests of fruitful discussion, were better avoided. But far from wishing the discussion to be fruitful, it
is the unfortunate peculiarity of this feminine intellect to seek
out a man's weak spots, fasten on them, and exasperate him.
This is not usually a conscious aim, but rather has the unconscious purpose of forcing a man into a superior position and thus
making him an object of admiration. The man does not as a rule
notice that he is having the role of the hero thrust upon him; he
merely finds her taunts so odious that in future he will go a long
way to avoid meeting the lady. In the end the only man who can
stand her is the one who gives in at the start, and therefore has
nothing wonderful about him.

248   My patient naturally found much to reflect upon in all this,
for she had no notion of the game she was playing. Moreover she
still had to gain insight into the regular romance that had been
enacted between her and her father ever since childhood. It
would lead us too far to describe in detail how, from her earliest
years, with unconscious sympathy, she had played upon the
shadow-side of her father which her mother never saw, and how,
far in advance of her years, she became her mother's rival. All
this came to light in the analysis of the personal unconscious.
Since, if only for professional reasons, I could not allow myself to
be irritated, I inevitably became the hero and father-lover. The
transference too consisted at first of contents from the personal
unconscious. My role as a hero was just a sham, and so, as it
turned me into the merest phantom, she was able to play her
traditional role of the supremely wise, very grown-up, all-under-
standing mother-daughter-beloved—an empty role, a persona
behind which her real and authentic being, her individual self,
lay hidden. Indeed, to the extent that she at first completely
identified herself with her role, she was altogether unconscious
of her real self. She was still in her nebulous infantile world and
had not yet discovered the real world at all. But as, through progressive analysis, she became conscious of the nature of her

159

transference, the dreams I spoke of in Chapter I began to materialize. They brought up bits of the collective unconscious, and that was the end of her infantile world and of all the heroics. She came to herself and to her own real potentialities. This is roughly the way things go in most cases, if the analysis is carried far enough. That the consciousness of her individuality should coincide exactly with the reactivation of an archaic god-image is not just an isolated coincidence, but a very frequent occurrence which, in my view, corresponds to an unconscious law.

249 After this digression, let us turn back to our earlier reflections.

250 Once the personal repressions are lifted, the individuality and the collective psyche begin to emerge in a coalescent state, thus releasing the hitherto repressed personal fantasies. The fantasies and dreams which now appear assume a somewhat different aspect. An infallible sign of collective images seems to be the appearance of the "cosmic" element, i.e., the images in the dream or fantasy are connected with cosmic qualities, such as temporal and spatial infinity, enormous speed and extension of movement, "astrological" associations, telluric, lunar, and solar analogies, changes in the proportions of the body, etc. The obvious occurrence of mythological and religious motifs in a dream also points to the activity of the collective unconscious. The collective element is very often announced by peculiar symptoms,[2] as for example by dreams where the dreamer is flying through space like a comet, or feels that he is the earth, or the sun, or a star; or else is of immense size, or dwarfishly small; or that he is dead, is in a strange place, is a stranger to himself, confused, mad, etc. Similarly, feelings of disorientation, of dizziness and the like, may appear along with symptoms of inflation.

251 The forces that burst out of the collective psyche have a confusing and blinding effect. One result of the dissolution of the persona is a release of involuntary fantasy, which is apparently nothing else than the specific activity of the collective psyche. This activity throws up contents whose existence one had never suspected before. But as the influence of the collective uncon-

---

[2] It may not be superfluous to note that collective elements in dreams are not restricted to this stage of the analytical treatment. There are many psychological situations in which the activity of the collective unconscious can come to the surface. But this is not the place to enlarge upon these conditions.

scious increases, so the conscious mind loses its power of leadership. Imperceptibly it becomes the led, while an unconscious and impersonal process gradually takes control. Thus, without noticing it, the conscious personality is pushed about like a figure on a chess-board by an invisible player. It is this player who decides the game of fate, not the conscious mind and its plans. This is how the resolution of the transference, apparently so impossible to the conscious mind, was brought about in my earlier example.

252   The plunge into this process becomes unavoidable whenever the necessity arises of overcoming an apparently insuperable difficulty. It goes without saying that this necessity does not occur in every case of neurosis, since perhaps in the majority the prime consideration is only the removal of temporary difficulties of adaptation. Certainly severe cases cannot be cured without a far-reaching change of character or of attitude. In by far the greater number, adaptation to external reality demands so much work that inner adaptation to the collective unconscious cannot be considered for a very long time. But when this inner adaptation becomes a problem, a strange, irresistible attraction proceeds from the unconscious and exerts a powerful influence on the conscious direction of life. The predominance of unconscious influences, together with the associated disintegration of the persona and the deposition of the conscious mind from power, constitute a state of psychic disequilibrium which, in analytical treatment, is artificially induced for the therapeutic purpose of resolving a difficulty that might block further development. There are of course innumerable obstacles that can be overcome with good advice and a little moral support, aided by goodwill and understanding on the part of the patient. Excellent curative results can be obtained in this way. Cases are not uncommon where there is no need to breathe a word about the unconscious. But again, there are difficulties for which one can foresee no satisfactory solution. If in these cases the psychic equilibrium is not already disturbed before treatment begins, it will certainly be upset during the analysis, and sometimes without any interference by the doctor. It often seems as though these patients had only been waiting to find a trustworthy person in order to give up and collapse. Such a loss of balance is similar in principle to a psychotic disturbance; that is, it differs from the

initial stages of mental illness only by the fact that it leads in the end to greater health, while the latter leads to yet greater destruction. It is a condition of panic, a letting go in face of apparently hopeless complications. Mostly it was preceded by desperate efforts to master the difficulty by force of will; then came the collapse, and the once guiding will crumbles completely. The energy thus freed disappears from consciousness and falls into the unconscious. As a matter of fact, it is at these moments that the first signs of unconscious activity appear. (I am thinking of the example of that young man who was weak in the head.) Obviously the energy that fell away from consciousness has activated the unconscious. The immediate result is a change of attitude. One can easily imagine that a stronger head would have taken that vision of the stars as a healing apparition, and would have looked upon human suffering *sub specie aeternitatis,* in which case his senses would have been restored.[3]

253   Had this happened, an apparently insurmountable obstacle would have been removed. Hence I regard the loss of balance as purposive, since it replaces a defective consciousness by the automatic and instinctive activity of the unconscious, which is aiming all the time at the creation of a new balance and will moreover achieve this aim, provided that the conscious mind is capable of assimilating the contents produced by the unconscious, i.e., of understanding and digesting them. If the unconscious simply rides roughshod over the conscious mind, a psychotic condition develops. If it can neither completely prevail nor yet be understood, the result is a conflict that cripples all further advance. But with this question, namely the understanding of the collective unconscious, we come to a formidable difficulty which I have made the theme of my next chapter.

[3] Cf. Flournoy, "Automatisme téléologique antisuicide: un cas de suicide empêché par une hallucination" (1907), 113–37; and Jung, "The Psychology of Dementia Praecox," pars. 304ff.

IV

NEGATIVE ATTEMPTS TO FREE
THE INDIVIDUALITY FROM
THE COLLECTIVE PSYCHE

a. *Regressive Restoration of the Persona*

254   A collapse of the conscious attitude is no small matter. It always feels like the end of the world, as though everything had tumbled back into original chaos. One feels delivered up, disoriented, like a rudderless ship that is abandoned to the moods of the elements. So at least it seems. In reality, however, one has fallen back upon the collective unconscious, which now takes over the leadership. We could multiply examples of cases where, at the critical moment, a "saving" thought, a vision, an "inner voice," came with an irresistible power of conviction and gave life a new direction. Probably we could mention just as many cases where the collapse meant a catastrophe that destroyed life, for at such moments morbid ideas are also liable to take root, or ideals wither away, which is no less disastrous. In the one case some psychic oddity develops, or a psychosis; in the other, a state of disorientation and demoralization. But once the unconscious contents break through into consciousness, filling it with their uncanny power of conviction, the question arises of how the individual will react. Will he be overpowered by these contents? Will he credulously accept them? Or will he reject them? (I am disregarding the ideal reaction, namely critical understanding.) The first case signifies paranoia or schizophrenia; the second may either become an eccentric with a taste for prophecy, or he may revert to an infantile attitude and be cut off from human society; the third signifies the *regressive restoration of the persona*. This formulation sounds very technical, and the reader may justifiably suppose that it has something to do with a com-

163

plicated psychic reaction such as can be observed in the course of analytical treatment. It would, however, be a mistake to think that cases of this kind make their appearance only in analytical treatment. The process can be observed just as well, and often better, in other situations of life, namely in all those careers where there has been some violent and destructive intervention of fate. Every one, presumably, has suffered adverse turns of fortune, but mostly they are wounds that heal and leave no crippling mark. But here we are concerned with experiences that are destructive, that can smash a man completely or at least cripple him for good. Let us take as an example a businessman who takes too great a risk and consequently becomes bankrupt. If he does not allow himself to be discouraged by this depressing experience, but, undismayed, keeps his former daring, perhaps with a little salutary caution added, his wound will be healed without permanent injury. But if, on the other hand, he goes to pieces, abjures all further risks, and laboriously tries to patch up his social reputation within the confines of a much more limited personality, doing inferior work with the mentality of a scared child, in a post far below him, then, technically speaking, he will have restored his persona in a regressive way. He will as a result of his fright have slipped back to an earlier phase of his personality; he will have demeaned himself, pretending that he is as he was *before* the crucial experience, though utterly unable even to think of repeating such a risk. Formerly perhaps he wanted more than he could accomplish; now he does not even dare to attempt what he has it in him to do.

255   Such experiences occur in every walk of life and in every possible form, hence in psychological treatment also. Here again it is a question of widening the personality, of taking a risk on one's circumstances or on one's nature. What the critical experience is in actual treatment can be seen from the case of our philosophy student: it is the transference. As I have already indicated, it is possible for the patient to slip over the reef of the transference unconsciously, in which case it does not become an experience and nothing fundamental happens. The doctor, for the sake of mere convenience, might well wish for such patients. But if they are intelligent, the patients soon discover the existence of this problem for themselves. If then the doctor, as in the above case, is exalted into the father-lover and consequently has

a flood of demands let loose against him, he must perforce think out ways and means of parrying the onslaught, without himself getting drawn into the maelstrom and without injury to the patient. A violent rupture of the transference may bring on a complete relapse, or worse; so the problem must be handled with great tact and foresight. Another possibility is the pious hope that "in time" the "nonsense" will stop of its own accord. Certainly everything stops in time, but it may be an unconscionably long time, and the difficulties may be so unbearable for both sides that one might as well give up the idea of time as a healing factor at once.

256   A far better instrument for "combatting" the transference would seem to be offered by the Freudian theory of neurosis. The dependence of the patient is explained as an infantile sexual demand that takes the place of a rational application of sexuality. Similar advantages are offered by the Adlerian theory,[1] which explains the transference as an infantile power-aim, and as a "security measure." Both theories fit the neurotic mentality so neatly that every case of neurosis can be explained by both theories at once.[2] This highly remarkable fact, which any unprejudiced observer is bound to corroborate, can only rest on the circumstance that Freud's "infantile eroticism" and Adler's "power drive" are one and the same thing, regardless of the clash of opinions between the two schools. It is simply a fragment of uncontrolled, and at first uncontrollable, primordial instinct that comes to light in the phenomenon of transference. The archaic fantasy-forms that gradually reach the surface of consciousness are only a further proof of this.

257   We can try both theories to make the patient see how infantile, impossible, and absurd his demands are, and perhaps in the end he will actually come to his senses again. My patient, however, was not the only one who did not do this. True enough, the doctor can always save his face with these theories and extricate himself from a painful situation more or less humanely. There are indeed patients with whom it is, or seems to be, unrewarding to go to greater lengths; but there are also cases where these procedures cause senseless psychic injury. In the case of my student I dimly felt something of the sort, and I therefore aban-

1 Adler, *The Neurotic Constitution* (orig. 1912).
2 Cf. supra, pars. 44ff., for an example of such a case.

doned my rationalistic attempts in order—with ill-concealed mistrust—to give nature a chance to correct what seemed to me to be her own foolishness. As already mentioned, this taught me something extraordinarily important, namely the existence of an unconscious self-regulation. Not only can the unconscious "wish," it can also cancel its own wishes. This realization, of such immense importance for the integrity of the personality, must remain sealed to anyone who cannot get over the idea that it is simply a question of infantilism. He will turn round on the threshold of this realization and tell himself: "It was all non-sense of course. I am a crazy visionary! The best thing to do would be to bury the unconscious or throw it overboard with all its works." The meaning and purpose he so eagerly desired he will see only as infantile maunderings. He will understand that his longing was absurd; he learns to be tolerant with himself, resigned. What can he do? Rather than face the conflict he will turn back and, as best he can, regressively restore his shattered persona, discounting all those hopes and expectations that had blossomed under the transference. He will become smaller, more limited, more rationalistic than he was before. One could not say that this result would be an unqualified misfortune in all cases, for there are all too many who, on account of their notorious ineptitude, thrive better in a rationalistic system than in freedom. Freedom is one of the more difficult things. Those who can stomach this way out can say with Faust:

> This earthly circle I know well enough.
> Towards the Beyond the view has been cut off;
> Fool—who directs that way his dazzled eye,
> Contrives himself a double in the sky!
> Let him look round him here, not stray beyond;
> To a sound man this world must needs respond.
> To roam into eternity is vain!
> What he perceives, he can attain.
> Thus let him walk along his earthlong day;
> Though phantoms haunt him, let him go his way.[3]

258   Such a solution would be perfect if a man were really able to shake off the unconscious, drain it of its energy and render it inactive. But experience shows that the unconscious can be de-

[3] *Faust,* trans. by Louis MacNeice, p. 283 (Part II, Act V).

prived of its energy only in part: it remains continually active, for it not only contains but is itself the source of the libido from which the psychic elements flow. It is therefore a delusion to think that by some kind of magical theory or method the unconscious can be finally emptied of libido and thus, as it were, eliminated. One may for a while play with this delusion, but the day comes when one is forced to say with Faust:

> But now such spectredom so throngs the air
> That none knows how to dodge it, none knows where.
> Though one day greet us with a rational gleam,
> The night entangles us in webs of dream.
> We come back happy from the fields of spring—
> And a bird croaks. Croaks what? Some evil thing.
> Enmeshed in superstition night and morn,
> It forms and shows itself and comes to warn.
> And we, so scared, stand without friend or kin,
> And the door creaks—and nobody comes in.[4]

Nobody, of his own free will, can strip the unconscious of its effective power. At best, one can merely deceive oneself on this point. For, as Goethe says:

> Unheard by the outward ear
> In the heart I whisper fear;
> Changing shape from hour to hour
> I employ my savage power.[5]

Only one thing is effective against the unconscious, and that is hard outer necessity. (Those with rather more knowledge of the unconscious will see behind the outer necessity the same face which once gazed at them from within.) An inner necessity can change into an outer one, and so long as the outer necessity is real, and not just faked, psychic problems remain more or less ineffective. This is why Mephisto offers Faust, who is sick of the "madness of magic," the following advice:

> Right. There is one way that needs
> No money, no physician, and no witch.

4 Ibid., p. 281 (Part II, Act V).
5 Ibid., p. 282 (Part II, Act V), modified.

Pack up your things and get back to the land
And there begin to dig and ditch;
Keep to the narrow round, confine your mind,
And live on fodder of the simplest kind,
A beast among the beasts; and don't forget
To use your own dung on the crops you set! [6]

It is a well-known fact that the "simple life" cannot be faked, and therefore the unproblematical existence of a poor man, who really is delivered over to fate, cannot be bought by such cheap imitations. Only the man who lives such a life not as a mere possibility, but is actually driven to it by the necessity of his own nature, will blindly pass over the problem of his soul, since he lacks the capacity to grasp it. But once he has seen the Faustian problem, the escape into the "simple life" is closed for ever. There is of course nothing to stop him from taking a two-room cottage in the country, or from pottering about in a garden and eating raw turnips. But his soul laughs at the deception. Only what is really oneself has the power to heal.

259   The regressive restoration of the persona is a possible course only for the man who owes the critical failure of his life to his own inflatedness. With diminished personality, he turns back to the measure he can fill. But in every other case resignation and self-belittlement are an evasion, which in the long run can be kept up only at the cost of neurotic sickliness. From the conscious point of view of the person concerned, his condition does not look like an evasion at all, but seems to be due to the impossibility of coping with the problem. Usually he is a lonely figure, with little or nothing to help him in our present-day culture. Even psychology has only purely reductive interpretations to offer, since it inevitably underlines the archaic and infantile character of these transitional states and makes them unacceptable to him. The fact that a medical theory may also serve the purpose of enabling the doctor to pull his own head more or less elegantly out of the noose does not occur to him. That is precisely why these reductive theories fit the essence of neurosis so beautifully—because they are of such great service to the doctor.

6 Ibid., p. 67 (Part I, Witch's Kitchen scene), modified.

b. *Identification with the Collective Psyche*

260   The second way leads to identification with the collective psyche. This would amount to an acceptance of inflation, but now exalted into a system. That is to say, one would be the fortunate possessor of *the* great truth which was only waiting to be discovered, of the eschatological knowledge which spells the healing of the nations. This attitude is not necessarily megalomania in direct form, but in the milder and more familiar form of prophetic inspiration and desire for martyrdom. For weak-minded persons, who as often as not possess more than their fair share of ambition, vanity, and misplaced naïveté, the danger of yielding to this temptation is very great. Access to the collective psyche means a renewal of life for the individual, no matter whether this renewal is felt as pleasant or unpleasant. Everybody would like to hold fast to this renewal: one man because it enhances his life-feeling, another because it promises a rich harvest of knowledge, a third because he has discovered the key that will transform his whole life. Therefore all those who do not wish to deprive themselves of the great treasures that lie buried in the collective psyche will strive by every means possible to maintain their newly won connection with the primal source of life.[7] Identification would seem to be the shortest road to this, for the dissolution of the persona in the collective psyche positively invites one to wed oneself with the abyss and blot out all memory in its embrace. This piece of mysticism is innate in all better men as the "longing for the mother," the nostalgia for the source from which we came.

261   As I have shown in my book on libido, there lie at the root of the regressive longing, which Freud conceives as "infantile fixation" or the "incest wish," a specific value and a specific need which are made explicit in myths. It is precisely the strongest and best among men, the heroes, who give way to their regres-

[7] I would like to call attention here to an interesting remark of Kant's. In his lectures on psychology (*Vorlesungen über Psychologie,* Leipzig, 1889) he speaks of the "treasure lying within the field of dim representations, that deep abyss of human knowledge forever beyond our reach." This treasure, as I have demonstrated in my *Symbols of Transformation,* is the aggregate of all those primordial images in which the libido is invested, or rather, which are self-representations of the libido.

sive longing and purposely expose themselves to the danger of being devoured by the monster of the maternal abyss. But if a man is a hero, he is a hero because, in the final reckoning, he did not let the monster devour him, but subdued it, not once but many times. Victory over the collective psyche alone yields the true value—the capture of the hoard, the invincible weapon, the magic talisman, or whatever it be that the myth deems most desirable. Anyone who identifies with the collective psyche—or, in mythological terms, lets himself be devoured by the monster—and vanishes in it, attains the treasure that the dragon guards, but he does so in spite of himself and to his own greatest harm.

262 Probably no one who was conscious of the absurdity of this identification would have the courage to make a principle of it. But the danger is that very many people lack the necessary humour, or else it fails them at this particular juncture; they are seized by a sort of pathos, everything seems pregnant with meaning, and all effective self-criticism is checked. I would not deny in general the existence of genuine prophets, but in the name of caution I would begin by doubting each individual case; for it is far too serious a matter for us lightly to accept a man as a genuine prophet. Every respectable prophet strives manfully against the unconscious pretensions of his role. When therefore a prophet appears at a moment's notice, we would be better advised to contemplate a possible psychic disequilibrium.

263 But besides the possibility of becoming a prophet, there is another alluring joy, subtler and apparently more legitimate: the joy of becoming a prophet's disciple. This, for the vast majority of people, is an altogether ideal technique. Its advantages are: the *odium dignitatis*, the superhuman responsibility of the prophet, turns into the so much sweeter *otium indignitatis*. The disciple is unworthy; modestly he sits at the Master's feet and guards against having ideas of his own. Mental laziness becomes a virtue; one can at least bask in the sun of a semidivine being. He can enjoy the archaism and infantilism of his unconscious fantasies without loss to himself, for all responsibility is laid at the Master's door. Through his deification of the Master, the disciple, apparently without noticing it, waxes in stature; moreover, does he not possess the great truth—not his own discovery, of course, but received straight from the Master's hands? Naturally the disciples always stick together, not out of love, but for

the very understandable purpose of effortlessly confirming their own convictions by engendering an air of collective agreement.

264 Now this is an identification with the collective psyche that seems altogether more commendable: somebody else has the honour of being a prophet, but also the dangerous responsibility. For one's own part, one is a mere disciple, but nonetheless a joint guardian of the great treasure which the Master has found. One feels the full dignity and burden of such a position, deeming it a solemn duty and a moral necessity to revile others not of a like mind, to enrol proselytes and to hold up a light to the Gentiles, exactly as though one were the prophet oneself. And these people, who creep about behind an apparently modest persona, are the very ones who, when inflated by identification with the collective psyche, suddenly burst upon the world scene. For, just as the prophet is a primordial image from the collective psyche, so also is the disciple of the prophet.

265 In both cases inflation is brought about by the collective unconscious, and the independence of the individuality suffers injury. But since by no means all individualities have the strength to be independent, the disciple-fantasy is perhaps the best they can accomplish. The gratifications of the accompanying inflation at least do something to make up for the loss of spiritual freedom. Nor should we underestimate the fact that the life of a real or imagined prophet is full of sorrows, disappointments, and privations, so that the hosanna-shouting band of disciples has the value of a compensation. All this is so humanly understandable that it would be a matter for astonishment if it led to any further destination whatever.

PART TWO

INDIVIDUATION

I

THE FUNCTION OF THE UNCONSCIOUS

266   There is a destination, a possible goal, beyond the alternative stages dealt with in our last chapter. That is the way of individuation. Individuation means becoming an "in-dividual," and, in so far as "individuality" embraces our innermost, last, and incomparable uniqueness, it also implies becoming one's own self. We could therefore translate individuation as "coming to selfhood" or "self-realization."

267   The possibilities of development discussed in the preceding chapters were, at bottom, alienations of the self, ways of divesting the self of its reality in favour of an external role or in favour of an imagined meaning. In the former case the self retires into the background and gives place to social recognition; in the latter, to the auto-suggestive meaning of a primordial image. In both cases the collective has the upper hand. Self-alienation in favour of the collective corresponds to a social ideal; it even passes for social duty and virtue, although it can also be misused for egotistical purposes. Egoists are called "selfish," but this, naturally, has nothing to do with the concept of "self" as I am using it here. On the other hand, self-realization seems to stand in opposition to self-alienation. This misunderstanding is quite general, because we do not sufficiently distinguish between individualism and individuation. Individualism means deliberately stressing and giving prominence to some supposed peculiarity rather than to collective considerations and obligations. But individuation means precisely the better and more complete ful-

173

filment of the collective qualities of the human being, since adequate consideration of the peculiarity of the individual is more conducive to a better social performance than when the peculiarity is neglected or suppressed. The idiosyncrasy of an individual is not to be understood as any strangeness in his substance or in his components, but rather as a unique combination, or gradual differentiation, of functions and faculties which in themselves are universal. Every human face has a nose, two eyes, etc., but these universal factors are variable, and it is this variability which makes individual peculiarities possible. Individuation, therefore, can only mean a process of psychological development that fulfils the individual qualities given; in other words, it is a process by which a man becomes the definite, unique being he in fact is. In so doing he does not become "selfish" in the ordinary sense of the word, but is merely fulfilling the peculiarity of his nature, and this, as we have said, is vastly different from egotism or individualism.

268   Now in so far as the human individual, as a living unit, is composed of purely universal factors, he is wholly collective and therefore in no sense opposed to collectivity. Hence the individualistic emphasis on one's own peculiarity is a contradiction of this basic fact of the living being. Individuation, on the other hand, aims at a living co-operation of all factors. But since the universal factors always appear only in individual form, a full consideration of them will also produce an individual effect, and one which cannot be surpassed by anything else, least of all by individualism.

269   The aim of individuation is nothing less than to divest the self of the false wrappings of the persona on the one hand, and of the suggestive power of primordial images on the other. From what has been said in the previous chapters it should be sufficiently clear what the persona means psychologically. But when we turn to the other side, namely to the influence of the collective unconscious, we find we are moving in a dark interior world that is vastly more difficult to understand than the psychology of the persona, which is accessible to everyone. Everyone knows what is meant by "putting on official airs" or "playing a social role." Through the persona a man tries to appear as this or that, or he hides behind a mask, or he may even build up a definite persona as a barricade. So the problem of the persona should

present no great intellectual difficulties.

270   It is, however, another thing to describe, in a way that can be generally understood, those subtle inner processes which invade the conscious mind with such suggestive force. Perhaps we can best portray these influences with the help of examples of mental illness, creative inspiration, and religious conversion. A most excellent account—taken from life, so to speak—of such an inner transformation is to be found in H. G. Wells' *Christina Alberta's Father*.[a] Changes of a similar kind are described in Léon Daudet's eminently readable *L'Hérédo*. A wide range of material is contained in William James' *Varieties of Religious Experience*. Although in many cases of this kind there are certain external factors which either directly condition the change, or at least provide the occasion for it, yet it is not always the case that the external factor offers a sufficient explanation of these changes of personality. We must recognize the fact that they can also arise from subjective inner causes, opinions, convictions, where external stimuli play no part at all, or a very insignificant one. In pathological changes of personality this can even be said to be the rule. The cases of psychosis that present a clear and simple reaction to some overwhelming outside event belong to the exceptions. Hence, for psychiatry, the essential aetiological factor is the inherited or acquired pathological disposition. The same is probably true of most creative intuitions, for we are hardly likely to suppose a purely causal connection between the falling apple and Newton's theory of gravitation. Similarly all religious conversions that cannot be traced back directly to suggestion and contagious example rest upon independent interior processes culminating in a change of personality. As a rule these processes have the peculiarity of being subliminal, i.e., unconscious, in the first place and of reaching consciousness only gradually. The moment of irruption can, however, be very sudden, so that consciousness is instantaneously flooded with extremely strange and apparently quite unsuspected contents. That is how it looks to the layman and even to the person concerned, but the experienced observer knows that psychological events are never sudden. In reality the irruption has been preparing for many years, often for half a lifetime, and already in childhood all sorts

a [Concerning the origin of this novel in a conversation between Wells and Jung, cf. Bennet, *What Jung Really Said*, p. 93.—EDITORS.]

of remarkable signs could have been detected which, in more or less symbolic fashion, hinted at abnormal future developments. I am reminded, for instance, of a mental case who refused all nourishment and created quite extraordinary difficulties in connection with nasal feeding. In fact an anaesthetic was necessary before the tube could be inserted. The patient was able in some remarkable way to swallow his tongue by pressing it back into the throat, a fact that was quite new and unknown to me at the time. In a lucid interval I obtained the following history from the man. As a boy he had often revolved in his mind the idea of how he could take his life, even if every conceivable measure were employed to prevent him. He first tried to do it by holding his breath, until he found that by the time he was in a semiconscious state he had already begun to breathe again. So he gave up these attempts and thought: perhaps it would work if he refused food. This fantasy satisfied him until he discovered that food could be poured into him through the nasal cavity. He therefore considered how this entrance might be closed, and thus it was that he hit upon the idea of pressing his tongue backwards. At first he was unsuccessful, and so he began a regular training, until at last he succeeded in swallowing his tongue in much the same way as sometimes happens accidentally during anaesthesia, evidently in his case by artificially relaxing the muscles at the root of the tongue.

271   In this strange manner the boy paved the way for his future psychosis. After the second attack he became incurably insane. This is only one example among many others, but it suffices to show how the subsequent, apparently sudden irruption of alien contents is really not sudden at all, but is rather the result of an unconscious development that has been going on for years.

272   The great question now is: in what do these unconscious processes consist? And how are they constituted? Naturally, so long as they are unconscious, nothing can be said about them. But sometimes they manifest themselves, partly through symptoms, partly through actions, opinions, affects, fantasies, and dreams. Aided by such observational material we can draw indirect conclusions as to the momentary state and constitution of the unconscious processes and their development. We should not, however, labour under the illusion that we have now dis-

176

covered the real nature of the unconscious processes. We never succeed in getting further than the hypothetical "as if."

273 "No mortal mind can plumb the depths of nature"—nor even the depths of the unconscious. We do know, however, that the unconscious never rests. It seems to be always at work, for even when asleep we dream. There are many people who declare that they never dream, but the probability is that they simply do not remember their dreams. It is significant that people who talk in their sleep mostly have no recollection either of the dream which started them talking, or even of the fact that they dreamed at all. Not a day passes but we make some slip of the tongue, or something slips our memory which at other times we know perfectly well, or we are seized by a mood whose cause we cannot trace, etc. These things are all symptoms of some consistent unconscious activity which becomes directly visible at night in dreams, but only occasionally breaks through the inhibitions imposed by our daytime consciousness.

274 So far as our present experience goes, we can lay it down that the unconscious processes stand in a compensatory relation to the conscious mind. I expressly use the word "compensatory" and not the word "contrary" because conscious and unconscious are not necessarily in opposition to one another, but complement one another to form a totality, which is the *self*. According to this definition the self is a quantity that is supraordinate to the conscious ego. It embraces not only the conscious but also the unconscious psyche, and is therefore, so to speak, a personality which we *also* are. It is easy enough to think of ourselves as possessing part-souls. Thus we can, for instance, see ourselves as a persona without too much difficulty. But it transcends our powers of imagination to form a clear picture of what we are as a self, for in this operation the part would have to comprehend the whole. There is little hope of our ever being able to reach even approximate consciousness of the self, since however much we may make conscious there will always exist an indeterminate and indeterminable amount of unconscious material which belongs to the totality of the self. Hence the self will always remain a supraordinate quantity.

275 The unconscious processes that compensate the conscious ego contain all those elements that are necessary for the self-

177

regulation of the psyche as a whole. On the personal level, these are the not consciously recognized personal motives which appear in dreams, or the meanings of daily situations which we have overlooked, or conclusions we have failed to draw, or affects we have not permitted, or criticisms we have spared ourselves. But the more we become conscious of ourselves through self-knowledge, and act accordingly, the more the layer of the personal unconscious that is superimposed on the collective unconscious will be diminished. In this way there arises a consciousness which is no longer imprisoned in the petty, oversensitive, personal world of the ego, but participates freely in the wider world of objective interests. This widened consciousness is no longer that touchy, egotistical bundle of personal wishes, fears, hopes, and ambitions which always has to be compensated or corrected by unconscious counter-tendencies; instead, it is a function of relationship to the world of objects, bringing the individual into absolute, binding, and indissoluble communion with the world at large. The complications arising at this stage are no longer egotistic wish-conflicts, but difficulties that concern others as much as oneself. At this stage it is fundamentally a question of collective problems, which have activated the collective unconscious because they require collective rather than personal compensation. We can now see that the unconscious produces contents which are valid not only for the person concerned, but for others as well, in fact for a great many people and possibly for all.

276   The Elgonyi, natives of the Elgon forests, of central Africa, explained to me that there are two kinds of dreams: the ordinary dream of the little man, and the "big vision" that only the great man has, e.g., the medicine-man or chief. Little dreams are of no account, but if a man has a "big dream" he summons the whole tribe in order to tell it to everybody.

277   How is a man to know whether his dream is a "big" or a "little" one? He knows it by an instinctive feeling of significance. He feels so overwhelmed by the impression it makes that he would never think of keeping the dream to himself. He *has* to tell it, on the psychologically correct assumption that it is of general significance. Even with us the collective dream has a feeling of importance about it that impels communication. It springs from a conflict of relationship and must therefore be

built into our conscious relations, because it compensates these and not just some inner personal quirk.

178 The processes of the collective unconscious are concerned not only with the more or less personal relations of an individual to his family or to a wider social group, but with his relations to society and to the human community in general. The more general and impersonal the condition that releases the unconscious reaction, the more significant, bizarre, and overwhelming will be the compensatory manifestation. It impels not just private communication, but drives people to revelations and confessions, and even to a dramatic representation of their fantasies.

179 I will explain by an example how the unconscious manages to compensate relationships. A somewhat arrogant gentleman once came to me for treatment. He ran a business in partnership with his younger brother. Relations between the two brothers were very strained, and this was one of the essential causes of my patient's neurosis. From the information he gave me, the real reason for the tension was not altogether clear. He had all kinds of criticisms to make of his brother, whose gifts he certainly did not show in a very favourable light. The brother frequently came into his dreams, always in the role of a Bismarck, Napoleon, or Julius Caesar. His house looked like the Vatican or Yildiz Kiosk. My patient's unconscious evidently had the need to exalt the rank of the younger brother. From this I concluded that he was setting himself too high and his brother too low. The further course of analysis entirely justified this inference.

180 Another patient, a young woman who clung to her mother in an extremely sentimental way, always had very sinister dreams about her. She appeared in the dreams as a witch, as a ghost, as a pursuing demon. The mother had spoilt her beyond all reason and had so blinded her by tenderness that the daughter had no conscious idea of her mother's harmful influence. Hence the compensatory criticism exercised by the unconscious.

181 I myself once happened to put too low a value on a patient, both intellectually and morally. In a dream I saw a castle perched on a high cliff, and on the topmost tower was a balcony, and there sat my patient. I did not hesitate to tell her this dream at once, naturally with the best results.

182 We all know how apt we are to make fools of ourselves in front of the very people we have unjustly underrated. Naturally

the case can also be reversed, as once happened to a friend of mine. While still a callow student he had written to Virchow, the pathologist, craving an audience with "His Excellency." When, quaking with fear, he presented himself and tried to give his name, he blurted out, "My name is Virchow." Whereupon His Excellency, smiling mischievously, said, "Ah! So your name is Virchow too?" The feeling of his own nullity was evidently too much for the unconscious of my friend, and in consequence it instantly prompted him to present himself as equal to Virchow in grandeur.

283   In these more personal relations there is of course no need for any very collective compensations. On the other hand, the figures employed by the unconscious in our first case are of a definitely collective nature: they are universally recognized heroes. Here there are two possible interpretations: either my patient's younger brother is a man of acknowledged and far-reaching collective importance, or my patient is overestimating his own importance not merely in relation to his brother but in relation to everybody else as well. For the first assumption there was no support at all, while for the second there was the evidence of one's own eyes. Since the man's extreme arrogance affected not only himself, but a far wider social group, the compensation availed itself of a collective image.

284   The same is true of the second case. The "witch" is a collective image; hence we must conclude that the blind dependence of the young woman applied as much to the wider social group as it did to her mother personally. This was indeed the case, in so far as she was still living in an exclusively infantile world, where the world was identical with her parents. These examples deal with relations within the personal orbit. There are, however, impersonal relations which occasionally need unconscious compensation. In such cases collective images appear with a more or less mythological character. Moral, philosophical, and religious problems are, on account of their universal validity, the most likely to call for mythological compensation. In the aforementioned novel by H. G. Wells we find a classical type of compensation: Mr. Preemby, a midget personality, discovers that he is really a reincarnation of Sargon, King of Kings. Happily, the genius of the author rescues poor old Sargon from pathological absurdity, and even gives the reader a chance to appre-

ciate the tragic and eternal meaning in this lamentable affray. Mr. Preemby, a complete nonentity, recognizes himself as the point of intersection of all ages past and future. This knowledge is not too dearly bought at the cost of a little madness, provided that Preemby is not in the end devoured by that monster of a primordial image—which is in fact what nearly happens to him.

285   The universal problem of evil and sin is another aspect of our impersonal relations to the world. Almost more than any other, therefore, this problem produces collective compensations. One of my patients, aged sixteen, had as the initial symptom of a severe compulsion neurosis the following dream: *He is walking along an unfamiliar street. It is dark, and he hears steps coming behind him. With a feeling of fear he quickens his pace. The footsteps come nearer, and his fear increases. He begins to run. But the footsteps seem to be overtaking him. Finally he turns round, and there he sees the devil. In deathly terror he leaps into the air and hangs there suspended.* This dream was repeated twice, a sign of its special urgency.

286   It is a notorious fact that the compulsion neuroses, by reason of their meticulousness and ceremonial punctilio, not only have the surface appearance of a moral problem but are indeed brimfull of inhuman beastliness and ruthless evil, against the integration of which the very delicately organized personality puts up a desperate struggle. This explains why so many things have to be performed in ceremonially "correct" style, as though to counteract the evil hovering in the background. After this dream the neurosis started, and its essential feature was that the patient had, as he put it, to keep himself in a "provisional" or "uncontaminated" state of purity. For this purpose he either severed or made "invalid" all contact with the world and with everything that reminded him of the transitoriness of human existence, by means of lunatic formalities, scrupulous cleansing ceremonies, and the anxious observance of innumerable rules and regulations of an unbelievable complexity. Even before the patient had any suspicion of the hellish existence that lay before him, the dream showed him that if he wanted to come down to earth again there would have to be a pact with evil.

287   Elsewhere I have described a dream that illustrates the compensation of a religious problem in a young theological student.[1]

1 "Archetypes of the Collective Unconscious," par. 71.

He was involved in all sorts of difficulties of belief, a not un-common occurrence in the man of today. In his dream he was the pupil of the "white magician," who, however, was dressed in black. After having instructed him up to a certain point, the white magician told him that they now needed the "black magi-cian." The black magician appeared, but clad in a white robe. He declared that he had found the keys of paradise, but needed the wisdom of the white magician in order to understand how to use them. This dream obviously contains the problem of oppo-sites which, as we know, has found in Taoist philosophy a solu-tion very different from the views prevailing in the West. The figures employed by the dream are impersonal collective images corresponding to the nature of the impersonal religious prob-lem. In contrast to the Christian view, the dream stresses the relativity of good and evil in a way that immediately calls to mind the Taoist symbol of Yin and Yang.

288   We should certainly not conclude from these compensations that, as the conscious mind becomes more deeply engrossed in universal problems, the unconscious will bring forth corre-spondingly far-reaching compensations. There is what one might call a legitimate and an illegitimate interest in imper-sonal problems. Excursions of this kind are legitimate only when they arise from the deepest and truest needs of the indi-vidual; illegitimate when they are either mere intellectual curi-osity or a flight from unpleasant reality. In the latter case the unconscious produces all too human and purely personal com-pensations, whose manifest aim is to bring the conscious mind back to ordinary reality. People who go illegitimately mooning after the infinite often have absurdly banal dreams which en-deavour to damp down their ebullience. Thus, from the nature of the compensation, we can at once draw conclusions as to the seriousness and rightness of the conscious strivings.

289   There are certainly not a few people who are afraid to admit that the unconscious could ever have "big" ideas. They will ob-ject, "But do you really believe that the unconscious is capable of offering anything like a constructive criticism of our Western mentality?" Of course, if we take the problem intellectually and impute rational intentions to the unconscious, the thing be-comes absurd. But it would never do to foist our conscious psy-chology upon the unconscious. Its mentality is an instinctive

one; it has no differentiated functions, and it does not "think" as we understand "thinking." It simply creates an image that answers to the conscious situation. This image contains as much thought as feeling, and is anything rather than a product of rationalistic reflection. Such an image would be better described as an artist's vision. We tend to forget that a problem like the one which underlies the dream last mentioned cannot, even to the conscious mind of the dreamer, be an intellectual problem, but is profoundly emotional. For a moral man the ethical problem is a passionate question which has its roots in the deepest instinctual processes as well as in his most idealistic aspirations. The problem for him is devastatingly real. It is not surprising, therefore, that the answer likewise springs from the depths of his nature. The fact that everyone thinks his psychology is the measure of all things, and, if he also happens to be a fool, will inevitably think that such a problem is beneath his notice, should not trouble the psychologist in the least, for he has to take things objectively, as he finds them, without twisting them to fit his subjective suppositions. The richer and more capacious natures may legitimately be gripped by an impersonal problem, and to the extent that this is so, their unconscious can answer in the same style. And just as the conscious mind can put the question, "Why is there this frightful conflict between good and evil?," so the unconscious can reply, "Look closer! Each needs the other. The best, just because it is the best, holds the seed of evil, and there is nothing so bad but good can come of it."

290   It might then dawn on the dreamer that the apparently insoluble conflict is, perhaps, a prejudice, a frame of mind conditioned by time and place. The seemingly complex dream-image might easily reveal itself as plain, instinctive common sense, as the tiny germ of a rational idea, which a maturer mind could just as well have thought consciously. At all events Chinese philosophy thought of it ages ago. The singularly apt, plastic configuration of thought is the prerogative of that primitive, natural spirit which is alive in all of us and is only obscured by a one-sided conscious development. If we consider the unconscious compensations from this angle, we might justifiably be accused of judging the unconscious too much from the conscious standpoint. And indeed, in pursuing these reflections, I have always started from the view that the unconscious simply reacts to the

conscious contents, albeit in a very significant way, but that it lacks initiative. It is, however, far from my intention to give the impression that the unconscious is merely reactive in all cases. On the contrary, there is a host of experiences which seem to prove that the unconscious is not only spontaneous but can actually take the lead. There are innumerable cases of people who lingered on in a pettifogging unconsciousness, only to become neurotic in the end. Thanks to the neurosis contrived by the unconscious, they are shaken out of their apathy, and this in spite of their own laziness and often desperate resistance.

291   Yet it would, in my view, be wrong to suppose that in such cases the unconscious is working to a deliberate and concerted plan and is striving to realize certain definite ends. I have found nothing to support this assumption. The driving force, so far as it is possible for us to grasp it, seems to be in essence only an urge towards self-realization. If it were a matter of some general teleological plan, then all individuals who enjoy a surplus of unconsciousness would necessarily be driven towards higher consciousness by an irresistible urge. That is plainly not the case. There are vast masses of the population who, despite their notorious unconsciousness, never get anywhere near a neurosis. The few who are smitten by such a fate are really persons of the "higher" type who, for one reason or another, have remained too long on a primitive level. Their nature does not in the long run tolerate persistence in what is for them an unnatural torpor. As a result of their narrow conscious outlook and their cramped existence they save energy; bit by bit it accumulates in the unconscious and finally explodes in the form of a more or less acute neurosis. This simple mechanism does not necessarily conceal a "plan." A perfectly understandable urge towards self-realization would provide a quite satisfactory explanation. We could also speak of a retarded maturation of the personality.

292   Since it is highly probable that we are still a long way from the summit of absolute consciousness, presumably everyone is capable of wider consciousness, and we may assume accordingly that the unconscious processes are constantly supplying us with contents which, if consciously recognized, would extend the range of consciousness. Looked at in this way, the unconscious appears as a field of experience of unlimited extent. If it were merely reactive to the conscious mind, we might aptly call it a

psychic mirror-world. In that case, the real source of all contents and activities would lie in the conscious mind, and there would be absolutely nothing in the unconscious except the distorted reflections of conscious contents. The creative process would be shut up in the conscious mind, and anything new would be nothing but conscious invention or cleverness. The empirical facts give the lie to this. Every creative man knows that spontaneity is the very essence of creative thought. Because the unconscious is not just a reactive mirror-reflection, but an independent, productive activity, its realm of experience is a self-contained world, having its own reality, of which we can only say that it affects us as we affect it—precisely what we say about our experience of the outer world. And just as material objects are the constituent elements of this world, so psychic factors constitute the objects of that other world.

293   The idea of psychic objectivity is by no means a new discovery. It is in fact one of the earliest and most universal acquisitions of humanity: it is nothing less than the conviction as to the concrete existence of a spirit-world. The spirit-world was certainly never an invention in the sense that fire-boring was an invention; it was far rather the experience, the conscious acceptance of a reality in no way inferior to that of the material world. I doubt whether primitives exist anywhere who are not acquainted with magical influence or a magical substance. ("Magical" is simply another word for "psychic.") It would also appear that practically all primitives are aware of the existence of spirits.[2] "Spirit" is a psychic fact. Just as we distinguish our own bodiliness from bodies that are strange to us, so primitives—if they have any notion of "souls" at all—distinguish between their own souls and the spirits, which are felt as strange and as "not belonging." They are objects of outward perception, whereas their own soul (or one of several souls where a plurality is assumed), though believed to be essentially akin to the spirits, is not usually an object of so-called sensible perception. After death the soul (or one of the plurality of souls) becomes a spirit which survives the dead man, and often it shows a marked dete-

---

[2] In cases of reports to the contrary, it must always be borne in mind that the fear of spirits is sometimes so great that people will actually deny that there are any spirits to fear. I have come across this myself among the dwellers on Mount Elgon.

rioration of character that partly contradicts the notion of personal immortality. The Bataks,[3] of Sumatra, go so far as to assert that the people who were good in this life turn into malign and dangerous spirits. Nearly everything that the primitives say about the tricks which the spirits play on the living, and the general picture they give of the *revenants*, corresponds down to the last detail with the phenomena established by spiritualistic experience. And just as the communications from the "Beyond" can be seen to be the activities of broken-off bits of the psyche, so these primitive spirits are manifestations of unconscious complexes.[4] The importance that modern psychology attaches to the "parental complex" is a direct continuation of primitive man's experience of the dangerous power of the ancestral spirits. Even the error of judgment which leads him unthinkingly to assume that the spirits are realities of the external world is carried on in our assumption (which is only partially correct) that the real parents are responsible for the parental complex. In the old trauma theory of Freudian psychoanalysis, and in other quarters as well, this assumption even passed for a scientific explanation. (It was in order to avoid this confusion that I advocated the term "parental imago." [5])

294   The simple soul is of course quite unaware of the fact that his nearest relations, who exercise immediate influence over him, create in him an image which is only partly a replica of themselves, while its other part is compounded of elements derived from himself. The imago is built up of parental influences plus the specific reactions of the child; it is therefore an image that reflects the object with very considerable qualifications. Naturally, the simple soul believes that his parents are as he sees them. The image is unconsciously projected, and when the parents die, the projected image goes on working as though it were a spirit existing on its own. The primitive then speaks of parental spirits who return by night (*revenants*), while the modern man calls it a father or mother complex.

295   The more limited a man's field of consciousness is, the more

---

3 Warnecke, *Die Religion der Batak* (1909).
4 Cf. "The Psychological Foundations of Belief in Spirits."
5 [This term was taken up by psychoanalysis, but in analytical psychology it has been largely replaced by "primordial image of the parent" or "parental archetype."—EDITORS.]

numerous the psychic contents (imagos) which meet him as quasi-external apparitions, either in the form of spirits, or as magical potencies projected upon living people (magicians, witches, etc.). At a rather higher stage of development, where the idea of the soul already exists, not all the imagos continue to be projected (where this happens, even trees and stones talk), but one or the other complex has come near enough to consciousness to be felt as no longer strange, but as somehow "belonging." Nevertheless, the feeling that it "belongs" is not at first sufficiently strong for the complex to be sensed as a subjective content of consciousness. It remains in a sort of no man's land between conscious and unconscious, in the half-shadow, in part belonging or akin to the conscious subject, in part an autonomous being, and meeting consciousness as such. At all events it is not necessarily obedient to the subject's intentions, it may even be of a higher order, more often than not a source of inspiration or warning, or of "supernatural" information. Psychologically such a content could be explained as a partly autonomous complex that is not yet fully integrated. The archaic souls, the *ba* and *ka* of the Egyptians, are complexes of this kind. At a still higher level, and particularly among the civilized peoples of the West, this complex is invariably of the feminine gender—anima and ψυχή—a fact for which deeper and cogent reasons are not lacking.

II

ANIMA AND ANIMUS

296   Among all possible spirits the spirits of the parents are in practice the most important; hence the universal incidence of the ancestor cult. In its original form it served to conciliate the *revenants,* but on a higher level of culture it became an essentially moral and educational institution, as in China. For the child, the parents are his closest and most influential relations. But as he grows older this influence is split off; consequently the parental imagos become increasingly shut away from consciousness, and on account of the restrictive influence they sometimes continue to exert, they easily acquire a negative aspect. In this way the parental imagos remain as alien elements somewhere "outside" the psyche. In place of the parents, woman now takes up her position as the most immediate environmental influence in the life of the adult man. She becomes his companion, she belongs to him in so far as she shares his life and is more or less of the same age. She is not of a superior order, either by virtue of age, authority, or physical strength. She is, however, a very influential factor and, like the parents, she produces an imago of a relatively autonomous nature—not an imago to be split off like that of the parents, but one that has to be kept associated with consciousness. Woman, with her very dissimilar psychology, is and always has been a source of information about things for which a man has no eyes. She can be his inspiration; her intuitive capacity, often superior to man's, can give him timely warning, and her feeling, always directed towards the personal, can show him ways which his own less personally accented feeling would never have discovered. What Tacitus says about the Germanic women is exactly to the point in this respect.[1]

297   Here, without a doubt, is one of the main sources for the feminine quality of the soul. But it does not seem to be the only

[1] *Germania* (Loeb edn.), pars. 18, 19.

source. No man is so entirely masculine that he has nothing feminine in him. The fact is, rather, that very masculine men have—carefully guarded and hidden—a very soft emotional life, often incorrectly described as "feminine." A man counts it a virtue to repress his feminine traits as much as possible, just as a woman, at least until recently, considered it unbecoming to be "mannish." The repression of feminine traits and inclinations naturally causes these contrasexual demands to accumulate in the unconscious. No less naturally, the imago of woman (the soul-image) becomes a receptacle for these demands, which is why a man, in his love-choice, is strongly tempted to win the woman who best corresponds to his own unconscious femininity—a woman, in short, who can unhesitatingly receive the projection of his soul. Although such a choice is often regarded and felt as altogether ideal, it may turn out that the man has manifestly married his own worst weakness. This would explain some highly remarkable conjunctions.

298   It seems to me, therefore, that apart from the influence of woman there is also the man's own femininity to explain the feminine nature of the soul-complex. There is no question here of any linguistic "accident," of the kind that makes the sun feminine in German and masculine in other languages. We have, in this matter, the testimony of art from all ages, and besides that the famous question: *habet mulier animam?* Most men, probably, who have any psychological insight at all will know what Rider Haggard means by "She-who-must-be-obeyed," and will also recognize the chord that is struck when they read Benoît's description of Antinéa.[2] Moreover they know at once the kind of woman who most readily embodies this mysterious factor, of which they have so vivid a premonition.

299   The wide recognition accorded to such books shows that there must be some supra-individual quality in this image of the anima,[3] something that does not owe a fleeting existence simply to its individual uniqueness, but is far more typical, with roots that go deeper than the obvious surface attachments I have pointed out. Both Rider Haggard and Benoît give unmistak-

---

2 Cf. Rider Haggard, *She;* Benoît, *L'Atlantide.*

3 Cf. *Psychological Types,* Def. 48, "Soul." [Also "Concerning the Archetypes, with Special Reference to the Anima Concept" and "The Psychological Aspects of the Kore."—EDITORS.]

able utterance to this supposition in the *historical* aspect of their anima figures.

300   As we know, there is no human experience, nor would experience be possible at all, without the intervention of a subjective aptitude. What is this subjective aptitude? Ultimately it consists in an innate psychic structure which allows man to have experiences of this kind. Thus the whole nature of man presupposes woman, both physically and spiritually. His system is tuned in to woman from the start, just as it is prepared for a quite definite world where there is water, light, air, salt, carbohydrates, etc. The form of the world into which he is born is already inborn in him as a virtual image. Likewise parents, wife, children, birth, and death are inborn in him as virtual images, as psychic aptitudes. These *a priori* categories have by nature a collective character; they are images of parents, wife, and children in general, and are not individual predestinations. We must therefore think of these images as lacking in solid content, hence as unconscious. They only acquire solidity, influence, and eventual consciousness in the encounter with empirical facts, which touch the unconscious aptitude and quicken it to life. They are in a sense the deposits of all our ancestral experiences, but they are not the experiences themselves. So at least it seems to us, in the present limited state of our knowledge. (I must confess that I have never yet found infallible evidence for the inheritance of memory images, but I do not regard it as positively precluded that in addition to these collective deposits which contain nothing specifically individual, there may also be inherited memories that are individually determined.)

301   An inherited collective image of woman exists in a man's unconscious, with the help of which he apprehends the nature of woman. This inherited image is the third important source for the femininity of the soul.

302   As the reader will have grasped, we are not concerned here with a philosophical, much less a religious, concept of the soul, but with the psychological recognition of the existence of a semiconscious psychic complex, having partial autonomy of function. Clearly, this recognition has as much or as little to do with philosophical or religious conceptions of the soul, as psychology has as much or as little to do with philosophy or religion. I have no wish to embark here on a "battle of the facul-

ties," nor do I seek to demonstrate either to the philosopher or to the theologian what exactly he means by "soul." I must, however, restrain both of them from prescribing what the psychologist *ought* to mean by "soul." The quality of personal immortality so fondly attributed to the soul by religion is, for science, no more than a psychological *indicium* which is already included in the idea of autonomy. The quality of personal immortality is by no means a constant attribute of the soul as the primitive sees it, nor even immortality as such. But setting this view aside as altogether inaccessible to science, the immediate meaning of "immortality" is simply a psychic activity that transcends the limits of consciousness. "Beyond the grave" or "on the other side of death" means, psychologically, "beyond consciousness." There is positively nothing else it could mean, since statements about immortality can only be made by the living, who, as such, are not exactly in a position to pontificate about conditions "beyond the grave."

303　　The autonomy of the soul-complex naturally lends support to the notion of an invisible, personal entity that apparently lives in a world very different from ours. Consequently, once the activity of the soul is felt to be that of an autonomous entity having no ties with our mortal substance, it is but a step to imagining that this entity must lead an entirely independent existence, perhaps in a world of invisible things. Yet it is not immediately clear why the *invisibility* of this independent entity should simultaneously imply its *immortality*. The quality of immortality might easily derive from another fact to which I have already alluded, namely the characteristically historical aspect of the soul. Rider Haggard has given one of the best descriptions of this in *She*. When the Buddhists say that progressive perfection through meditation awakens memories of former incarnations, they are no doubt referring to the same psychological reality, the only difference being that they ascribe the historical factor not to the soul but to the Self (*atman*). It is altogether in keeping with the thoroughly extraverted attitude of the Western mind so far, that immortality should be ascribed, both by feeling and by tradition, to a soul which we distinguish more or less from our ego, and which also differs from the ego on account of its feminine qualities. It would be entirely logical if, by deepening that neglected, introverted side of our spiritual culture, there were to take place in us a transformation more akin to the Eastern frame of mind, where the quality of immortality would transfer itself from the ambiguous figure of the soul (*anima*) to the self. For it is essentially the overvaluation of the material object without that constellates a spiritual and immortal figure within (obviously for the purpose of compensation and self-regulation). Fundamentally, the historical factor does not attach only to the archetype of the feminine, but to all archetypes whatsoever, i.e., to every inherited unit, mental as well as physical. Our life is indeed the same as it ever was. At all events, in our sense of the word it is not transitory; for the same physiological and psychological processes that have been man's for hundreds of thousands of years still endure, instilling into our inmost hearts this profound intuition of the "eternal" continuity of the living. But the self, as an inclusive term that embraces our whole living organism, not only contains the deposit and totality of all past life, but is also a point of departure, the fertile soil from which all future life will spring. This premonition of futurity is as clearly impressed upon our innermost feelings as is the historical aspect. The idea of immortality follows legitimately from these psychological premises.

304   In the Eastern view the concept of the anima, as we have stated it here, is lacking, and so, logically, is the concept of a persona. This is certainly no accident, for, as I have already indicated, a compensatory relationship exists between persona and anima.

305   The persona is a complicated system of relations between the individual consciousness and society, fittingly enough a kind of mask, designed on the one hand to make a definite impression upon others, and, on the other, to conceal the true nature of the individual. That the latter function is superfluous could be maintained only by one who is so identified with his persona that he no longer knows himself; and that the former is unnecessary could only occur to one who is quite unconscious of the true nature of his fellows. Society expects, and indeed must expect, every individual to play the part assigned to him as perfectly as possible, so that a man who is a parson must not only carry out his official functions objectively, but must at all times and in all circumstances play the role of parson in a flawless manner. Society demands this as a kind of surety; each must stand at his

post, here a cobbler, there a poet. No man is expected to be both. Nor is it advisable to be both, for that would be "odd." Such a man would be "different" from other people, not quite reliable. In the academic world he would be a dilettante, in politics an "unpredictable" quantity, in religion a free-thinker—in short, he would always be suspected of unreliability and incompetence, because society is persuaded that only the cobbler who is not a poet can supply workmanlike shoes. To present an unequivocal face to the world is a matter of practical importance: the average man—the only kind society knows anything about—must keep his nose to one thing in order to achieve anything worth while, two would be too much. Our society is undoubtedly set on such an ideal. It is therefore not surprising that everyone who wants to get on must take these expectations into account. Obviously no one could completely submerge his individuality in these expectations; hence the construction of an artificial personality becomes an unavoidable necessity. The demands of propriety and good manners are an added inducement to assume a becoming mask. What goes on behind the mask is then called "private life." This painfully familiar division of consciousness into two figures, often preposterously different, is an incisive psychological operation that is bound to have repercussions on the unconscious.

306   The construction of a collectively suitable persona means a formidable concession to the external world, a genuine self-sacrifice which drives the ego straight into identification with the persona, so that people really do exist who believe they are what they pretend to be. The "soullessness" of such an attitude is, however, only apparent, for under no circumstances will the unconscious tolerate this shifting of the centre of gravity. When we examine such cases critically, we find that the excellence of the mask is compensated by the "private life" going on behind it. The pious Drummond once lamented that "bad temper is the vice of the virtuous." Whoever builds up too good a persona for himself naturally has to pay for it with irritability. Bismarck had hysterical weeping fits, Wagner indulged in correspondence about the belts of silk dressing-gowns, Nietzsche wrote letters to his "dear lama," Goethe held conversations with Eckermann, etc. But there are subtler things than the banal lapses of heroes. I once made the acquaintance of a very venerable personage—in

fact, one might easily call him a saint. I stalked round him for three whole days, but never a mortal failing did I find in him. My feeling of inferiority grew ominous, and I was beginning to think seriously of how I might better myself. Then, on the fourth day, his wife came to consult me. . . . Well, nothing of the sort has ever happened to me since. But this I did learn: that any man who becomes one with his persona can cheerfully let all disturbances manifest themselves through his wife without her noticing it, though she pays for her self-sacrifice with a bad neurosis.

307   These identifications with a social role are a very fruitful source of neuroses. A man cannot get rid of himself in favour of an artificial personality without punishment. Even the attempt to do so brings on, in all ordinary cases, unconscious reactions in the form of bad moods, affects, phobias, obsessive ideas, backslidings, vices, etc. The social "strong man" is in his private life often a mere child where his own states of feeling are concerned; his discipline in public (which he demands quite particularly of others) goes miserably to pieces in private. His "happiness in his work" assumes a woeful countenance at home; his "spotless" public morality looks strange indeed behind the mask—we will not mention deeds, but only fantasies, and the wives of such men would have a pretty tale to tell. As to his selfless altruism, his children have decided views about that.

308   To the degree that the world invites the individual to identify with the mask, he is delivered over to influences from within. "High rests on low," says Lao-tzu. An opposite forces its way up from inside; it is exactly as though the unconscious suppressed the ego with the very same power which drew the ego into the persona. The absence of resistance outwardly against the lure of the persona means a similar weakness inwardly against the influence of the unconscious. Outwardly an effective and powerful role is played, while inwardly an effeminate weakness develops in face of every influence coming from the unconscious. Moods, vagaries, timidity, even a limp sexuality (culminating in impotence) gradually gain the upper hand.

309   The persona, the ideal picture of a man as he should be, is inwardly compensated by feminine weakness, and as the individual outwardly plays the strong man, so he becomes inwardly a woman, i.e., the anima, for it is the anima that reacts to the

persona. But because the inner world is dark and invisible to the extraverted consciousness, and because a man is all the less capable of conceiving his weaknesses the more he is identified with the persona, the persona's counterpart, the anima, remains completely in the dark and is at once projected, so that our hero comes under the heel of his wife's slipper. If this results in a considerable increase of her power, she will acquit herself none too well. She becomes inferior, thus providing her husband with the welcome proof that it is not he, the hero, who is inferior in private, but his wife. In return the wife can cherish the illusion, so attractive to many, that at least she has married a hero, unperturbed by her own uselessness. This little game of illusion is often taken to be the whole meaning of life.

310   Just as, for the purpose of individuation, or self-realization, it is essential for a man to distinguish between what he is and how he appears to himself and to others, so it is also necessary for the same purpose that he should become conscious of his invisible system of relations to the unconscious, and especially of the anima, so as to be able to distinguish himself from her. One cannot of course distinguish oneself from something unconscious. In the matter of the persona it is easy enough to make it clear to a man that he and his office are two different things. But it is very difficult for a man to distinguish himself from his anima, the more so because she is invisible. Indeed, he has first to contend with the prejudice that everything coming from inside him springs from the truest depths of his being. The "strong man" will perhaps concede that in private life he is singularly undisciplined, but that, he says, is just his "weakness" with which, as it were, he proclaims his solidarity. Now there is in this tendency a cultural legacy that is not to be despised; for when a man recognizes that his ideal persona is responsible for his anything but ideal anima, his ideals are shattered, the world becomes ambiguous, he becomes ambiguous even to himself. He is seized by doubts about goodness, and what is worse, he doubts his own good intentions. When one considers how much our private idea of good intentions is bound up with vast historical assumptions, it will readily be understood that it is pleasanter and more in keeping with our present view of the world to deplore a personal weakness than to shatter ideals.

311   But since the unconscious factors act as determinants no less

than the factors that regulate the life of society, and are no less collective, I might just as well learn to distinguish between what *I* want and what the unconscious thrusts upon me, as to see what my office demands of me and what I myself desire. At first the only thing that is at all clear is the incompatibility of the demands coming from without and from within, with the ego standing between them, as between hammer and anvil. But over against this ego, tossed like a shuttlecock between the outer and inner demands, there stands some scarcely definable arbiter, which I would on no account label with the deceptive name "conscience," although, taken in its best sense, the word fits that arbiter very aptly indeed. What we have made of this "conscience" Spitteler has described with unsurpassable humour.[4] Hence we should strenuously avoid this particular signification. We should do far better to realize that the tragic counterplay between inside and outside (depicted in Job and *Faust* as the wager with God) represents, at bottom, the energetics of the life process, the polar tension that is necessary for self-regulation. However different, to all intents and purposes, these opposing forces may be, their fundamental meaning and desire is the life of the individual: they always fluctuate round this centre of balance. Just because they are inseparably related through opposition, they also unite in a mediatory meaning, which, willingly or unwillingly, is born out of the individual and is therefore divined by him. He has a strong feeling of what should be and what could be. To depart from this divination means error, aberration, illness.

312   It is probably no accident that our modern notions of "personal" and "personality" derive from the word *persona*. I can assert that my ego is personal or a personality, and in exactly the same sense I can say that my persona is a personality with which I identify myself more or less. The fact that I then possess two personalities is not so remarkable, since every autonomous or even relatively autonomous complex has the peculiarity of appearing as a personality, i.e., of being personified. This can be observed most readily in the so-called spiritualistic manifestations of automatic writing and the like. The sentences produced are always personal statements and are propounded in the first person singular, as though behind every utterance there stood

[4] *Psychological Types,* pars. 282ff.

an actual personality. A naïve intelligence at once thinks of spirits. The same sort of thing is also observable in the hallucinations of the insane, although these, more clearly than the first, can often be recognized as mere thoughts or fragments of thoughts whose connection with the conscious personality is immediately apparent to everyone.

313   The tendency of the relatively autonomous complex to direct personification also explains why the persona exercises such a "personal" effect that the ego is all too easily deceived as to which is the "true" personality.

314   Now, everything that is true of the persona and of all autonomous complexes in general also holds true of the anima. She likewise is a personality, and this is why she is so easily projected upon a woman. So long as the anima is unconscious she is always projected, for everything unconscious is projected. The first bearer of the soul-image is always the mother; later it is borne by those women who arouse the man's feelings, whether in a positive or a negative sense. Because the mother is the first bearer of the soul-image, separation from her is a delicate and important matter of the greatest educational significance. Accordingly among primitives we find a large number of rites designed to organize this separation. The mere fact of becoming adult, and of outward separation, is not enough; impressive initiations into the "men's house" and ceremonies of rebirth are still needed in order to make the separation from the mother (and hence from childhood) entirely effective.

315   Just as the father acts as a protection against the dangers of the external world and thus serves his son as a model persona, so the mother protects him against the dangers that threaten from the darkness of his psyche. In the puberty rites, therefore, the initiate receives instruction about these things of "the other side," so that he is put in a position to dispense with his mother's protection.

316   The modern civilized man has to forgo this primitive but nonetheless admirable system of education. The consequence is that the anima, in the form of the mother-imago, is transferred to the wife; and the man, as soon as he marries, becomes childish, sentimental, dependent, and subservient, or else truculent, tyrannical, hypersensitive, always thinking about the prestige of his superior masculinity. The last is of course merely the reverse

of the first. The safeguard against the unconscious, which is what his mother meant to him, is not replaced by anything in the modern man's education; unconsciously, therefore, his ideal of marriage is so arranged that his wife has to take over the magical role of the mother. Under the cloak of the ideally exclusive marriage he is really seeking his mother's protection, and thus he plays into the hands of his wife's possessive instincts. His fear of the dark incalculable power of the unconscious gives his wife an illegitimate authority over him, and forges such a dangerously close union that the marriage is permanently on the brink of explosion from internal tension—or else, out of protest, he flies to the other extreme, with the same results.

317   I am of the opinion that it is absolutely essential for a certain type of modern man to recognize his distinction not only from the persona, but from the anima as well. For the most part our consciousness, in true Western style, looks outwards, and the inner world remains in darkness. But this difficulty can be overcome easily enough, if only we will make the effort to apply the same concentration and criticism to the psychic material which manifests itself, not outside, but in our private lives. So accustomed are we to keep a shamefaced silence about this other side —we even tremble before our wives, lest they betray us!—and, if found out, to make rueful confessions of "weakness," that there would seem to be only one method of education, namely, to crush or repress the weaknesses as much as possible or at least hide them from the public. But that gets us nowhere.

318   Perhaps I can best explain what has to be done if I use the persona as an example. Here everything is plain and straightforward, whereas with the anima all is dark, to Western eyes anyway. When the anima continually thwarts the good intentions of the conscious mind, by contriving a private life that stands in sorry contrast to the dazzling persona, it is exactly the same as when a naïve individual, who has not the ghost of a persona, encounters the most painful difficulties in his passage through the world. There are indeed people who lack a developed persona— "Canadians who know not Europe's sham politeness"—blundering from one social solecism to the next, perfectly harmless and innocent, soulful bores or appealing children, or, if they are women, spectral Cassandras dreaded for their tactlessness, eternally misunderstood, never knowing what they are about, al-

ways taking forgiveness for granted, blind to the world, hopeless dreamers. From them we can see how a neglected persona works, and what one must do to remedy the evil. Such people can avoid disappointments and an infinity of sufferings, scenes, and social catastrophes only by learning to see how men behave in the world. They must learn to understand what society expects of them; they must realize that there are factors and persons in the world far above them; they must know that what they do has a meaning for others, and so forth. Naturally all this is child's play for one who has a properly developed persona. But if we reverse the picture and confront the man who possesses a brilliant persona with the anima, and, for the sake of comparison, set him beside the man with no persona, then we shall see that the latter is just as well informed about the anima and her affairs as the former is about the world. The use which either makes of his knowledge can just as easily be abused, in fact it is more than likely that it will be.

319   The man with the persona is blind to the existence of inner realities, just as the other is blind to the reality of the world, which for him has merely the value of an amusing or fantastic playground. But the fact of inner realities and their unqualified recognition is obviously the *sine qua non* for a serious consideration of the anima problem. If the external world is, for me, simply a phantasm, how should I take the trouble to establish a complicated system of relationship and adaptation to it? Equally, the "nothing but fantasy" attitude will never persuade me to regard my anima manifestations as anything more than fatuous weakness. If, however, I take the line that the world is outside *and* inside, that reality falls to the share of both, I must logically accept the upsets and annoyances that come to me from inside as symptoms of faulty adaptation to the conditions of that inner world. No more than the blows rained on the innocent abroad can be healed by moral repression will it help him resignedly to catalogue his "weaknesses." Here are reasons, intentions, consequences, which can be tackled by will and understanding. Take, for example, the "spotless" man of honour and public benefactor, whose tantrums and explosive moodiness terrify his wife and children. What is the anima doing here?

320   We can see it at once if we just allow things to take their natural course. Wife and children will become estranged; a vac-

uum will form about him. At first he will bewail the hard-heartedness of his family, and will behave if possible even more vilely than before. That will make the estrangement absolute. If the good spirits have not utterly forsaken him, he will after a time notice his isolation, and in his loneliness he will begin to understand how he caused the estrangement. Perhaps, aghast at himself, he will ask, "What sort of devil has got into me?"—without of course seeing the meaning of this metaphor. Then follow remorse, reconciliation, oblivion, repression, and, in next to no time, a new explosion. Clearly, the anima is trying to enforce a separation. This tendency is in nobody's interest. The anima comes between them like a jealous mistress who tries to alienate the man from his family. An official post or any other advantageous social position can do the same thing, but there we can understand the force of the attraction. Whence does the anima obtain the power to wield such enchantment? On the analogy with the persona there must be values or some other important and influential factors lying in the background like seductive promises. In such matters we must guard against rationalizations. Our first thought is that the man of honour is on the look-out for another woman. That might be—it might even be arranged by the anima as the most effective means to the desired end. Such an arrangement should not be misconstrued as an end in itself, for the blameless gentleman who is correctly married according to the law can be just as correctly divorced according to the law, which does not alter his fundamental attitude one iota. The old picture has merely received a new frame.

321   As a matter of fact, this arrangement is a very common method of implementing a separation—and of hampering a final solution. Therefore it is more reasonable not to assume that such an obvious possibility is the end-purpose of the separation. We would be better advised to investigate what is behind the tendencies of the anima. The first step is what I would call the objectivation of the anima, that is, the strict refusal to regard the trend towards separation as a weakness of one's own. Only when this has been done can one face the anima with the question, "Why do you want this separation?" To put the question in this personal way has the great advantage of recognizing the anima as a personality, and of making a relationship possible. The more personally she is taken the better.

322   To anyone accustomed to proceed purely intellectually and
rationally, this may seem altogether too ridiculous. It would indeed be the height of absurdity if a man tried to have a conversation with his persona, which he recognized merely as a psychological means of relationship. But it is absurd only for the man
who *has* a persona. If he has none, he is in this point no different
from the primitive who, as we know, has only one foot in what
we commonly call reality. With the other foot he stands in a
world of spirits, which is quite real to him. Our model case behaves, in the world, like a modern European; but in the world
of spirits he is the child of a troglodyte. He must therefore submit to living in a kind of prehistoric kindergarten until he has
got the right idea of the powers and factors which rule that other
world. Hence he is quite right to treat the anima as an autonomous personality and to address personal questions to her.

323   I mean this as an actual technique. We know that practically
every one has not only the peculiarity, but also the faculty, of
holding a conversation with himself. Whenever we are in a pre-
dicament we ask ourselves (or whom else?), "What shall I do?"
either aloud or beneath our breath, and we (or who else?) supply the answer. Since it is our intention to learn what we can
about the foundations of our being, this little matter of living in
a metaphor should not bother us. We have to accept it as a symbol of our primitive backwardness (or of such naturalness as is
still, mercifully, left to us) that we can, like the Negro, discourse
personally with our "snake." The psyche not being a unity but
a contradictory multiplicity of complexes, the dissociation required for our dialectics with the anima is not so terribly difficult. The art of it consists only in allowing our invisible partner
to make herself heard, in putting the mechanism of expression
momentarily at her disposal, without being overcome by the dis-
taste one naturally feels at playing such an apparently ludicrous
game with oneself, or by doubts as to the genuineness of the
voice of one's interlocutor. This latter point is technically very
important: we are so in the habit of identifying ourselves with
the thoughts that come to us that we invariably assume we have
made them. Curiously enough, it is precisely the most impossible thoughts for which we feel the greatest subjective responsibility. If we were more conscious of the inflexible universal laws
that govern even the wildest and most wanton fantasy, we

might perhaps be in a better position to see these thoughts above all others as objective occurrences, just as we see dreams, which nobody supposes to be deliberate or arbitrary inventions. It certainly requires the greatest objectivity and absence of prejudice to give the "other side" the opportunity for perceptible psychic activity. As a result of the repressive attitude of the conscious mind, the other side is driven into indirect and purely symptomatic manifestations, mostly of an emotional kind, and only in moments of overwhelming affectivity can fragments of the unconscious come to the surface in the form of thoughts or images. The inevitable accompanying symptom is that the ego momentarily identifies with these utterances, only to revoke them in the same breath. And, indeed, the things one says when in the grip of an affect sometimes seem very strange and daring. But they are easily forgotten, or wholly denied. This mechanism of deprecation and denial naturally has to be reckoned with if one wants to adopt an objective attitude. The habit of rushing in to correct and criticize is already strong enough in our tradition, and it is as a rule further reinforced by fear—a fear that can be confessed neither to oneself nor to others, a fear of insidious truths, of dangerous knowledge, of disagreeable verifications, in a word, fear of all those things that cause so many of us to flee from being alone with ourselves as from the plague. We say that it is egoistic or "morbid" to be preoccupied with oneself; one's own company is the worst, "it makes you melancholy"—such are the glowing testimonials accorded to our human make-up. They are evidently deeply ingrained in our Western minds. Whoever thinks in this way has obviously never asked himself what possible pleasure other people could find in the company of such a miserable coward. Starting from the fact that in a state of affect one often surrenders involuntarily to the truths of the other side, would it not be far better to make use of an affect so as to give the other side an opportunity to speak? It could therefore be said just as truly that one should cultivate the art of conversing with oneself in the setting provided by an affect, as though the affect itself were speaking without regard to our rational criticism. So long as the affect is speaking, criticism must be withheld. But once it has presented its case, we should begin criticizing as conscientiously as though a real person closely connected with us were our interlocutor. Nor should the matter rest there, but statement and answer must follow one another until a satisfactory end to the discussion is reached. Whether the result is satisfactory or not, only subjective feeling can decide. Any humbug is of course quite useless. Scrupulous honesty with oneself and no rash anticipation of what the other side might conceivably say are the indispensable conditions of this technique for educating the anima.

324　There is, however, something to be said for this characteristically Western fear of the other side. It is not entirely without justification, quite apart from the fact that it is real. We can understand at once the fear that the child and the primitive have of the great unknown. We have the same childish fear of our inner side, where we likewise touch upon a great unknown world. All we have is the affect, the fear, without knowing that this is a world-fear—for the world of affects is invisible. We have either purely theoretical prejudices against it, or superstitious ideas. One cannot even talk about the unconscious before many educated people without being accused of mysticism. The fear is legitimate in so far as our rational *Weltanschauung* with its scientific and moral certitudes—so hotly believed in because so deeply questionable—is shattered by the facts of the other side. If only one could avoid them, then the emphatic advice of the Philistine to "let sleeping dogs lie" would be the only truth worth advocating. And here I would expressly point out that I am not recommending the above technique as either necessary or even useful to any person not driven to it by necessity. The stages, as I said, are many, and there are greybeards who die as innocent as babes in arms, and in this year of grace troglodytes are still being born. There are truths which belong to the future, truths which belong to the past, and truths which belong to no time.

325　I can imagine someone using this technique out of a kind of holy inquisitiveness, some youth, perhaps, who would like to set wings to his feet, not because of lameness, but because he yearns for the sun. But a grown man, with too many illusions dissipated, will submit to this inner humiliation and surrender only if forced, for why should he let the terrors of childhood again have their way with him? It is no light matter to stand between a day-world of exploded ideals and discredited values, and a night-world of apparently senseless fantasy. The weirdness of this standpoint is in fact so great that there is probably nobody who does not reach out for security, even though it be a reaching back to the mother who shielded his childhood from the terrors of night. Whoever is afraid must needs be dependent; a weak thing needs support. That is why the primitive mind, from deep psychological necessity, begot religious instruction and embodied it in magician and priest. *Extra ecclesiam nulla salus* is still a valid truth today—for those who can go back to it. For the few who cannot, there is only dependence upon a human being, a humbler and a prouder dependence, a weaker and a stronger support, so it seems to me, than any other. What can one say of the Protestant? He has neither church nor priest, but only God—and even God becomes doubtful.

326   The reader may ask in some consternation, "But what on earth does the anima do, that such double insurances are needed before one can come to terms with her?" I would recommend my reader to study the comparative history of religion so intently as to fill these dead chronicles with the emotional life of those who lived these religions. Then he will get some idea of what lives on the other side. The old religions with their sublime and ridiculous, their friendly and fiendish symbols did not drop from the blue, but were born of this human soul that dwells within us at this moment. All those things, their primal forms, live on in us and may at any time burst in upon us with annihilating force, in the guise of mass-suggestions against which the individual is defenceless. Our fearsome gods have only changed their names: they now rhyme with *ism*. Or has anyone the nerve to claim that the World War or Bolshevism was an ingenious invention? Just as outwardly we live in a world where a whole continent may be submerged at any moment, or a pole be shifted, or a new pestilence break out, so inwardly we live in a world where at any moment something similar may occur, albeit in the form of an idea, but no less dangerous and untrustworthy for that. Failure to adapt to this inner world is a negligence entailing just as serious consequences as ignorance and ineptitude in the outer world. It is after all only a tiny fraction of humanity, living mainly on that thickly populated peninsula of Asia which juts out into the Atlantic Ocean, and calling themselves "cultured," who, because they lack all contact with nature, have hit upon the idea that religion is a peculiar kind of

mental disturbance of undiscoverable purport. Viewed from a safe distance, say from central Africa or Tibet, it would certainly look as if this fraction had projected its own unconscious mental derangements upon nations still possessed of healthy instincts.

327   Because the things of the inner world influence us all the more powerfully for being unconscious, it is essential for anyone who intends to make progress in self-culture (and does not all culture begin with the individual?) to objectivate the effects of the anima and then try to understand what contents underlie those effects. In this way he adapts to, and is protected against, the invisible. No adaptation can result without concessions to both worlds. From a consideration of the claims of the inner and outer worlds, or rather, from the conflict between them, the possible and the necessary follows. Unfortunately our Western mind, lacking all culture in this respect, has never yet devised a concept, nor even a name, for the *union of opposites through the middle path,* that most fundamental item of inward experience, which could respectably be set against the Chinese concept of Tao. It is at once the most individual fact and the most universal, the most legitimate fulfilment of the meaning of the individual's life.

328   In the course of my exposition so far, I have kept exclusively to *masculine* psychology. The anima, being of feminine gender, is exclusively a figure that compensates the masculine consciousness. In woman the compensating figure is of a masculine character, and can therefore appropriately be termed the *animus.* If it was no easy task to describe what is meant by the anima, the difficulties become almost insuperable when we set out to describe the psychology of the animus.

329   The fact that a man naïvely ascribes his anima reactions to himself, without seeing that he really cannot identify himself with an autonomous complex, is repeated in feminine psychology, though if possible in even more marked form. This identification with an autonomous complex is the essential reason why it is so difficult to understand and describe the problem, quite apart from its inherent obscurity and strangeness. We always start with the naïve assumption that we are masters in our own house. Hence we must first accustom ourselves to the thought that, in our most intimate psychic life as well, we live in a kind of house which has doors and windows to the world, but that,

although the objects or contents of this world act upon us, they do not belong to us. For many people this hypothesis is by no means easy to conceive, just as they do not find it at all easy to understand and to accept the fact that their neighbour's psychology is not necessarily identical with their own. My reader may think that the last remark is something of an exaggeration, since in general one is aware of individual differences. But it must be remembered that our individual conscious psychology develops out of an original state of unconsciousness and therefore of non-differentiation (termed by Lévy-Bruhl *participation mystique*). Consequently, consciousness of differentiation is a relatively late achievement of mankind, and presumably but a relatively small sector of the indefinitely large field of original identity. Differentiation is the essence, the *sine qua non* of consciousness. Everything unconscious is undifferentiated, and everything that happens unconsciously proceeds on the basis of non-differentiation—that is to say, there is no determining whether it belongs or does not belong to oneself. It cannot be established *a priori* whether it concerns me, or another, or both. Nor does feeling give us any sure clues in this respect.

330   An inferior consciousness cannot *eo ipso* be ascribed to women; it is merely different from masculine consciousness. But, just as a woman is often clearly conscious of things which a man is still groping for in the dark, so there are naturally fields of experience in a man which, for woman, are still wrapped in the shadows of non-differentiation, chiefly things in which she has little interest. Personal relations are as a rule more important and interesting to her than objective facts and their interconnections. The wide fields of commerce, politics, technology, and science, the whole realm of the applied masculine mind, she relegates to the penumbra of consciousness; while, on the other hand, she develops a minute consciousness of personal relationships, the infinite nuances of which usually escape the man entirely.

331   We must therefore expect the unconscious of woman to show aspects essentially different from those found in man. If I were to attempt to put in a nutshell the difference between man and woman in this respect, i.e., what it is that characterizes the animus as opposed to the anima, I could only say this: as the anima produces *moods,* so the animus produces *opinions;* and as the

moods of a man issue from a shadowy background, so the opinions of a woman rest on equally unconscious prior assumptions. Animus opinions very often have the character of solid convictions that are not lightly shaken, or of principles whose validity is seemingly unassailable. If we analyse these opinions, we immediately come upon unconscious assumptions whose existence must first be inferred; that is to say, the opinions are apparently conceived *as though* such assumptions existed. But in reality the opinions are not thought out at all; they exist ready made, and they are held so positively and with so much conviction that the woman never has the shadow of a doubt about them.

332 One would be inclined to suppose that the animus, like the anima, personifies itself in a single figure. But this, as experience shows, is true only up to a point, because another factor unexpectedly makes its appearance, which brings about an essentially different situation from that existing in a man. The animus does not appear as one person, but as a plurality of persons. In H. G. Wells' novel *Christina Alberta's Father,* the heroine, in all that she does or does not do, is constantly under the surveillance of a supreme moral authority, which tells her with remorseless precision and dry matter-of-factness what she is doing and for what motives. Wells calls this authority a "Court of Conscience." This collection of condemnatory judges, a sort of College of Preceptors, corresponds to a personification of the animus. The animus is rather like an assembly of fathers or dignitaries of some kind who lay down incontestable, "rational," *ex cathedra* judgments. On closer examination these exacting judgments turn out to be largely sayings and opinions scraped together more or less unconsciously from childhood on, and compressed into a canon of average truth, justice, and reasonableness, a compendium of preconceptions which, whenever a conscious and competent judgment is lacking (as not infrequently happens), instantly obliges with an opinion. Sometimes these opinions take the form of so-called sound common sense, sometimes they appear as principles which are like a travesty of education: "People have always done it like this," or "Everybody says it is like that."

333 It goes without saying that the animus is just as often projected as the anima. The men who are particularly suited to these projections are either walking replicas of God himself, who know all about everything, or else they are misunderstood

207

word-addicts with a vast and windy vocabulary at their command, who translate common or garden reality into the terminology of the sublime. It would be insufficient to characterize the animus merely as a conservative, collective conscience; he is also a neologist who, in flagrant contradiction to his correct opinions, has an extraordinary weakness for difficult and unfamiliar words which act as a pleasant substitute for the odious task of reflection.

334   Like the anima, the animus is a jealous lover. He is an adept at putting, in place of the real man, an opinion about him, the exceedingly disputable grounds for which are never submitted to criticism. Animus opinions are invariably collective, and they override individuals and individual judgments in exactly the same way as the anima thrusts her emotional anticipations and projections between man and wife. If the woman happens to be pretty, these animus opinions have for the man something rather touching and childlike about them, which makes him adopt a benevolent, fatherly, professorial manner. But if the woman does not stir his sentimental side, and competence is expected of her rather than appealing helplessness and stupidity, then her animus opinions irritate the man to death, chiefly because they are based on nothing but opinion for opinion's sake, and "everybody has a right to his own opinions." Men can be pretty venomous here, for it is an inescapable fact that the animus always plays up the anima—and *vice versa*, of course—so that all further discussion becomes pointless.

335   In intellectual women the animus encourages a critical disputatiousness and would-be highbrowism, which, however, consists essentially in harping on some irrelevant weak point and nonsensically making it the main one. Or a perfectly lucid discussion gets tangled up in the most maddening way through the introduction of a quite different and if possible perverse point of view. Without knowing it, such women are solely intent upon exasperating the man and are, in consequence, the more completely at the mercy of the animus. "Unfortunately I am always right," one of these creatures once confessed to me.

336   However, all these traits, as familiar as they are unsavoury, are simply and solely due to the extraversion of the animus. The animus does not belong to the function of conscious relationship; his function is rather to facilitate relations with the uncon-

scious. Instead of the woman merely associating opinions with external situations—situations which she ought to think about consciously—the animus, as an associative function, should be directed inwards, where it could associate the contents of the unconscious. The technique of coming to terms with the animus is the same in principle as in the case of the anima; only here the woman must learn to criticize and hold her opinions at a distance; not in order to repress them, but, by investigating their origins, to penetrate more deeply into the background, where she will then discover the primordial images, just as the man does in his dealings with the anima. The animus is the deposit, as it were, of all woman's ancestral experiences of man—and not only that, he is also a creative and procreative being, not in the sense of masculine creativity, but in the sense that he brings forth something we might call the λόγος σπερματικός, the spermatic word. Just as a man brings forth his work as a complete creation out of his inner feminine nature, so the inner masculine side of a woman brings forth creative seeds which have the power to fertilize the feminine side of the man. This would be the *femme inspiratrice* who, if falsely cultivated, can turn into the worst kind of dogmatist and high-handed pedagogue—a regular "animus hound," as one of my women patients aptly expressed it.

337   A woman possessed by the animus is always in danger of losing her femininity, her adapted feminine persona, just as a man in like circumstances runs the risk of effeminacy. These psychic changes of sex are due entirely to the fact that a function which belongs inside has been turned outside. The reason for this perversion is clearly the failure to give adequate recognition to an inner world which stands autonomously opposed to the outer world, and makes just as serious demands on our capacity for adaptation.

338   With regard to the plurality of the animus as distinguished from what we might call the "uni-personality" of the anima, this remarkable fact seems to me to be a correlate of the conscious attitude. The conscious attitude of woman is in general far more exclusively personal than that of man. Her world is made up of fathers and mothers, brothers and sisters, husbands and children. The rest of the world consists likewise of families, who nod to each other but are, in the main, interested essentially in

themselves. The man's world is the nation, the state, business concerns, etc. His family is simply a means to an end, one of the foundations of the state, and his wife is not necessarily *the* woman for him (at any rate not as the woman means it when she says "my man"). The general means more to him than the personal; his world consists of a multitude of co-ordinated factors, whereas her world, outside her husband, terminates in a sort of cosmic mist. A passionate exclusiveness therefore attaches to the man's anima, and an indefinite variety to the woman's animus. Whereas the man has, floating before him, in clear outlines, the alluring form of a Circe or a Calypso, the animus is better expressed as a bevy of Flying Dutchmen or unknown wanderers from over the sea, never quite clearly grasped, protean, given to persistent and violent motion. These personifications appear especially in dreams, though in concrete reality they can be famous tenors, boxing champions, or great men in far-away, unknown cities.

339　　These two crepuscular figures from the dark hinterland of the psyche—truly the semi-grotesque "guardians of the threshold," to use the pompous jargon of theosophy—can assume an almost inexhaustible number of shapes, enough to fill whole volumes. Their complicated transformations are as rich and strange as the world itself, as manifold as the limitless variety of their conscious correlate, the persona. They inhabit the twilight sphere, and we can just make out that the autonomous complex of anima and animus is essentially a psychological function that has usurped, or rather retained, a "personality" only because this function is itself autonomous and undeveloped. But already we can see how it is possible to break up the personifications, since by making them conscious we convert them into bridges to the unconscious. It is because we are not using them purposefully as functions that they remain personified complexes. So long as they are in this state they must be accepted as relatively independent personalities. They cannot be integrated into consciousness while their contents remain unknown. The purpose of the dialectical process is to bring these contents into the light; and only when this task has been completed, and the conscious mind has become sufficiently familiar with the unconscious processes reflected in the anima, will the anima be felt simply as a function.

340   I do not expect every reader to grasp right away what is meant by animus and anima. But I hope he will at least have gained the impression that it is not a question of anything "metaphysical," but far rather of empirical facts which could equally well be expressed in rational and abstract language. I have purposely avoided too abstract a terminology because, in matters of this kind, which hitherto have been so inaccessible to our experience, it is useless to present the reader with an intellectual formulation. It is far more to the point to give him some conception of what the actual possibilities of experience are. Nobody can really understand these things unless he has experienced them himself. I am therefore much more interested in pointing out the possible ways to such experience than in devising intellectual formulae which, for lack of experience, must necessarily remain an empty web of words. Unfortunately there are all too many who learn the words by heart and add the experiences in their heads, thereafter abandoning themselves, according to temperament, either to credulity or to criticism. We are concerned here with a new questioning, a new—and yet age-old— field of psychological experience. We shall be able to establish relatively valid theories about it only when the corresponding psychological facts are known to a sufficient number of people. The first things to be discovered are always facts, not theories. Theory-building is the outcome of discussion among many.

III

THE TECHNIQUE OF DIFFERENTIATION
BETWEEN THE EGO AND
THE FIGURES OF THE
UNCONSCIOUS

341   I owe it to the reader to give him a detailed example of the specific activity of animus and anima. Unfortunately this material is so enormous and demands so much explanation of symbols that I cannot include such an account within the compass of this essay. I have, however, published some of these products with all their symbolical associations in a separate work,[1] and to this I must refer the reader. In that book I said nothing about the animus, because at that time this function was still unknown to me. Nevertheless, if I advise a woman patient to associate her unconscious contents, she will always produce the same kind of fantasy. The masculine hero figure who almost unfailingly appears is the animus, and the succession of fantasy-experiences demonstrates the gradual transformation and dissolution of the autonomous complex.

342   This transformation is the aim of the analysis of the unconscious. If there is no transformation, it means that the determining influence of the unconscious is unabated, and that it will in some cases persist in maintaining neurotic symptoms in spite of all our analysis and all our understanding. Alternatively, a compulsive transference will take hold, which is just as bad as a neurosis. Obviously in such cases no amount of suggestion, good will, and purely reductive understanding has helped to break the power of the unconscious. This is not to say—once again I would like to emphasize this point very clearly—that all psychotherapeutic methods are, by and large, useless. I merely want to stress the fact that there are not a few cases where the doctor has to make up his mind to deal fundamentally with the uncon-

1 *Symbols of Transformation.*

scious, to come to a real settlement with it. This is of course something very different from interpretation. In the latter case it is taken for granted that the doctor *knows* beforehand, so as to be able to interpret. But in the case of a real settlement it is not a question of interpretation: it is a question of releasing unconscious processes and letting them come into the conscious mind in the form of fantasies. We can try our hand at interpreting these fantasies if we like. In many cases it may be quite important for the patient to have some idea of the meaning of the fantasies produced. But it is of vital importance that he should experience them to the full and, in so far as intellectual understanding belongs to the totality of experience, also understand them. Yet I would not give priority to understanding. Naturally the doctor must be able to assist the patient in his understanding, but, since he will not and indeed cannot understand everything, the doctor should assiduously guard against clever feats of interpretation. For the important thing is not to interpret and understand the fantasies, but primarily to experience them. Alfred Kubin has given a very good description of the unconscious in his book *Die andere Seite;* that is, he has described what he, as an artist, experienced of the unconscious. It is an artistic experience which, in the deeper meaning of human experience, is incomplete. I would like to recommend an attentive reading of this book to everybody who is interested in these questions. He will then discover the incompleteness I speak of: the vision is experienced artistically, but not humanly. By "human" experience I mean that the person of the author should not just be included passively in the vision, but that he should face the figures of the vision actively and reactively, with full consciousness. I would level the same criticism at the authoress of the fantasies dealt with in the book mentioned above; she, too, merely stands opposite the fantasies forming themselves out of the unconscious, perceiving them, or at best passively enduring them. But a real settlement with the unconscious demands a firmly opposed conscious standpoint.

343   I will try to explain what I mean by an example. One of my patients had the following fantasy: *He sees his fiancée running down the road towards the river. It is winter, and the river is frozen. She runs out on the ice, and he follows her. She goes right out, and then the ice breaks, a dark fissure appears, and he*

is afraid she is going to jump in. And that is what happens: she jumps into the crack, and he watches her sadly.

344   This fragment, although torn out of its context, clearly shows the attitude of the conscious mind: it perceives and passively endures, the fantasy-image is merely seen and felt, it is two-dimensional, as it were, because the patient is not sufficiently involved. Therefore the fantasy remains a flat image, concrete and agitating perhaps, but unreal, like a dream. This unreality comes from the fact that he himself is not playing an active part. If the fantasy happened in reality, he would not be at a loss for some means to prevent his fiancée from committing suicide. He could, for instance, easily overtake her and restrain her bodily from jumping into the crack. Were he to act in reality as he acted in the fantasy, he would obviously be paralysed, either with horror, or because of the unconscious thought that he really has no objection to her committing suicide. The fact that he remains passive in the fantasy merely expresses his attitude to the activity of the unconscious in general: he is fascinated and stupefied by it. In reality he suffers from all sorts of depressive ideas and convictions; he thinks he is no good, that he has some hopeless hereditary taint, that his brain is degenerating, etc. These negative feelings are so many auto-suggestions which he accepts without argument. Intellectually, he can understand them perfectly and recognize them as untrue, but nevertheless the feelings persist. They cannot be attacked by the intellect because they have no intellectual or rational basis; they are rooted in an unconscious, irrational fantasy-life which is not amenable to conscious criticism. In these cases the unconscious must be given an opportunity to produce its fantasies, and the above fragment is just such a product of unconscious fantasy activity. Since the case was one of psychogenic depression, the depression itself was due to fantasies of whose existence the patient was totally unconscious. In genuine melancholia, extreme exhaustion, poisoning, etc., the situation would be reversed: the patient has such fantasies because he is in a depressed condition. But in a case of psychogenic depression he is depressed because he has such fantasies. My patient was a very clever young man who had been intellectually enlightened as to the cause of his neurosis by a lengthy analysis. However, intellectual understanding made no difference to his depression. In cases of this sort the doctor

should spare himself the useless trouble of delving still further into the causality; for, when a more or less exhaustive understanding is of no avail, the discovery of yet another little bit of causality will be of no avail either. The unconscious has simply gained an unassailable ascendency; it wields an attractive force that can invalidate all conscious contents—in other words, it can withdraw libido from the conscious world and thereby produce a "depression," an *abaissement du niveau mental* (Janet). But as a result of this we must, according to the law of energy, expect an accumulation of value—i.e., libido—in the unconscious.

345   Libido can never be apprehended except in a definite form; that is to say, it is identical with fantasy-images. And we can only release it from the grip of the unconscious by bringing up the corresponding fantasy-images. That is why, in a case like this, we give the unconscious a chance to bring its fantasies to the surface. This is how the foregoing fragment was produced. It is a single episode from a long and very intricate series of fantasy-images, corresponding to the quota of energy that was lost to the conscious mind and its contents. The patient's conscious world has become cold, empty, and grey; but his unconscious is activated, powerful, and rich. It is characteristic of the nature of the unconscious psyche that it is sufficient unto itself and knows no human considerations. Once a thing has fallen into the unconscious it is retained there, regardless of whether the conscious mind suffers or not. The latter can hunger and freeze, while everything in the unconscious becomes verdant and blossoms.

346   So at least it appears at first. But when we look deeper, we find that this unconcern of the unconscious has a meaning, indeed a purpose and a goal. There are psychic goals that lie beyond the conscious goals; in fact, they may even be inimical to them. But we find that the unconscious has an inimical or ruthless bearing towards the conscious only when the latter adopts a false or pretentious attitude.

347   The conscious attitude of my patient is so one-sidedly intellectual and rational that nature herself rises up against him and annihilates his whole world of conscious values. But he cannot de-intellectualize himself and make himself dependent on another function, e.g., feeling, for the very simple reason that he has not got it. The unconscious has it. Therefore we have no alternative but to hand over the leadership to the unconscious

and give it the opportunity of becoming a conscious content in the form of fantasies. If, formerly, my patient clung to his intellectual world and defended himself with rationalizations against what he regarded as his illness, he must now yield himself up to it entirely, and when a fit of depression comes upon him, he must no longer force himself to some kind of work in order to forget, but must accept his depression and give it a hearing.

348   Now this is the direct opposite of succumbing to a mood, which is so typical of neurosis. It is no weakness, no spineless surrender, but a hard achievement, the essence of which consists in keeping your objectivity despite the temptations of the mood, and in making the mood your object, instead of allowing it to become in you the dominating subject. So the patient must try to get his mood to speak to him; his mood must tell him all about itself and show him through what kind of fantastic analogies it is expressing itself.

349   The foregoing fragment is a bit of visualized mood. If he had not suceeded in keeping his objectivity in relation to his mood, he would have had, in place of the fantasy-image, only a crippling sense that everything was going to the devil, that he was incurable, etc. But because he gave his mood a chance to express itself in an image, he succeeded in converting at least a small sum of libido, of unconscious creative energy in eidetic form, into a conscious content and thus withdrawing it from the sphere of the unconscious.

350   But this effort is not enough, for the fantasy, to be completely experienced, demands not just perception and passivity, but active participation. The patient would comply with this demand if he conducted himself in the fantasy as he would doubtless conduct himself in reality. He would never remain an idle spectator while his fiancée tried to drown herself; he would leap up and stop her. This should also happen in the fantasy. If he succeeds in behaving in the fantasy as he would behave in a similar situation in reality, he would prove that he was taking the fantasy seriously, i.e., assigning absolute reality value to the unconscious. In this way he would have won a victory over his one-sided intellectualism and, indirectly, would have asserted the validity of the irrational standpoint of the unconscious.

351   That would be the complete experience of the unconscious

216

demanded of him. But one must not underestimate what that actually means: your whole world is menaced by fantastic irreality. It is almost insuperably difficult to forget, even for a moment, that all this is only fantasy, a figment of the imagination that must strike one as altogether arbitrary and artificial. How can one assert that anything of this kind is "real" and take it seriously?

352   We can hardly be expected to believe in a sort of double life, in which we conduct ourselves on one plane as modest average citizens, while on another we have unbelievable adventures and perform heroic deeds. In other words, we must not concretize our fantasies. But there is in man a strange propensity to do just this, and all his aversion to fantasy and his critical depreciation of the unconscious come solely from the deep-rooted fear of this tendency. Concretization and the fear of it are both primitive superstitions, but they still survive in the liveliest form among so-called enlightened people. In his civic life a man may follow the trade of a shoemaker, but as the member of a sect he puts on the dignity of an archangel. To all appearances he is a small tradesman, but among the freemasons he is a mysterious grandee. Another sits all day in his office; at evening, in his circle, he is a reincarnation of Julius Caesar, fallible as a man, but in his official capacity infallible. These are all unintentional concretizations.

353   As against this, the scientific credo of our time has developed a superstitious phobia about fantasy. But the real is what works. And the fantasies of the unconscious work, there can be no doubt about that. Even the cleverest philosopher can be the victim of a thoroughly idiotic agoraphobia. Our famous scientific reality does not afford us the slightest protection against the so-called irreality of the unconscious. Something works behind the veil of fantastic images, whether we give this something a good name or a bad. It is something real, and for this reason its manifestations must be taken seriously. But first the tendency to concretization must be overcome; in other words, we must not take the fantasies literally when we approach the question of interpreting them. While we are in the grip of the actual experience, the fantasies cannot be taken literally enough. But when it comes to understanding them, we must on no account mistake

the semblance, the fantasy-image as such, for the operative process underlying it. The semblance is not the thing itself, but only its expression.

354 Thus my patient is not experiencing the suicide scene "on another plane" (though in every other respect it is just as concrete as a real suicide); he experiences something real which looks like a suicide. The two opposing "realities," the world of the conscious and the world of the unconscious, do not quarrel for supremacy, but each makes the other relative. That the reality of the unconscious is very relative indeed will presumably arouse no violent contradiction; but that the reality of the conscious world could be doubted will be accepted with less alacrity. And yet both "realities" are psychic experience, psychic semblances painted on an inscrutably dark back-cloth. To the critical intelligence, nothing is left of *absolute* reality.

355 Of the essence of things, of absolute being, we know nothing. But we experience various effects: from "outside" by way of the senses, from "inside" by way of fantasy. We would never think of asserting that the colour "green" had an independent existence; similarly we ought never to imagine that a fantasy-experience exists in and for itself, and is therefore to be taken quite literally. It is an expression, an appearance standing for something unknown but real. The fantasy-fragment I have mentioned coincides in time with a wave of depression and desperation, and this event finds expression in the fantasy. The patient really does have a fiancée; for him she represents the one emotional link with the world. Snap that link, and it would be the end of his relation to the world. This would be an altogether hopeless aspect. But his fiancée is also a symbol for his anima, that is, for his relation to the unconscious. Hence the fantasy simultaneously expresses the fact that, without any hindrance on his part, his anima is disappearing again into the unconscious. This aspect shows that once again his mood is stronger than he is. It throws everything to the winds, while he looks on without lifting a hand. But he could easily step in and arrest the anima.

356 I give preference to this latter aspect, because the patient is an introvert whose life-relationship is ruled by inner facts. Were he an extravert, I would have to give preference to the first aspect, because for the extravert life is governed primarily by his

relation to human beings. He might in the trough of a mood do away with his fiancée and himself too, whereas the introvert harms himself most when he casts off his relation to the anima, i.e., to the object within.

357 So my patient's fantasy clearly reveals the negative movement of the unconscious, a tendency to recoil from the conscious world so energetically that it sucks away the libido from consciousness and leaves the latter empty. But, by making the fantasy conscious, we stop this process from happening unconsciously. If the patient were himself to participate actively in the way described above, he would possess himself of the libido invested in the fantasy, and would thus gain added influence over the unconscious.

358 Continual conscious realization of unconscious fantasies, together with active participation in the fantastic events, has, as I have witnessed in a very large number of cases, the effect firstly of extending the conscious horizon by the inclusion of numerous unconscious contents; secondly of gradually diminishing the dominant influence of the unconscious; and thirdly of bringing about a change of personality.

359 This change of personality is naturally not an alteration of the original hereditary disposition, but rather a transformation of the general attitude. Those sharp cleavages and antagonisms between conscious and unconscious, such as we see so clearly in the endless conflicts of neurotic natures, nearly always rest on a noticeable one-sidedness of the conscious attitude, which gives absolute precedence to one or two functions, while the others are unjustly thrust into the background. Conscious realization and experience of fantasies assimilates the unconscious inferior functions to the conscious mind—a process which is naturally not without far-reaching effects on the conscious attitude.

360 For the moment I will refrain from discussing the nature of this change of personality, since I only want to emphasize the fact that an important change does take place. I have called this change, which is the aim of our analysis of the unconscious, the transcendent function. This remarkable capacity of the human psyche for change, expressed in the transcendent function, is the principal object of late medieval alchemical philosophy, where it was expressed in terms of alchemical symbolism. Herbert Silberer, in his very able book *Problems of Mysticism and Its Sym-*

bolism, has already pointed out the psychological content of alchemy. It would be an unpardonable error to accept the current view and reduce these "alchymical" strivings to a mere matter of alembics and melting-pots. This side certainly existed; it represented the tentative beginnings of exact chemistry. But alchemy also had a spiritual side which must not be underestimated and whose psychological value has not yet been sufficiently appreciated: there was an "alchymical" philosophy, the groping precursor of the most modern psychology. The secret of alchemy was in fact the transcendent function, the transformation of personality through the blending and fusion of the noble with the base components, of the differentiated with the inferior functions, of the conscious with the unconscious.

361 But, just as the beginnings of scientific chemistry were hopelessly distorted and confused by fantastic conceits and whimsicalities, so alchemical philosophy, hampered by the inevitable concretizations of the still crude and undifferentiated intellect, never advanced to any clear psychological formulation, despite the fact that the liveliest intuition of profound truths kept the medieval thinker passionately attached to the problems of alchemy. No one who has undergone the process of assimilating the unconscious will deny that it gripped his very vitals and changed him.

362 I would not blame my reader at all if he shakes his head dubiously at this point, being quite unable to imagine how such a *quantité négligeable* as the footling fantasy given above could ever have the slightest influence on anybody. I admit at once that in considering the transcendent function and the extraordinary influence attributed to it, the fragment we have quoted is anything but illuminating. But it is—and here I must appeal to the benevolent understanding of my reader—exceedingly difficult to give any examples, because every example has the unfortunate characteristic of being impressive and significant only to the individual concerned. Therefore I always advise my patients not to cherish the naïve belief that what is of the greatest significance to them personally also has objective significance.

363 The vast majority of people are quite incapable of putting themselves individually into the mind of another. This is indeed a singularly rare art, and, truth to tell, it does not take us very far. Even the man whom we think we know best and who assures

us himself that we understand him through and through is at bottom a stranger to us. He is *different*. The most we can do, and the best, is to have at least some inkling of his otherness, to respect it, and to guard against the outrageous stupidity of wishing to interpret it.

364   I can, therefore, produce nothing convincing, nothing that would convince the reader as it convinces the man whose deepest experience it is. We must simply believe it by reason of its analogy with our own experience. Ultimately, when all else fails, the end-result is plain beyond a doubt: the perceptible change of personality. With these reservations in mind, I would like to present the reader with another fantasy-fragment, this time from a woman. The difference from the previous example leaps to the eye: here the experience is total, the observer takes an active part and thus makes the process her own. The material in this case is very extensive, culminating in a profound transformation of personality. The fragment comes from a late phase of personal development and is an organic part of a long and continuous series of transformations which have as their goal the attainment of the mid-point of the personality.

365   It may not be immediately apparent what is meant by a "mid-point of the personality." I will therefore try to outline this problem in a few words. If we picture the conscious mind, with the ego as its centre, as being opposed to the unconscious, and if we now add to our mental picture the process of assimilating the unconscious, we can think of this assimilation as a kind of approximation of conscious and unconscious, where the centre of the total personality no longer coincides with the ego, but with a point midway between the conscious and the unconscious. This would be the point of new equilibrium, a new centering of the total personality, a virtual centre which, on account of its focal position between conscious and unconscious, ensures for the personality a new and more solid foundation. I freely admit that visualizations of this kind are no more than the clumsy attempts of the unskilled mind to give expression to inexpressible, and well-nigh indescribable, psychological facts. I could say the same thing in the words of St. Paul: "Yet not I live, but Christ liveth in me." Or I might invoke Lao-tzu and appropriate his concept of Tao, the Middle Way and creative centre of all things. In all these the same thing is meant. Speak-

ing as a psychologist with a scientific conscience, I must say at once that these things are psychic factors of undeniable power; they are not the inventions of an idle mind, but definite psychic events obeying definite laws and having their legitimate causes and effects, which can be found among the most widely differing peoples and races today, as thousands of years ago. I have no theory as to what constitutes the nature of these processes. One would first have to know what constitutes the nature of the psyche. I am content simply to state the facts.

366   Coming now to our example: it concerns a fantasy of intensely visual character, something which in the language of the ancients would be called a "vision." Not a "vision seen in a dream," but a vision perceived by intense concentration on the background of consciousness, a technique that is perfected only after long practice.[2] Told in her own words, this is what the patient saw:

"I climbed the mountain and came to a place where I saw seven red stones in front of me, seven on either side, and seven behind me. I stood in the middle of this quadrangle. The stones were flat like steps. I tried to lift the four stones nearest me. In doing so I discovered that these stones were the pedestals of four statues of gods buried upside down in the earth. I dug them up and arranged them about me so that I was standing in the middle of them. Suddenly they leaned towards one another until their heads touched, forming something like a tent over me. I myself fell to the ground and said, 'Fall upon me if you must! I am tired.' Then I saw that beyond, encircling the four gods, a ring of flame had formed. After a time I got up from the ground and overthrew the statues of the gods. Where they fell, four trees shot up. At that blue flames leapt up from the ring of fire and began to burn the foliage of the trees. Seeing this I said, 'This must stop. I must go into the fire myself so that the leaves shall not be burned.' Then I stepped into the fire. The trees vanished and the fiery ring drew together to one immense blue flame that carried me up from the earth."

367   Here the vision ended. Unfortunately I cannot see how I can make conclusively clear to the reader the extraordinarily inter-

2 [This technique is elsewhere called "active imagination." Cf. "The Transcendent Function," pars. 166ff., and *Mysterium Coniunctionis*, pars. 706 and 749ff. —EDITORS.]

esting meaning of this vision. The fragment is an excerpt from a long sequence, and one would have to explain everything that happened before and afterwards, in order to grasp the significance of the picture. At all events the unprejudiced reader will recognize at once the idea of a "mid-point" that is reached by a kind of climb (mountaineering, effort, struggle, etc.). He will also recognize without difficulty the famous medieval conundrum of the squaring of the circle, which belongs to the field of alchemy. Here it takes its rightful place as a symbol of individuation. The total personality is indicated by the four cardinal points, the four gods, i.e., the four functions which give bearings in psychic space, and also by the circle enclosing the whole. Overcoming the four gods who threaten to smother the individual signifies liberation from identification with the four functions, a fourfold *nirdvandva* ("free from opposites") followed by an approximation to the circle, to undivided wholeness. This in its turn leads to further exaltation.

368   I must content myself with these hints. Anyone who takes the trouble to reflect upon the matter will be able to form a rough idea of how the transformation of personality proceeds. Through her active participation the patient merges herself in the unconscious processes, and she gains possession of them by allowing them to possess her. In this way she joins the conscious to the unconscious. The result is ascension in the flame, transmutation in the alchemical heat, the genesis of the "subtle spirit." That is the transcendent function born of the union of opposites.

369   I must recall at this point a serious misunderstanding to which my readers often succumb, and doctors most commonly. They invariably assume, for reasons unknown, that I never write about anything except my method of treatment. This is far from being the case. I write about *psychology*. I must therefore expressly emphasize that my method of treatment does not consist in causing my patients to indulge in strange fantasies for the purpose of changing their personality, and other nonsense of that kind. I merely put it on record that there are certain cases where such a development occurs, not because I force anyone to it, but because it springs from inner necessity. For many of my patients these things are and must remain double Dutch. Indeed, even if it were possible for them to tread this path, it

would be a disastrously wrong turning, and I would be the first to hold them back. The way of the transcendent function is an individual destiny. But on no account should one imagine that this way is equivalent to the life of a psychic anchorite, to alienation from the world. Quite the contrary, for such a way is possible and profitable only when the specific worldly tasks which these individuals set themselves are carried out in reality. Fantasies are no substitute for living; they are fruits of the spirit which fall to him who pays his tribute to life. The shirker experiences nothing but his own morbid fear, and it yields him no meaning. Nor will this way ever be known to the man who has found his way back to Mother Church. There is no doubt that the *mysterium magnum* is hidden in her forms, and in these he can live his life sensibly. Finally, the normal man will never be burdened, either, with this knowledge, for he is everlastingly content with the little that lies within his reach. Wherefore I entreat my reader to understand that I write about things which actually happen, and am not propounding methods of treatment.

370   These two examples of fantasy represent the positive activity of anima and animus. To the degree that the patient takes an active part, the personified figure of anima or animus will disappear. It becomes the function of relationship between conscious and unconscious. But when the unconscious contents—these same fantasies—are not "realized," they give rise to a negative activity and personification, i.e., to the autonomy of animus and anima. Psychic abnormalities then develop, states of possession ranging in degree from ordinary moods and "ideas" to psychoses. All these states are characterized by one and the same fact that an unknown "something" has taken possession of a smaller or greater portion of the psyche and asserts its hateful and harmful existence undeterred by all our insight, reason, and energy, thereby proclaiming the power of the unconscious over the conscious mind, the sovereign power of possession. In this state the possessed part of the psyche generally develops an animus or anima psychology. The woman's incubus consists of a host of masculine demons; the man's succubus is a vampire.

371   This particular concept of a soul which, according to the conscious attitude, either exists by itself or disappears in a func-

tion, has, as anyone can see, not the remotest connection with the Christian concept of the soul.

372   The second fantasy is a typical example of the kind of content produced by the collective unconscious. Although the form is entirely subjective and individual, the substance is none the less collective, being composed of universal images and ideas common to the generality of men, components, therefore, by which the individual is assimilated to the rest of mankind. If these contents remain unconscious, the individual is, in them, unconsciously commingled with other individuals—in other words, he is not differentiated, not individuated.

373   Here one may ask, perhaps, why it is so desirable that a man should be individuated. Not only is it desirable, it is absolutely indispensable because, through his contamination with others, he falls into situations and commits actions which bring him into disharmony with himself. From all states of unconscious contamination and non-differentiation there is begotten a compulsion to be and to act in a way contrary to one's own nature. Accordingly a man can neither be at one with himself nor accept responsibility for himself. He feels himself to be in a degrading, unfree, unethical condition. But the disharmony with himself is precisely the neurotic and intolerable condition from which he seeks to be delivered, and deliverance from this condition will come only when he can be and act as he feels is conformable with his true self. People have a feeling for these things, dim and uncertain at first, but growing ever stronger and clearer with progressive development. When a man can say of his states and actions, "As I am, so I act," he can be at one with himself, even though it be difficult, and he can accept responsibility for himself even though he struggle against it. We must recognize that nothing is more difficult to bear with than oneself. ("You sought the heaviest burden, and found yourself," says Nietzsche.) Yet even this most difficult of achievements becomes possible if we can distinguish ourselves from the unconscious contents. The introvert discovers these contents in himself, the extravert finds them projected upon human objects. In both cases the unconscious contents are the cause of blinding illusions which falsify ourselves and our relations to our fellow men, making both unreal. For these reasons individuation is indispen-

sable for certain people, not only as a therapeutic necessity, but as a high ideal, an idea of the best we can do. Nor should I omit to remark that it is at the same time the primitive Christian ideal of the Kingdom of Heaven which "is within you." The idea at the bottom of this ideal is that right action comes from right thinking, and that there is no cure and no improving of the world that does not begin with the individual himself. To put the matter drastically: the man who is pauper or parasite will never solve the social question.

IV

THE MANA-PERSONALITY

374   My initial material for the discussion that now follows is taken from cases where the condition that was presented in the previous chapter as the immediate goal has been achieved, namely the conquest of the anima as an autonomous complex, and her transformation into a function of relationship between the conscious and the unconscious. With the attainment of this goal it becomes possible to disengage the ego from all its entanglements with collectivity and the collective unconscious. Through this process the anima forfeits the daemonic power of an autonomous complex; she can no longer exercise the power of possession, since she is depotentiated. She is no longer the guardian of treasures unknown; no longer Kundry, daemonic Messenger of the Grail, half divine and half animal; no longer is the soul to be called "Mistress," but a psychological function of an intuitive nature, akin to what the primitives mean when they say, "He has gone into the forest to talk with the spirits" or "My snake spoke with me" or, in the mythological language of infancy, "A little bird told me."

375   Those of my readers who know Rider Haggard's description of "She-who-must-be-obeyed" will surely recall the magical power of this personality. "She" is a mana-personality, a being full of some occult and bewitching quality (*mana*), endowed with magical knowledge and power. All these attributes naturally have their source in the naïve projection of an unconscious self-knowledge which, expressed in less poetic terms, would run somewhat as follows: "I recognize that there is some psychic factor active in me which eludes my conscious will in the most incredible manner. It can put extraordinary ideas into my head, induce in me unwanted and unwelcome moods and emotions, lead me to astonishing actions for which I can accept no responsibility, upset my relations with other people in a very irritating

way, etc. I feel powerless against this fact and, what is worse, I am in love with it, so that all I can do is marvel." (Poets often call this the "artistic temperament," unpoetical folk excuse themselves in other ways.)

376   Now when the anima loses her mana, what becomes of it? Clearly the man who has mastered the anima acquires her mana, in accordance with the primitive belief that when a man kills the mana-person he assimilates his mana into his own body.

377   Well then: who is it that has integrated the anima? Obviously the conscious ego, and therefore the ego has taken over the mana. Thus the ego becomes a mana-personality. But the mana-personality is a dominant of the collective unconscious, the well-known archetype of the mighty man in the form of hero, chief, magician, medicine-man, saint, the ruler of men and spirits, the friend of God.

378   This masculine collective figure who now rises out of the dark background and takes possession of the conscious personality entails a psychic danger of a subtle nature, for by inflating the conscious mind it can destroy everything that was gained by coming to terms with the anima. It is therefore of no little practical importance to know that in the hierarchy of the unconscious the anima occupies the lowest rank, only one of many possible figures, and that her subjection constellates another collective figure which now takes over her mana. Actually it is the figure of the magician, as I will call it for short, who attracts the mana to himself, i.e., the autonomous valency of the anima. Only in so far as I unconsciously identify with his figure can I imagine that I myself possess the anima's mana. But I will infallibly do so under these circumstances.

379   The figure of the magician has a no less dangerous equivalent in women: a sublime, matriarchal figure, the Great Mother, the All-Merciful, who understands everything, forgives everything, who always acts for the best, living only for others, and never seeking her own interests, the discoverer of the great love, just as the magician is the mouthpiece of the ultimate truth. And just as the great love is never appreciated, so the great wisdom is never understood. Neither, of course, can stand the sight of the other.

380   Here is cause for serious misunderstanding, for without a doubt it is a question of inflation. The ego has appropriated

something that does not belong to it. But how has it appropriated the mana? If it was really the ego that conquered the anima,
then the mana does indeed belong to it, and it would be correct
to conclude that one has become important. But why does not
this importance, the mana, work upon others? That would
surely be an essential criterion! It does not work because one has
not in fact become important, but has merely become adulter-
ated with an archetype, another unconscious figure. Hence we
must conclude that the ego never conquered the anima at all
and therefore has not acquired the mana. All that has happened
is a new adulteration, this time with a figure of the same sex
corresponding to the father-imago, and possessed of even greater
power.

> From the power that binds all creatures none is free
> Except the man who wins self-mastery! [1]

Thus he becomes a superman, superior to all powers, a demigod
at the very least. "I and the Father are one"—this mighty avowal
in all its awful ambiguity is born of just such a psychological
moment.

81   In the face of this, our pitiably limited ego, if it has but a
spark of self-knowledge, can only draw back and rapidly drop
all pretence of power and importance. It was a delusion: the
conscious mind has not become master of the unconscious, and
the anima has forfeited her tyrannical power only to the extent
that the ego was able to come to terms with the unconscious.
This accommodation, however, was not a victory of the conscious over the unconscious, but the establishment of a balance
of power between the two worlds.

82   Hence the "magician" could take possession of the ego only
because the ego dreamed of victory over the anima. That dream
was an encroachment, and every encroachment of the ego is followed by an encroachment from the unconscious:

> Changing shape from hour to hour
> I employ my savage power.[2]

[1] Goethe, "Die Geheimnisse: Ein Fragment," lines 191-92.
[2] *Faust,* trans. by Louis MacNeice, p. 282 (Part II, Act V), modified.

Consequently, if the ego drops its claim to victory, possession by the magician ceases automatically. But what happens to the mana? Who or what becomes mana when even the magician can no longer work magic? So far we only know that neither the conscious nor the unconscious has mana, for it is certain that when the ego makes no claim to power there is no possession, that is to say, the unconscious too loses its ascendency. In this situation the mana must have fallen to something that is both conscious and unconscious, or else neither. This something is the desired "mid-point" of the personality, that ineffable something betwixt the opposites, or else that which unites them, or the result of conflict, or the product of energic tension: the coming to birth of personality, a profoundly individual step forward, the next stage.

383   I do not expect the reader to have followed this rapid survey of the whole problem in all its parts. He may regard it as a kind of preliminary statement leading up to the more closely reasoned analysis which now follows.

384   The starting-point of our problem is the condition which results when the unconscious contents that are the efficient cause of the animus and anima phenomenon have become sufficiently assimilated to the conscious mind. This can best be represented in the following way: the unconscious contents are, in the first instance, things belonging to the personal sphere, similar perhaps to the fantasy of the male patient quoted above. Subsequently, fantasies from the impersonal unconscious develop, containing essentially collective symbols more or less similar to the vision of my woman patient. These fantasies are not so wild and unregulated as a naïve intelligence might think; they pursue definite, unconscious lines of direction which converge upon a definite goal. We could therefore most fittingly describe these later series of fantasies as processes of initiation, since these form the closest analogy. All primitive groups and tribes that are in any way organized have their rites of initiation, often very highly developed, which play an extraordinarily important part in their social and religious life.[3] Through these ceremonies boys are made men, and girls women. The Kavirondos stigmatize those who do not submit to circumcision and excision as "animals." This shows that the initiation ceremonies are a mag-

3 Cf. Webster, *Primitive Secret Societies* (1908).

ical means of leading man from the animal state to the human state. They are clearly transformation mysteries of the greatest spiritual significance. Very often the initiands are subjected to excruciating treatment, and at the same time the tribal mysteries are imparted to them, the laws and hierarchy of the tribe on the one hand, and on the other the cosmogonic and mythical doctrines. Initiations have survived among all cultures. In Greece the ancient Eleusinian mysteries were preserved, it seems, right into the seventh century of our era. Rome was flooded with mystery religions. Of these Christianity was one, and even in its present form it still preserves the old initiation ceremonies, somewhat faded and degenerated, in the rites of baptism, confirmation, and communion. Hence nobody is in a position to deny the enormous historical importance of initiations.

385   Modern men have absolutely nothing to compare with this (consider the testimonies of the ancients in regard to the Eleusinian mysteries). Freemasonry, *l'Église gnostique de la France,* legendary Rosicrucians, theosophy, and so forth are all feeble substitutes for something that were better marked up in red letters on the historical casualty list. The fact is that the whole symbolism of initiation rises up, clear and unmistakable, in the unconscious contents. The objection that this is antiquated superstition and altogether unscientific is about as intelligent as remarking, in the presence of a cholera epidemic, that it is merely an infectious disease and exceedingly unhygienic. The point is not—I cannot be too emphatic about this—whether the initiation symbols are objective truths, but whether these unconscious contents are or are not the equivalents of initiation practices, and whether they do or do not influence the human psyche. Nor is it a question of whether they are desirable or not. It is enough that they exist and that they work.

386   Since it is not possible in this connection to put before the reader in detail these sometimes very lengthy sequences of images, I trust he will be content with the few examples already given and, for the rest, accept my statement that they are logically constructed, purposive sequences. I must own that I use the word "purposive" with some hesitation. This word needs to be used cautiously and with reserve. For in mental cases we come across dream-sequences, and in neurotics fantasy-

sequences, which run on in themselves with no apparent aim or purpose. The young man whose suicide fantasy I gave above was in a fair way to produce a string of aimless fantasies, unless he could learn to take an active part and to intervene consciously. Only thus could there be orientation to a goal. From one point of view the unconscious is a purely natural process without design, but from another it has that potential directedness which is characteristic of all energy processes. When the conscious mind participates actively and experiences each stage of the process, or at least understands it intuitively, then the next image always starts off on the higher level that has been won, and purposiveness develops.

387   The immediate goal of the analysis of the unconscious, therefore, is to reach a state where the unconscious contents no longer remain unconscious and no longer express themselves indirectly as animus and anima phenomena; that is to say, a state in which animus and anima become functions of relationship to the unconscious. So long as they are not this, they are autonomous complexes, disturbing factors that break through the conscious control and act like true "disturbers of the peace." Because this is such a well-known fact my term "complex," as used in this sense, has passed into common speech. The more "complexes" a man has, the more he is possessed; and when we try to form a picture of the personality which expresses itself through his complexes we must admit that it resembles nothing so much as an hysterical woman—i.e., the anima! But if such a man makes himself conscious of his unconscious contents, as they appear firstly in the factual contents of his personal unconscious, and then in the fantasies of the collective unconscious, he will get to the roots of his complexes, and in this way rid himself of his possession. With that the anima phenomenon comes to a stop.

388   That superior power, however, which caused the possession —for what I cannot shake off must in some sense be superior to me—should, logically, disappear with the anima. One should then be "complex-free," psychologically house-trained, so to speak. Nothing more should happen that is not sanctioned by the ego, and when the ego wants something, nothing should be capable of interfering. The ego would thus be assured of an impregnable position, the steadfastness of a superman or the sublimity of a perfect sage. Both figures are ideal images: Napoleon

on the one hand, Lao-tzu on the other. Both are consistent with the idea of "the extraordinarily potent," which is the term that Lehmann, in his celebrated monograph,[4] uses for his definition of mana. I therefore call such a personality simply the *mana-personality*. It corresponds to a dominant of the collective unconscious, to an archetype which has taken shape in the human psyche through untold ages of just that kind of experience. Primitive man does not analyse and does not work out why another is superior to him. If another is cleverer and stronger than he, then he has mana, he is possessed of a stronger power; and by the same token he can lose this power, perhaps because someone has walked over him in his sleep, or stepped on his shadow.

389   Historically, the mana-personality evolves into the hero and the godlike being,[5] whose earthly form is the priest. How very much the doctor is still mana is the whole plaint of the analyst! But in so far as the ego apparently draws to itself the power belonging to the anima, the ego does become a mana-personality. This development is an almost regular phenomenon. I have never yet seen a fairly advanced development of this kind where at least a temporary identification with the archetype of the mana-personality did not take place. It is the most natural thing in the world that this should happen, for not only does one expect it oneself, but everybody else expects it too. One can scarcely help admiring oneself a little for having seen more deeply into things than others, and the others have such an urge to find a tangible hero somewhere, or a superior wise man, a leader and father, some undisputed authority, that they build temples to little tin gods with the greatest promptitude and burn incense upon the altars. This is not just the lamentable stupidity of idolaters incapable of judging for themselves, but a natural psychological law which says that what has once been will always be in the future. And so it will be, unless consciousness puts an end to the naïve concretization of primordial images. I do not know whether it is desirable that consciousness should alter the eternal laws; I only know that occasionally it does alter them, and that this measure is a vital necessity for some people—which, however, does not always prevent these

4 Lehmann, *Mana* (1922).
5 According to popular belief, the Most Christian King could cure epilepsy with his mana by the laying on of hands.

same people from setting themselves up on the father's throne and making the old rule come true. It is indeed hard to see how one can escape the sovereign power of the primordial images.

390   Actually I do not believe it can be escaped. One can only alter one's attitude and thus save oneself from naïvely falling into an archetype and being forced to act a part at the expense of one's humanity. Possession by an archetype turns a man into a flat collective figure, a mask behind which he can no longer develop as a human being, but becomes increasingly stunted. One must therefore beware of the danger of falling victim to the dominant of the mana-personality. The danger lies not only in oneself becoming a father-mask, but in being overpowered by this mask when worn by another. Master and pupil are in the same boat in this respect.

391   The dissolution of the anima means that we have gained insight into the driving forces of the unconscious, but not that we have made these forces ineffective. They can attack us at any time in new form. And they will infallibly do so if the conscious attitude has a flaw in it. It's a question of might against might. If the ego presumes to wield power over the unconscious, the unconscious reacts with a subtle attack, deploying the dominant of the mana-personality, whose enormous prestige casts a spell over the ego. Against this the only defence is full confession of one's weakness in face of the powers of the unconscious. By opposing no force to the unconscious we do not provoke it to attack.

392   It may sound rather comical to the reader if I speak of the unconscious in this personal way. I hope I shall not arouse the prejudice that I regard the unconscious as something personal. The unconscious consists of natural processes that lie outside the sphere of the human personality. Only our conscious mind is "personal." Therefore when I speak of "provoking" the unconscious I do not mean that it is offended and—like the gods of old—rises up to smite the offender in jealous anger or revenge. What I mean is more like an error in psychic diet which upsets the equilibrium of my digestion. The unconscious reacts automatically like my stomach which, in a manner of speaking, wreaks its revenge upon me. When I presume to have power over the unconscious, that is like a dietary solecism, an unseemly attitude which in the interests of one's own well-being were better avoided. My unpoetical comparison is, if anything, far too

mild in view of the far-reaching and devastating moral effects of a disordered unconscious. In this regard it would be more fitting to speak of the wrath of offended gods.

393   In differentiating the ego from the archetype of the mana-personality one is now forced, exactly as in the case of the anima, to make conscious those contents which are specific of the mana-personality. Historically, the mana-personality is always in possession of the secret name, or of some esoteric knowledge, or has the prerogative of a special way of acting—*quod licet Jovi, non licet bovi*—in a word, it has an individual distinction. Conscious realization of the contents composing it means, for the man, the second and real liberation from the father, and, for the woman, liberation from the mother, and with it comes the first genuine sense of his or her true individuality. This part of the process corresponds exactly to the aim of the concretistic primitive initiations up to and including baptism, namely, severance from the "carnal" (or animal) parents, and rebirth *in novam infantiam,* into a condition of immortality and spiritual childhood, as formulated by certain mystery religions of the ancient world, among them Christianity.

394   It is now quite possible that, instead of identifying with the mana-personality, one will concretize it as an extramundane "Father in Heaven," complete with the attribute of absoluteness —something that many people seem very prone to do. This would be tantamount to giving the unconscious a supremacy that was just as absolute (if one's faith could be pushed that far!), so that all value would flow over to that side.[6] The logical result is that the only thing left behind here is a miserable, inferior, worthless, and sinful little heap of humanity. This so-

6 "Absolute" means "cut off," "detached." To assert that God is absolute amounts to placing him outside all connection with mankind. Man cannot affect him, or he man. Such a God would be of no consequence at all. We can in fairness only speak of a God who is relative to man, as man is to God. The Christian idea of God as a "Father in Heaven" puts God's relativity in exquisite form. Quite apart from the fact that a man can know even less about God than an ant can know of the contents of the British Museum, this urge to regard God as "absolute" derives solely from the fear that God might become "psychological." This would naturally be dangerous. An absolute God, on the other hand, does not concern us in the least, whereas a "psychological" God would be *real.* This kind of God could reach man. The Church seems to be a magical instrument for protecting man against this eventuality, since it is written: "It is a fearful thing to fall into the hands of the living God."

lution, as we know, has become an historical world view. As I am moving here on psychological ground only, and feel no inclination whatever to dictate my eternal truths to the world at large, I must observe, by way of criticizing this solution, that if I shift all the highest values over to the side of the unconscious, thus converting it into a *summum bonum,* I am then placed in the unfortunate position of having to discover a devil of equal weight and dimensions who could act as the psychological counterbalance to my *summum bonum.* Under no circumstances, however, will my modesty allow me to identify myself with the devil. That would be altogether too presumptuous and would, moreover, bring me into unbearable conflict with my highest values. Nor, with my moral deficit, can I possibly afford it.

395   On psychological grounds, therefore, I would recommend that no God be constructed out of the archetype of the mana-personality. In other words, he must not be concretized, for only thus can I avoid projecting my values and non-values into God and Devil, and only thus can I preserve my human dignity, my specific gravity, which I need so much if I am not to become the unresisting shuttlecock of unconscious forces. In his dealings with the visible world, a man must certainly be mad to suppose that he is master of this world. Here we follow, quite naturally, the principle of non-resistance to all superior forces, up to a certain individual limit, beyond which the most peaceful citizen becomes a bloody revolutionary. Our bowing down before law and order is a commendable example of what our general attitude to the collective unconscious should be. ("Render unto Caesar. . . .") Thus far our obeisance would not be too difficult. But there are other factors in the world to which our conscience does not give unqualified assent—and yet we bow to them. Why? Because in practice it is more expedient than the reverse. Similarly there are factors in the unconscious with regard to which we must be worldly-wise ("Resist not evil." "Make to yourselves friends of the mammon of unrighteousness." "The children of this world are in their generation wiser than the children of light." *Ergo:* "Be ye therefore wise as serpents and harmless as doves.")

396   The mana-personality is on one side a being of superior wis-

dom, on the other a being of superior will. By making conscious the contents that underlie this personality, we find ourselves obliged to face the fact that we have learnt more and want more than other people. This uncomfortable kinship with the gods, as we know, struck so deep into poor Angelus Silesius' bones that it sent him flying out of his super-Protestantism, past the precarious halfway house of the Lutherans, back to the nethermost womb of the dark Mother—unfortunately very much to the detriment of his lyrical gifts and the health of his nerves.

97 And yet Christ, and Paul after him, wrestled with these same problems, as a number of clues still make evident. Meister Eckhart, Goethe in his *Faust*, Nietzsche in his *Zarathustra*, have again brought this problem somewhat closer to us. Goethe and Nietzsche try to solve it by the idea of mastery, the former through the figure of the magician and ruthless man of will who makes a pact with the devil, the latter through the masterman and supreme sage who knows neither God nor devil. With Nietzsche man stands alone, as he himself did, neurotic, financially dependent, godless, and worldless. This is no ideal for a real man who has a family to support and taxes to pay. Nothing can argue the reality of the world out of existence, there is no miraculous way round it. Similarly, nothing can argue the effects of the unconscious out of existence. Or can the neurotic philosopher prove to us that he has no neurosis? He cannot prove it even to himself. Therefore we stand with our soul suspended between formidable influences from within and from without, and somehow we must be fair to both. This we can do only after the measure of our individual capacities. Hence we must bethink ourselves not so much of what we "ought" to do as of what we *can* and *must* do.

98 Thus the dissolution of the mana-personality through conscious assimilation of its contents leads us, by a natural route, back to ourselves as an actual, living something, poised between two world-pictures and their darkly discerned potencies. This "something" is strange to us and yet so near, wholly ourselves and yet unknowable, a virtual centre of so mysterious a constitution that it can claim anything—kinship with beasts and gods, with crystals and with stars—without moving us to wonder, without even exciting our disapprobation. This "something"

237

claims all that and more, and having nothing in our hands that could fairly be opposed to these claims, it is surely wiser to listen to this voice.

399 I have called this centre the *self*. Intellectually the self is no more than a psychological concept, a construct that serves to express an unknowable essence which we cannot grasp as such, since by definition it transcends our powers of comprehension. It might equally well be called the "God within us." The beginnings of our whole psychic life seem to be inextricably rooted in this point, and all our highest and ultimate purposes seem to be striving towards it. This paradox is unavoidable, as always, when we try to define something that lies beyond the bourn of our understanding.

400 I hope it has become sufficiently clear to the attentive reader that the self has as much to do with the ego as the sun with the earth. They are not interchangeable. Nor does it imply a deification of man or a dethronement of God. What is beyond our understanding is in any case beyond its reach. When, therefore, we make use of the concept of a God we are simply formulating a definite psychological fact, namely the independence and sovereignty of certain psychic contents which express themselves by their power to thwart our will, to obsess our consciousness and to influence our moods and actions. We may be outraged at the idea of an inexplicable mood, a nervous disorder, or an uncontrollable vice being, so to speak, a manifestation of God. But it would be an irreparable loss for religious experience if such things, perhaps even evil things, were artificially segregated from the sum of autonomous psychic contents. It is an apotropaic euphemism[7] to dispose of these things with a "nothing but" explanation. In that way they are merely repressed, and as a rule only an apparent advantage is gained, a new twist given to illusion. The personality is not enriched by it, only impoverished and smothered. What seems evil, or at least meaningless and valueless to contemporary experience and knowledge, might on a higher level of experience and knowledge appear as the source of the best—everything depending, naturally, on the use one makes of one's seven devils. To explain them as meaningless robs the personality of its proper shadow, and with this it loses its form. The living form needs deep shadow if it is to

7 Giving a bad thing a good name in order to avert its disfavour.

appear plastic. Without shadow it remains a two-dimensional phantom, a more or less well brought-up child.

01 Here I am alluding to a problem that is far more significant than these few simple words would seem to suggest: mankind is, in essentials, psychologically still in a state of childhood—a stage that cannot be skipped. The vast majority needs authority, guidance, law. This fact cannot be overlooked. The Pauline overcoming of the law falls only to the man who knows how to put his soul in the place of conscience. Very few are capable of this ("Many are called, but few are chosen"). And these few tread this path only from inner necessity, not to say suffering, for it is sharp as the edge of a razor.

02 The conception of God as an autonomous psychic content makes God into a moral problem—and that, admittedly, is very uncomfortable. But if this problem does not exist, God is not real, for nowhere can he touch our lives. He is then either an historical and intellectual bogey or a philosophical sentimentality.

03 If we leave the idea of "divinity" quite out of account and speak only of "autonomous contents," we maintain a position that is intellectually and empirically correct, but we silence a note which, psychologically, should not be missing. By using the concept of a divine being we give apt expression to the peculiar way in which we experience the workings of these autonomous contents. We could also use the term "daemonic," provided that this does not imply that we are still holding up our sleeves some concretized God who conforms exactly to our wishes and ideas. Our intellectual conjuring tricks do not help us to make a reality of the God we desire, any more than the world accommodates itself to our expectations. Therefore, by affixing the attribute "divine" to the workings of autonomous contents, we are admitting their relatively superior force. And it is this superior force which has at all times constrained men to ponder the inconceivable, and even to impose the greatest sufferings upon themselves in order to give these workings their due. It is a force as real as hunger and the fear of death.

04 The self could be characterized as a kind of compensation of the conflict between inside and outside. This formulation would not be unfitting, since the self has somewhat the character of a result, of a goal attained, something that has come to pass very

gradually and is experienced with much travail. So too the self is our life's goal, for it is the completest expression of that fateful combination we call individuality, the full flowering not only of the single individual, but of the group, in which each adds his portion to the whole.

405   Sensing the self as something irrational, as an indefinable existent, to which the ego is neither opposed nor subjected, but merely attached, and about which it revolves very much as the earth revolves round the sun—thus we come to the goal of individuation. I use the word "sensing" in order to indicate the apperceptive character of the relation between ego and self. In this relation nothing is knowable, because we can say nothing about the contents of the self. The ego is the only content of the self that we do know. The individuated ego senses itself as the object of an unknown and supraordinate subject. It seems to me that our psychological inquiry must come to a stop here, for the idea of a self is itself a transcendental postulate which, although justifiable psychologically, does not allow of scientific proof. This step beyond science is an unconditional requirement of the psychological development I have sought to depict, because without this postulate I could give no adequate formulation of the psychic processes that occur empirically. At the very least, therefore, the self can claim the value of an hypothesis analogous to that of the structure of the atom. And even though we should once again be enmeshed in an image, it is none the less powerfully alive, and its interpretation quite exceeds my powers. I have no doubt at all that it is an image, but one in which we are contained.

406   I am deeply conscious that in this essay I have made no ordinary demands on the understanding of my reader. Though I have done my utmost to smooth the path of understanding, there is one great difficulty which I could not eliminate, namely the fact that the experiences which form the basis of my discussion are unknown to most people and are bound to seem strange. Consequently I cannot expect my readers to follow all my conclusions. Although every author naturally prefers to be understood by his public, yet the interpretation of my observations is of less moment to me than the disclosure of a wide field of experience, at present hardly explored, which it is the aim of this book to bring within reach of many. In this field, hitherto so

dark, it seems to me that there lie the answers to many riddles which the psychology of consciousness has never even approached. I would not pretend to have formulated these answers with any degree of finality. I shall, therefore, be well satisfied if my essay may be counted as a tentative attempt at an answer.

APPENDICES

I

NEW PATHS IN PSYCHOLOGY [1]

407   Like all sciences, psychology has gone through its epoch of
scholasticism, and something of this spirit has lasted on into the
present. Against this kind of philosophical psychology it must be
objected that it decides *ex cathedra* how the psyche shall be constituted, and what qualities must belong to it in this world and
in the next. The spirit of modern scientific investigation has to a
large extent disposed of these fantasies and put in their place an
exact empirical method. From this there arose the experimental
psychology of today, or what the French call "psychophysiol-
ogy." The father of this movement was the dual-minded Fechner, who, in his *Elemente der Psychophysik,* dared to introduce
the physical point of view into the conception of psychic phenomena. This idea [, and not least the brilliant errors in this

[1] [First published as "Neue Bahnen der Psychologie" in *Raschers Jahrbuch für
Schweizer Art und Kunst* (Zurich, 1912); trans. as "New Paths in Psychology,"
Collected Papers on Analytical Psychology (1st edn., London, 1916). Subsequently
revised and expanded (more than threefold) and published under the title *Die
Psychologie der unbewussten Prozesse* (Zurich, 1917); trans. as "The Psychology
of the Unconscious Processes," *Collected Papers on Analytical Psychology* (2nd
edn., London, 1917; New York, 1920). This work, after further revision and expansion (see Prefaces, supra, pp. 3–7), finally appeared as *Ueber die Psychologie
des Unbewussten* (Zurich, 1943), a translation of which forms Part I of the present volume.

[In reworking "Neue Bahnen der Psychologie" for the first (1917) edition of
Die Psychologie der unbewussten Prozesse, the author deleted or modified a
number of passages, and these passages were similarly treated in the text of
"New Paths in Psychology" as it appeared in the first edition of the present
volume. (It should be noted that, except for pars. 440 and 441 and a few other
brief passages, they were not deleted in the equivalent opening section of "The
Psychology of the Unconscious Processes" in the 1917 edition of *Collected Papers
on Analytical Psychology.*) In this revised edition of *Collected Works,* vol. 7,
the deleted passages have been restored and are indicated by square brackets.
They are similarly but not identically treated in Vol. 7 of the *Gesammelte
Werke* (Zurich, 1964).—EDITORS.]

work,] was a fertilizing force. Fechner's younger contemporary and, we might say, the perfecter of his work, was Wundt, whose great erudition, industry, and genius for devising new methods of experimental research have created the dominant trend in modern psychology.

408   Until quite recently experimental psychology was essentially academic. The first notable attempt to enlist at least some of its numerous experimental methods in the service of practical psychology came from the psychiatrists of the former Heidelberg school (Kraepelin, Aschaffenburg, and others); for, as may easily be imagined, the psychiatrist was the first to feel the pressing need for exact knowledge of the psychic processes. Next came pedagogy, making its own demands on psychology. From this there has recently grown up an "experimental pedagogy," in which field Meumann in Germany and Binet in France have rendered signal service.

409   If he wants to help his patient, the doctor, and above all the "specialist for nervous diseases," must have psychological knowledge; for nervous disorders and all that is embraced by the terms "nervousness," hysteria, etc. are of psychic origin and therefore logically require psychic treatment. Cold water, light, fresh air, electricity, and so forth have at best a transitory effect and sometimes none at all. Often they are disreputable artifices, calculated to work upon suggestibility. But the patient is sick in mind, in the highest and most complex of the mind's functions, and these can hardly be said to belong any more to the province of medicine. Here the doctor must also be a psychologist, which means that he must have knowledge of the human psyche. The doctor cannot evade this demand. So he naturally turns for help to psychology, since his psychiatry text-books have nothing to offer him. The experimental psychology of today, however, does not even begin to give him any coherent insight into what are, practically, the most important psychic processes. That is not its aim: it tries to isolate the very simplest and most elementary processes which border on physiology, and studies them in isolation. It is ill-disposed towards the infinite variety and mobility of individual psychic life, and for this reason its findings and its facts are so many details lacking organic cohesion. Therefore anyone who wants to know the human psyche will learn next to nothing from experimental psychology. He would be better ad-

vised to [abandon exact science] put away his scholar's gown, bid farewell to his study, and wander with human heart through the world. There, in the horrors of prisons, lunatic asylums and hospitals, in drab suburban pubs, in brothels and gambling-hells, in the salons of the elegant, the Stock Exchanges, Socialist meetings, churches, revivalist gatherings and ecstatic sects, through love and hate, through the experience of passion in every form in his own body, he would reap richer stores of knowledge than text-books a foot thick could give him, and he will know how to doctor the sick with real knowledge of the human soul. He may be pardoned if his respect for the so-called cornerstones of experimental psychology is no longer excessive. For between what science calls psychology and what the practical needs of daily life demand from psychology there is a great gulf fixed.

410   This deficiency became the starting-point for a new psychology, whose inception we owe first and foremost to Sigmund Freud of Vienna, the brilliant physician and investigator of functional nervous disorders. One could describe the psychology inaugurated by him as "analytical psychology." Bleuler has suggested the name "depth psychology," [2] in order to indicate that Freudian psychology was concerned with the deeper regions or hinterland of the psyche, also called the unconscious. Freud himself was content just to name his method of investigation: he called it psychoanalysis. And such is the name by which this movement is generally known.

411   Before we enter upon a closer presentation of our subject, something must be said about its relation to science as known hitherto. Here we encounter a curious spectacle which proves yet again the truth of Anatole France's remark, "Les savants ne sont pas curieux." The first work of any magnitude[3] in this field awakened only the faintest echo, in spite of the fact that it introduced an entirely new and fundamental conception of the neuroses. A few writers spoke of it appreciatively and then, on the next page, proceeded to explain their hysterical cases in the same old way. They behaved very much like a man who, having eulogized the idea or fact that the earth was a sphere, calmly continues to represent it as flat. Freud's next publications[4] re-

2 ["Die Psychoanalyse Freuds" (1910).]
3 Breuer and Freud, *Studies on Hysteria* (orig. 1895).
4 *Early Psycho-Analytic Publications* (orig. 1906), Standard Edition, vol. 3.

mained absolutely unnoticed, although they put forward obser-vations which were of incalculable importance for psychiatry. When, in the year 1899, Freud wrote the first real psychology of dreams[5] (a Stygian darkness had hitherto reigned over this field), people began to laugh, and when about the middle of the last decade he started to throw light on the psychology of sexual-ity itself,[6] [and at the same time the Zurich school decided to range itself on his side,] laughter turned to insult, sometimes of the nastiest kind, and this has lasted until very recently. [Even a layman like Förster insinuated himself among the denigrators. (I hope the ugliness and impertinence of his tone came from his ignorance of the actual facts.) At the last South-West German Congress of Alienists the adherents of the new psychology also had the pleasure of hearing Hoche, University Professor of Psy-chiatry at Freiburg im Breisgau, describe the movement in a long and loudly applauded address as an epidemic of insanity among doctors. The old adage "Medicus medicum non decimat" was here quite put to shame.] How carefully the works had been studied is shown by the naïve remark of one of the most emi-nent neurologists of Paris at an International Congress in 1907, which I heard with my own ears: "I have not read Freud's works" (he knew no German) "but as for his theories, they are nothing but a *mauvaise plaisanterie.*" [Freud, the dignified old master, once said to me: "I first became clearly conscious of what I had discovered when it was met everywhere with resistance and indignation, and since that time I have learnt to judge the value of my work by the degree of resistance it provoked. It is the sexual theory that raises the greatest outcry, so it would seem that therein lies my best work. Perhaps after all the real benefac-tors of mankind are its false teachers, for opposition to the false teachings pushes men willy-nilly into truth. Your truth-teller is a pernicious fellow, he drives men into error."]

412   [The reader must now calmly accept the idea that in this psychology he is dealing with something quite unique, if not indeed some altogether irrational, sectarian, or occult wisdom; for what else could possibly provoke all the scientific authorities to pooh-pooh it from the start?]

413   Accordingly we must look more closely into this new psy-

5 *The Interpretation of Dreams* (orig. 1900).
6 "Three Essays on the Theory of Sexuality" (orig. 1905).

chology. Already in Charcot's time it was known that the neurotic symptom is "psychogenic," i.e., originates in the psyche. It was also known, thanks mainly to the work of the Nancy school, that all hysterical symptoms can be produced in exactly the same way by suggestion. But it was not known *how* an hysterical symptom originates in the psyche; the psychic causal factors were completely unknown. In the early eighties Dr. Breuer, an old Viennese practitioner, made a discovery which became the real starting-point of the new psychology. He had a young, very intelligent woman patient suffering from hysteria, who manifested the following symptoms among others: she had a spastic (rigid) paralysis of the right arm, and occasional fits of absent-mindedness or twilight states; she had also lost the power of speech inasmuch as she could no longer command her mother tongue but could only express herself in English (systematic aphasia). They tried at that time, and still try, to account for these disorders with anatomical theories, although the cortical centre for the arm function is as little disturbed here as in the corresponding centre of a normal person [who gives somebody a box on the ears]. The symptomatology of hysteria is full of anatomical impossibilities. One lady, who had completely lost her hearing because of an hysterical affection, often used to sing. Once, when she was singing, her doctor seated himself unobserved at the piano and softly accompanied her. In passing from one stanza to the next he made a sudden change of key, whereupon the patient, without noticing it, went on singing in the changed key. Thus she hears—and does not hear. The various forms of systematic blindness offer similar phenomena: a man suffering from total hysterical blindness recovered his sight in the course of treatment, but it was only partial at first and remained so for a long time. He could see everything with the exception of people's heads. He saw all the people round him without heads. Thus he sees—and does not see. From a large number of like experiences it has long been concluded that only the conscious mind of the patient does not see and hear, but that the sense-function is otherwise in working order. This state of affairs directly contradicts the nature of an organic disorder, which always affects the function in some way.

414   After this digression, let us come back to the Breuer case. There were no organic causes for the disorder, so it had to be

regarded as hysterical, i.e., psychogenic. Breuer had observed that if, during her twilight states (whether spontaneous or artificially induced), he got the patient to tell him of the reminiscences and fantasies that thronged in upon her, her condition was eased for several hours afterwards. He made systematic use of this discovery for further treatment. The patient devised the appropriate name "talking cure" for it, or, jokingly, "chimney-sweeping."

415   The patient had become ill when nursing her father in his fatal illness. Naturally her fantasies were chiefly concerned with these disturbing days. Reminiscences of this period came to the surface during her twilight states with photographic fidelity; so vivid were they, down to the last detail, that we can hardly assume the waking memory to have been capable of such plastic and exact reproduction. (The name "hypermnesia" has been given to this intensification of the powers of memory which may easily occur in restricted states of consciousness.) Remarkable things now came to light. One of the many stories told ran somewhat as follows:

One night, watching by the sick man, who had a high fever, she was tense with anxiety because a surgeon was expected from Vienna to perform an operation. Her mother had left the room for a while, and Anna, the patient, sat by the sick-bed with her right arm hanging over the back of the chair. She fell into a sort of waking dream and saw a black snake coming, apparently out of the wall, towards the sick man as though to bite him. (It is quite likely that there really were snakes in the meadow at the back of the house, which had already given the girl a fright and which now provided the material for the hallucination.) She wanted to drive the creature away, but felt paralysed; her right arm, hanging over the back of the chair, had "gone to sleep": it had become anaesthetic and paretic, and as she looked at it, the fingers changed into little serpents with death's-heads [the fingernails]. Probably she made efforts to drive away the snake with her paralysed right hand, so that the anaesthesia and paralysis became associated with the snake hallucination. When the snake had disappeared, she was so frightened that she wanted to pray; but all speech failed her, she could not utter a word until finally she remembered an English nursery rhyme, and then she was able to go on thinking and praying in English.

416   Such was the scene in which the paralysis and the speech disturbance originated, and with the narration of this scene the disturbance itself was removed. In this manner the case was finally cured.

417   I must content myself with this one example. In the book I have mentioned by Breuer and Freud there is a wealth of similar examples. It can readily be understood that scenes of this kind make a powerful impression, and people are therefore inclined to impute causal significance to them in the genesis of the symptom. The view of hysteria then current, which derived from the English theory of the "nervous shock" energetically championed by Charcot, was well qualified to explain Breuer's discovery. Hence there arose the so-called trauma theory, which says that the hysterical symptom, and, in so far as the symptoms constitute the illness, hysteria in general, derive from psychic injuries or traumata whose imprint persists unconsciously for years. Freud, now collaborating with Breuer, was able to furnish abundant confirmation of this discovery. It turned out that none of the hundreds of hysterical symptoms arose by chance—they were always caused by psychic occurrences. So far the new conception opened up an extensive field for empirical work. But Freud's inquiring mind could not remain long on this superficial level, for already deeper and more difficult problems were beginning to emerge. It is obvious enough that moments of extreme anxiety such as Breuer's patient experienced may leave an abiding impression. But how did she come to experience them at all, since they already clearly bear a morbid stamp? Could the strain of nursing bring this about? If so, there ought to be many more occurrences of the kind, for there are unfortunately very many exhausting cases to nurse, and the nervous health of the nurse is not always of the best. To this problem medicine gives an excellent answer: "The x in the calculation is predisposition." One is just "predisposed" that way. But for Freud the problem was: what constitutes the predisposition? This question leads logically to an examination of the previous history of the psychic trauma. It is a matter of common observation that exciting scenes have quite different effects on the various persons involved, or that things which are indifferent or even agreeable to one person arouse the greatest horror in others—witness frogs, snakes, mice, cats, etc. There are cases of women who will assist

at bloody operations without turning a hair, while they tremble all over with fear and loathing at the touch of a cat. I remember a young woman who suffered from acute hysteria following a sudden fright. She had been to an evening party and was on her way home about midnight in the company of several acquaintances, when a cab came up behind them at full trot. The others got out of the way, but she, as though spellbound with terror, kept to the middle of the road and ran along in front of the horses. The cabman cracked his whip and swore; it was no good, she ran down the whole length of the road, which led across a bridge. There her strength deserted her, and to avoid being trampled on by the horses she would in her desperation have leapt into the river had not the passers-by prevented her. Now, this same lady had happened to be in St. Petersburg on the bloody twenty-second of January [1905], in the very street which was cleared by the volleys of the soldiers. All round her people were falling to the ground dead or wounded; she, however, quite calm and clear-headed, espied a gate leading into a yard through which she made her escape into another street. These dreadful moments caused her no further agitation. She felt perfectly well afterwards—indeed, rather better than usual.

418   This failure to react to an apparent shock can frequently be observed. Hence it necessarily follows that the intensity of a trauma has very little pathogenic significance in itself; everything depends on the particular circumstances. Here we have the key to the predisposition [, or at least to one of its anterooms]. We have therefore to ask ourselves: what are the particular circumstances of the scene with the cab? The patient's fear began with the sound of the trotting horses; for an instant it seemed to her that this portended some terrible doom—her death, or something as dreadful; the next moment she lost all sense of what she was doing.

419   The real shock evidently came from the horses. The patient's predisposition to react in so unaccountable a way to this unremarkable incident might therefore consist in the fact that horses have some special significance for her. We might conjecture, for instance, that she once had a dangerous accident with horses. This was actually found to be the case. As a child of about seven she was out for a drive with the coachman, when suddenly the horses took fright and at a wild gallop made for the precipitous

bank of a deep river-gorge. The coachman jumped down and shouted to her to do likewise, but she was in such deadly fear that she could hardly make up her mind. Nevertheless she jumped in the nick of time, while the horses crashed with the carriage into the depths below. That such an event would leave a very deep impression scarcely needs proof. Yet it does not explain why at a later date such an insensate reaction should follow a perfectly harmless stimulus. So far we know only that the later symptom had a prelude in childhood, but the pathological aspect of it still remains in the dark. In order to penetrate this mystery, further knowledge is needed. For it had become clear with increasing experience that in all the cases analysed so far, there existed, apart from the traumatic experiences, another, special class of disturbance which can only be described as a disturbance in the province of love. Admittedly "love" is an elastic concept that stretches from heaven to hell and combines in itself good and evil, high and low.[7] With this discovery Freud's views underwent a considerable change. If, more or less under the spell of Breuer's trauma theory, he had formerly sought the cause of the neurosis in traumatic experiences, now the centre of gravity of the problem shifted to an entirely different point. This may be best illustrated by our case: we can understand well enough why horses should play a special part in the life of the patient, but we do not understand the later reaction, so exaggerated and uncalled for. The pathological peculiarity of this story does not lie in the fact that she is frightened of horses. Remembering the empirical discovery mentioned above, that besides the traumatic experiences there is [invariably] a disturbance in the province of love, we might inquire whether perhaps there is something not quite in order in this connection.

420   The lady knows a young man to whom she thinks of becoming engaged; she loves him and hopes to be happy with him. At first nothing more is discoverable. But it would never do to be deterred from investigation by the negative results of the preliminary questioning. There are indirect ways of reaching the goal when the direct way fails. We therefore return to that sin-

---

7 We may apply to love the old mystic saying: "Heaven above, heaven below, sky above, sky below, all above, all below, accept this and rejoice." [Mephistopheles expresses the same idea when he speaks of the "power that produces good whilst ever scheming evil."]

gular moment when the lady ran headlong in front of the horses. We inquire about her companions and what sort of festive occasion it was in which she had just taken part. It had been a farewell party for her best friend, who was going abroad to a health resort on account of her nerves. This friend is married and, we are told, happily; she is also the mother of a child. We may take leave to doubt the statement that she is happy; for, were she really so, she would presumably have no reason to be "nervous" and in need of a cure. Shifting my angle of approach, I learned that after her friends had rescued her they brought the patient back to the house of her host, as this was the nearest shelter. There she was hospitably received in her exhausted state. At this point the patient broke off her narrative, became embarrassed, fidgeted, and tried to change the subject. Evidently some disagreeable reminiscence had suddenly bobbed up. After the most obstinate resistance had been overcome, it appeared that yet another very remarkable incident had occurred that night: the amiable host had made her a fiery declaration of love, thus precipitating a situation which, in the absence of the lady of the house, might well be considered both difficult and distressing. Ostensibly this declaration of love came to her like a bolt from the blue. [A small dose of criticism teaches us that these things never do drop from the sky but always have their previous history.] It was now the task of the next few weeks to dig out bit by bit a long love story, until at last a complete picture emerged which I attempt to outline somewhat as follows:

As a child the patient had been a regular tomboy, caring only for wild boys' games, scorning her own sex and avoiding all feminine ways and occupations. After puberty, when the erotic problem might have come too close, she began to shun all society, hated and despised everything that even remotely reminded her of the biological destiny of woman, and lived in a world of fantasies which had nothing in common with rude reality. Thus, until about her twenty-fourth year, she evaded all those little adventures, hopes, and expectations which ordinarily move a girl's heart at this age. (In these matters women are often amazingly insincere with themselves and with the doctor.) Then she got to know two men who were destined to break through the thorny hedge that had grown up around her. Mr. A was her best friend's husband, and Mr. B was his bachelor friend. She liked them both. Nevertheless it soon began to look as though she liked Mr. B a vast deal better. An intimacy quickly sprang up between them and before long there was talk of a possible engagement. Through her relations with Mr. B and through her friend she often came into contact with Mr. A, whose presence sometimes disturbed her in the most unaccountable way and made her nervous. About this time the patient went to a large party. Her friends were also there. She became lost in thought and was dreamily playing with her ring when it suddenly slipped off her finger and rolled under the table. Both gentlemen looked for it and Mr. B succeeded in finding it. He placed the ring on her finger with an arch smile and said, "You know what that means!" Overcome by a strange and irresistible feeling, she tore the ring from her finger and flung it through the open window. A painful moment ensued, as may be imagined, and soon she left the party in deep dejection. Not long after this, so-called chance brought it about that she should spend her summer holidays at a health resort where Mr. and Mrs. A were also staying. Mrs. A then began to grow visibly nervous, and frequently stayed indoors because she felt out of sorts. The patient was thus in a position to go out for walks alone with Mr. A. On one occasion they went boating. So boisterous was she in her merriment that she suddenly fell overboard. She could not swim, and it was only with great difficulty that Mr. A pulled her half-unconscious into the boat. And then it was that he kissed her. With this romantic episode the bonds were tied fast. To excuse herself in her own eyes she pursued her engagement to Mr. B all the more energetically, telling herself every day that it was Mr. B whom she loved. Naturally this curious little game had not escaped the keen glances of wifely jealousy. Mrs. A, her friend, had guessed the secret and fretted accordingly, so that her nerves only got worse. Hence it became necessary for Mrs. A to go abroad for a cure. At the farewell party the evil spirit stepped up to our patient and whispered in her ear, "Tonight he is alone. Something must happen to you so that you can go to his house." And so indeed it happened: through her own strange behaviour she came back to his house, and thus she attained her desire.

421   After this explanation everyone will probably be inclined to assume that only a devilish subtlety could devise such a chain of

circumstances and set it to work. There is no doubt about the subtlety, but its moral evaluation remains a doubtful matter, because I must emphasize that the motives leading to this dramatic dénouement were in no sense conscious. To the patient, the whole story seemed to happen of itself, without her being conscious of any motive. But the previous history makes it perfectly clear that everything was [most ingeniously] directed to this end, while the conscious mind was struggling to bring about the engagement to Mr. B. The unconscious drive in the other direction was stronger.

422   So once more we return to our original question, namely, whence comes the pathological (i.e., peculiar or exaggerated) nature of the reaction to the trauma? On the basis of a conclusion drawn from analogous experiences we conjectured that in this case too there must be, in addition to the trauma, a disturbance in the erotic sphere. This conjecture has been entirely confirmed, and we have learned that the trauma, the ostensible cause of the illness, is no more than an occasion for something previously not conscious to manifest itself, i.e., an important erotic conflict. Accordingly the trauma loses its pathogenic significance and is replaced by a much deeper and more comprehensive conception which sees the pathogenic agent as an erotic conflict. [This conception might be called the *sexual theory of neurosis.*]

423   I often hear the question: why should the erotic conflict be the cause of the neurosis rather than any other conflict? To this we can only answer: no one asserts that it must be so, but in point of fact it [always] is so [, notwithstanding all the cousins and aunts, parents, godparents, and teachers who rage against it]. In spite of all indignant protestations to the contrary, the fact remains that love,[8] its problems and its conflicts, is of fundamental importance in human life, and, as careful inquiry consistently shows, is of far greater significance than the individual suspects.

424   The trauma theory has therefore been abandoned as antiquated; for with the discovery that not the trauma but a hidden erotic conflict is the [true] root of the neurosis, the trauma completely loses its pathogenic significance.

[8] Using the word in the wider sense which belongs to it by right and embraces more than sexuality.

425   [The theory was thus shifted onto an entirely different plane.] The question of the trauma was solved and disposed of; but in its place the investigator was faced with the problem of the erotic conflict, which, as our example shows, contains a wealth of abnormal elements and cannot at first sight be compared with an ordinary erotic conflict. What is peculiarly striking and almost incredible is that only the pose should be conscious, while the patient's real passion remained hidden from her. In this case certainly, it is beyond dispute that the real erotic relationship was shrouded in darkness, while the pose largely dominated the field of consciousness. If we formulate these facts theoretically, we arrive at the following result: there are in a neurosis two [erotic] tendencies standing in strict opposition to one another, one of which at least is unconscious. [Against this formula it might be objected that it obviously fits only this particular case and therefore lacks general validity. The objection will be urged the more readily because no one is willing to admit that the erotic conflict is of universal prevalence. On the contrary, it is assumed that the erotic conflict belongs more properly to the sphere of novels, since it is generally understood as something in the nature of such extra-marital adventures as are described in the novels of Karin Michaelis, or by Forel in *The Sexual Question*. But this is not so at all, for we know that the wildest and most moving dramas are played not in the theatre but in the hearts of ordinary men and women who pass by without exciting attention, and who betray to the world nothing of the conflicts that rage within them except possibly by a nervous breakdown. What is so difficult for the layman to grasp is the fact that in most cases the patients themselves have no suspicion whatever of the internecine war raging in their unconscious. If we remember that there are many people who understand nothing at all about themselves, we shall be less surprised at the realization that there are also people who are utterly unaware of their actual conflicts.]

426   [Now even if the reader is ready to admit the possible existence of pathogenic, and perhaps even of unconscious conflicts, he will still protest that they are not *erotic* conflicts. If this kind reader should happen himself to be somewhat nervous, the mere suggestion will arouse his indignation; for we are all accustomed, through our education at school and at home, to cross

ourselves three times when we meet words like "erotic" and "sexual"—and so we are conveniently able to think that nothing of the sort exists, or at least very seldom, and at a great distance from ourselves. But it is just this attitude that brings about neurotic conflicts in the first place.]

427   The growth of culture consists, as we know, in a progressive subjugation of the animal in man. It is a process of domestication which cannot be accomplished without rebellion on the part of the animal nature that thirsts for freedom. From time to time there passes as it were a wave of frenzy through the ranks of men too long constrained within the limitations of their culture. Antiquity experienced it in the Dionysian orgies that surged over from the East and became an essential and characteristic ingredient of classical culture. The spirit of these orgies contributed not a little towards the development of the stoic ideal of asceticism in the innumerable sects and philosophical schools of the last century before Christ, which produced from the polytheistic chaos of that epoch the twin ascetic religions of Mithraism and Christianity. A second wave of Dionysian licentiousness swept over the West at the Renaissance. It is difficult to gauge the spirit of one's own time; but, if we observe the trend of art, of style, and of public taste, and see what people read and write, what sort of societies they found, what "questions" are the order of the day, what the Philistines fight against, we shall find that in the long catalogue of our present social questions by no means the last is the so-called "sexual question." This is discussed by men and women who challenge the existing sexual morality and who seek to throw off the burden of moral guilt which past centuries have heaped upon Eros. One cannot simply deny the existence of these endeavours nor condemn them as indefensible; they exist, and probably have adequate grounds for their existence. It is more interesting and more useful to examine carefully the underlying causes of these contemporary movements than to join in the lamentations of the professional mourners of morality who [with hysterical unction] prophesy the moral downfall of humanity. It is the way of moralists not to put the slightest trust in God, as if they thought that the good tree of humanity flourished only by dint of being pruned, tied back, and trained on a trellis; whereas in fact Father Sun and Mother

Earth have allowed it to grow for their delight in accordance with deep, wise laws.

428   Serious-minded people know that there is something of a sexual problem today. They know that the rapid development of the towns, with the specialization of work brought about by the extraordinary division of labour, the increasing industrialization of the countryside, and the growing sense of insecurity, deprive men of many opportunities for giving vent to their affective energies. The peasant's alternating rhythm of work secures him unconscious satisfactions through its symbolical content—satisfactions which the factory workers and office employees do not know and can never enjoy. What do these know of his life with nature, of those grand moments when, as lord and fructifier of the earth, he drives his plough through the soil, and with a kingly gesture scatters the seed for the future harvest; of his rightful fear of the destructive power of the elements, of his joy in the fruitfulness of his wife who bears him the daughters and sons who mean increased working-power and prosperity? [Alas!] From all this we city-dwellers, we modern machine-minders, are far removed. Is not the fairest and most natural of all satisfactions beginning to fail us, when we can no longer regard with unmixed joy the harvest of our own sowing, the "blessing" of children? [Marriages where no artifices are resorted to are rare. Is not this an all-important departure from the joys which Mother Nature gave her first-born son?] Can such a state of affairs bring satisfaction? See how men slink to work, only observe the faces in trains at 7:30 in the morning! One man makes his little wheels go round, another writes things that interest him not at all. What wonder that nearly every man belongs to as many clubs as there are days in the week, or that there are flourishing little societies for women where they can pour out, on the hero of the latest cult, those inarticulate longings which the man drowns at the pub in big talk and small beer? To these sources of discontent there is added a further and graver difficulty. Nature has armed defenceless and weaponless man with a vast store of energy, to enable him not only passively to endure the rigours of existence but also to overcome them. She has equipped her son for tremendous hardships [and has placed a costly premium on the overcoming of them, as Scho-

penhauer well understood when he said that happiness is merely the cessation of unhappiness]. As a rule we are protected from the most pressing necessities, and for that reason we are daily tempted to excess; for the animal in man always becomes rampant unless hard necessity presses. But if we are high-spirited, in what orgiastic feasts and revels can we let off our surplus of energy? Our moral views forbid this outlet.

429   [Let us reckon up the many sources of discontent: the denial of continual procreation and giving birth, for which purpose nature has endowed us with vast quantities of energy; the monotony of our highly differentiated methods of labour, which exclude any interest in the work itself; our effortless security against war, lawlessness, robbery, plague, child and female mortality—all this gives a sum of surplus energy which needs must find an outlet. But how? Relatively few create quasi-natural dangers for themselves in reckless sport; many more, seeking for some equivalent of the hard life in order to siphon off dangerous accumulations of energy that might burst out even more crazily, are driven to alcoholic excess, or expend themselves in the rush of money-making, or in the frenzied performance of duties, or in perpetual overwork. It is for such reasons that we have today a sexual question. The pent-up energy would like to get out here, as it has done since time immemorial in periods of security and abundance. Under such circumstances it is not only rabbits that multiply; men and women, too, are made the sport of these whims of nature—the sport, because their moral views have shut them up in a narrow cage, the excessive narrowness of which was not felt so long as harsh necessity pressed with even greater constraint. But now it is too tight even for the city-dweller. Temptation surrounds him on all sides, and like an invisible procurer there slinks through society the knowledge of the preventive methods that make everything unhappened.]

430   Why then the moral restriction? Out of religious consideration for a wrathful God? Irrespective of the widespread unbelief, even the believer might quietly ask himself whether, if he were God, he would punish every Jack-and-Jill escapade with everlasting damnation. Such ideas are no longer compatible with our comfortable conception of God. Our God is far too tolerant to make a great fuss about it. [Mean-mindedness and hypocrisy are a thousand times worse.] Thus the ascetically in-

spired and markedly hypocritical [9] sexual morality of our time is robbed of any effective background. Or can we say that we are protected from excess by our superior wisdom and our insight into the nullity of human behaviour? Unfortunately we are very far from that. [The hypnotic power of tradition still holds us in thrall, and out of cowardice and thoughtlessness the herd goes trudging along the same old path.] But man possesses in the unconscious a fine flair for the spirit of his time; he divines his possibilities and feels in his heart the instability of present-day morality, no longer supported by living religious conviction. Here is the source of most of our [erotic] conflicts. The urge to freedom beats upon the weakening barriers of morality: we are in a state of temptation, we want and do not want. And because we want and yet cannot think out what it is we really want, the [erotic] conflict is largely unconscious, and thence comes neurosis. Neurosis, therefore, is intimately bound up with the problem of our time and really represents an unsuccessful attempt on the part of the individual to solve the general problem in his own person. Neurosis is self-division. In most people the cause of the division is that the conscious mind wants to hang on to its moral ideal, while the unconscious strives after its—in the contemporary sense—unmoral ideal which the conscious mind [steadfastly] tries to deny. Men of this type want to be more respectable than they really are. But the conflict can easily be the other way about: there are men who to all appearances are very disreputable and do not put the least restraint upon [their sexuality], but at bottom this is only a pose of wickedness [assumed for heaven knows what reasons], for in the background they have [a highly respectable soul] which has fallen into the unconscious just as surely as the immoral side in the case of the moral man. (Extremes should therefore be avoided as far as possible, because they always arouse suspicion of their opposite.)

431 　This general discussion was necessary in order to clarify the idea of an "erotic conflict" [in analytical psychology, for it is the

[9] [The abolition of houses of prostitution is also one of the hypocritical pests of our famous sexual morality. Prostitution exists anyway; the less it is organized and looked after, the more scandalous and dangerous it becomes. Since this evil nevertheless exists and always will, we should be more tolerant and make the thing as hygienic as possible. If people had not worn moral blinkers, syphilis would have been put down long ago.] [Note omitted in both editions of Collected Papers.—EDITORS.]

key to the whole conception of neurosis]. Thence we can proceed to discuss firstly the technique of psychoanalysis and secondly the question of therapy. [Obviously the latter question would involve us in details and complicated case material which far exceed the scope of this short introduction. We must therefore be content to cast a glance at the technique of psychoanalysis.]

432 Obviously the great question for this technique is: How are we to arrive by the shortest and best path at a knowledge of what is happening in the unconscious of the patient? The original method was hypnotism: either interrogation in a state of hypnotic concentration or else the spontaneous production of fantasies by the patient while in this state. This method is still occasionally employed, but compared with the present technique it is too primitive and therefore unsatisfactory. A second method was evolved by the Psychiatric Clinic, in Zurich, the so-called association method,[10] the value of which is primarily theoretical and experimental. Its results give one a comprehensive though superficial grasp of the unconscious conflict or "complex." [11] The more penetrating method is that of dream-analysis, discovered by [the genius of Sigmund] Freud.

433 Of the dream it can indeed be said that "the stone which the builders rejected has become the head of the corner." It is only in modern times that the dream, this fleeting and insignificant-looking product of the psyche, has met with such profound contempt. Formerly it was esteemed as a harbinger of fate, a portent and comforter, a messenger of the gods. Now we see it as an emissary of the unconscious, whose task it is to reveal the secrets [which our unconscious jealously hides] from the conscious mind, and this it does with astounding completeness.

434 From the analytical study of the dream it was found that the dream, as it appears to us, is only a façade which conceals the interior of the house. If, however, while observing certain technical rules, we induce the dreamer to talk about the details of his dream, it soon becomes evident that his associations tend in a particular direction and group themselves round particular topics. These appear to be of personal significance and yield a

10 Jung and others, *Studies in Word Association*, trans. by M. D. Eder.
11 The theory of complexes is set out in Jung, "The Psychology of Dementia Praecox."

meaning which could never have been conjectured to lie behind the dream, but which, as careful comparison has shown, stands in an extremely delicate and meticulously exact [symbolic] relation to the dream façade.[12] This particular complex of ideas, wherein are united all the threads of the dream, is the conflict we are looking for, or rather a variation of it conditioned by circumstances. The painful and incompatible elements in the conflict are in this way so covered up or obliterated that one may speak of a "wish-fulfilment"; though we must immediately add that the wishes fulfilled in the dream do not seem to be ours, but are of a kind that often runs directly counter to them. Thus, for instance, a daughter loves her mother tenderly, but dreams to her great distress that her mother is dead. Such dreams, in which there is apparently no trace of wish-fulfilment, are innumerable, and are a constant stumbling-block to our learned critics, for [—incredible to relate—] they still cannot grasp the elementary distinction between the manifest and the latent content of the dream. We must guard against this error: the conflict worked out in the dream is unconscious, and so is the resultant wish for a solution. Our dreamer does in fact have the wish to be rid of her mother; expressed in the language of the unconscious, she wants her mother to die. Now we know that a certain compartment of the unconscious contains everything that has passed beyond the recall of memory, including all those infantile instinctual impulses which could find no outlet in adult life, that is, a succession of ruthless childish desires. We can say that the bulk of what comes out of the unconscious has an infantile character, as for instance this wish, which is simplicity itself: "When Mummy dies you will marry me, won't you, Daddy?" This expression of an infantile wish is the substitute for a recent desire to marry, a desire in this case painful to the dreamer, for reasons still to be discovered. The idea of marriage, or rather the seriousness of the corresponding impulse, is, as they say, "repressed into the unconscious" and from there must necessarily express itself in an infantile fashion, because the material at the disposal

12 [The rules of dream analysis, the laws governing the structure of the dream, and its symbolism together form almost a science, or at any rate one of the most important chapters of the psychology of the unconscious and one requiring particularly arduous study.]

of the unconscious consists largely of infantile reminiscences. [As the latest researches of the Zurich school have shown,[13] besides the infantile reminiscences there are also "race memories" extending far beyond the limits of the individual.]

435 [This is not the place to elucidate the extraordinarily complicated field of dream analysis. We must content ourselves with the results of research: dreams are a symbolic substitute for a personally important wish which was not sufficiently appreciated during the day and was "repressed." In consequence of the predominant moral tendencies, the insufficiently appreciated wishes that strive to realize themselves symbolically in dreams are, as a rule, erotic ones. It is therefore inadvisable to tell one's dreams to a knowledgeable person, for the symbolism is often quite transparent to one who knows the rules. The clearest in this respect are anxiety dreams, which are so common, and which invariably symbolize a strong erotic wish.]

436 The dream is often occupied with apparently very silly details, thus producing an impression of absurdity, or else it is on the surface so unintelligible as to leave us thoroughly bewildered. Hence we always have to overcome a certain resistance before we can seriously set about disentangling the [symbolic] web through patient work. But when at last we penetrate to its real meaning, we find ourselves deep in the dreamer's secrets and discover with astonishment that an apparently quite senseless dream is in the highest degree significant, and that in reality it speaks only of extraordinarily important and serious things of the soul. This discovery compels rather more respect for the old superstition that dreams have a meaning, to which the rationalistic temper of our age has hitherto given short shrift.

437 As Freud says, dream-analysis is the *via regia* to the unconscious. It leads straight to the deepest personal secrets, and is, therefore, an invaluable instrument in the hand of the physician and educator of the soul. The attacks of the opposition against this method are, as might be expected, based upon arguments which—setting aside the undercurrents of personal feeling—derive chiefly from the very strong scholastic streak that still exists in the learned thought of our day. Dream-analysis above all else mercilessly uncovers the lying morality and hypocritical pretences of man, showing him, for once, the other side of his

13 [Jung, *Wandlungen und Symbole der Libido.*]

character in the most vivid light; can we wonder if many feel that their toes have been heavily trodden upon? In this connection I am always reminded of the striking statue of Carnal Pleasure outside Basel Cathedral, the front exhibiting the sweet archaic smile, the rear covered with toads and serpents. Dream-analysis reverses the picture and shows the other side. The ethical value of this reality-corrective can hardly be denied. It is a painful but extremely useful operation which makes great demands on both doctor and patient. Psychoanalysis, considered as a therapeutic technique, consists in the main of numerous dream-analyses. In the course of treatment the dreams successively throw up the dregs of the unconscious in order to expose them to the disinfecting power of daylight, and in this way much that is valuable and believed lost is found again. It is a catharsis of a special kind, something like the maieutics of Socrates, the "art of the midwife." It is only to be expected that for many people who have adopted a certain pose towards themselves, in which they violently believe, psychoanalysis is a veritable torture. For, in accordance with the old mystical saying, "Give up what thou hast, then shalt thou receive!" they are called upon to abandon all their cherished illusions in order that something deeper, fairer, and more embracing may arise within them. Only through the mystery of self-sacrifice can a man find himself anew. It is a genuine old wisdom that comes to light again in psychoanalytical treatment, and it is especially curious that this kind of psychic education should prove necessary in the heyday of our culture. In more than one respect it may be compared with the Socratic method, though it must be said that psychoanalysis penetrates to far greater depths.

438   We always find in the patient a conflict which at a certain point is connected with the great problems of society. Hence, when the analysis is pushed to this point, the apparently individual conflict of the patient is revealed as a universal conflict of his environment and epoch. Neurosis is thus nothing less than an individual attempt, however unsuccessful, to solve a universal problem; indeed it cannot be otherwise, for a general problem, a "question," is not an *ens per se*, but exists only in the hearts of individuals. ["The question" that troubles the patient is— whether you like it or not—the "sexual" question, or more precisely, the problem of present-day sexual morality. His increased

demand for life and the joy of life, for glowing reality, can stand the necessary limitations that reality itself imposes, but not the arbitrary, ill-supported prohibitions of present-day morality, which would curb too much the creative spirit rising up from the depths of the animal darkness.] The neurotic has the soul of a child who bears ill with arbitrary restrictions whose meaning he does not see; he tries to make this morality his own, but falls into profound division and disunity with himself: one side of him wants to suppress, the other longs to be free—and this struggle goes by the name of neurosis. Were the conflict clearly conscious in all its parts, it would never give rise to neurotic symptoms; these occur only when we cannot see the other side of our nature and the urgency of its problems. Only under these conditions does the symptom appear, and it helps to give expression to the unrecognized side of the psyche. The symptom is therefore an indirect expression of unrecognized desires which, when conscious, come into violent conflict with our moral convictions. As already observed, this shadow-side of the psyche, being withdrawn from conscious scrutiny, cannot be dealt with by the patient. He cannot correct it, cannot come to terms with it, nor yet disregard it; for in reality he does not "possess" the unconscious impulses at all. Thrust out from the hierarchy of the conscious psyche, they have become *autonomous complexes* which can be brought under control again through the analysis of the unconscious, though not without great resistances. There are very many patients who boast that for them the erotic conflict does not exist; they assure us that the sexual question is all nonsense, for they say they possess no sexuality whatever. These people do not see that other things of unknown origin cumber their path—hysterical moods, underhand tricks which they play on themselves and their neighbours, a nervous catarrh of the stomach, pains in various places, irritability for no reason, and a whole host of nervous symptoms. [That is where the trouble lies. Only a few especially favoured by fate escape the great conflict of modern man; the majority are caught in it from sheer necessity.]

439   Psychoanalysis has been accused of liberating man's (fortunately) repressed animal instincts and thus causing incalculable harm. This [childish] apprehension shows how little trust we place in the efficacy of our moral principles. People pretend that *only* morality holds men back from unbridled licence; but a

much more effective regulator is necessity, which sets bounds far more real and persuasive than any moral precepts. It is true that analysis liberates the animal instincts, though not, as many would have it, with a view to giving them unbridled power, but rather to put them to higher uses, so far as this is possible for the individual concerned and so far as he requires such "sublimation." It is under all circumstances an advantage to be in full possession of one's personality, otherwise the repressed portions of the personality will only crop up as a hindrance elsewhere, not just at some unimportant point, but at the very spot where we are most sensitive: this worm always rots the core. [Instead of waging war on himself it is surely better for a man to learn to tolerate himself, and to convert his inner difficulties into real experiences instead of expending them in useless fantasies. Then at least he lives, and does not waste his life in fruitless struggles.] If people can be educated to see the lowly side of their own natures, it may be hoped that they will also learn to understand and to love their fellow men better. A little less hypocrisy and a little more tolerance towards oneself can only have good results in respect for our neighbour; for we are all too prone to transfer to our fellows the injustice and violence we inflict upon our own natures.

440   [This funnelling of the individual conflict into the general moral problem puts psychoanalysis far outside the confines of a merely medical therapy. It gives the patient a working philosophy of life based on empirical insights, which, besides affording him a knowledge of his own nature, also make it possible for him to fit himself into this scheme of things. Wherein these very varied insights consist cannot be discussed here. It is also not at all easy to form an adequate picture of an actual analysis from the existing literature, since by no means everything has been published that relates to the technique of a deep analysis. Very great problems still remain to be solved in this field. Unfortunately the number of scientific works on this subject is still rather small, because too many prejudices still prevent most of the specialists from collaborating in this important endeavour. Many, especially in Germany, are also held back by the fear of ruining their careers if they venture to set foot on this territory.]

441   [All these weird and wonderful phenomena that congregate round psychoanalysis allow us to conjecture—in accordance with

psychoanalytic principles—that something extremely significant is going on here, which the learned public will (as usual) first combat by displays of the liveliest affect. But: *magna est vis veritatis et praevalebit.*]

II

THE STRUCTURE OF THE UNCONSCIOUS [1]

1. *The Distinction between the Personal and the Impersonal Unconscious*

442   Since we parted company with the Viennese school on the question of the interpretive principle in psychoanalysis, namely, whether it be *sexuality* or simply *energy*, our concepts have undergone considerable development. Once the prejudice regarding the explanatory cause had been removed by accepting a purely abstract one, the nature of which was not postulated in advance, our interest was directed to the concept of the unconscious.

[1] [First delivered as a lecture to the Zurich School for Analytical Psychology, 1916, and published the same year, in a French translation by M. Marsen, in the *Archives de Psychologie* (XVI, pp. 152–79) under the title "La Structure de l'inconscient." The lecture appeared in English with the title "The Conception of the Unconscious" in *Collected Papers on Analytical Psychology* (2nd edn., 1917), and had evidently been translated from a German MS, which subsequently disappeared. For the first edition of the present volume a translation was made by Philip Mairet from the French version. The German MS, titled "Über das Unbewusste und seine Inhalte," came to light again only after Jung's death in 1961. It contained a stratum of revisions and additions, in a later hand of the author's, most of which were incorporated in the revised and expanded version, titled *Die Beziehungen zwischen dem Ich und dem Unbewussten* (1928), a translation of which forms Part II of the present volume. The MS did not, however, contain all the new material that was added in the 1928 version. In particular, section 5 (infra, pars. 480–521) was replaced by Part Two of that essay.

[The text that now follows is a new translation from the newly discovered German MS. Additions that found their way into the 1928 version have not been included; additions that are not represented in that version are given in square brackets. To facilitate comparison between the 1916 and the final versions, the corresponding paragraph numbers of the latter are likewise given in square brackets. A similar but not identical presentation of the rediscovered MS is given in Vol. 7 of the Swiss edition.—EDITORS.]

[202] 443   In Freud's view, as most people know, the contents of the unconscious are reducible to infantile tendencies which are repressed because of their incompatible character. Repression is a process that begins in early childhood under the moral influence of the environment and continues throughout life. By means of analysis the repressions are removed and the repressed wishes are made conscious again. Theoretically the unconscious would thus find itself emptied and, so to speak, done away with; but in reality the production of infantile-sexual wish-fantasies continues right into old age.

[203] 444   According to this theory, the unconscious would contain only those elements of the personality which could just as well be conscious, and have in fact been suppressed only through the process of education. It follows that the essential content of the unconscious would be of a personal character. Although from one point of view the infantile tendencies of the unconscious are the most conspicuous, it would none the less be a mistake to define or evaluate the unconscious entirely in these terms. The unconscious has still another side to it: it includes not only repressed contents, but also all psychic material that lies below the threshold of consciousness. It is impossible to explain the subliminal nature of all this material on the principle of repression, for in that case the removal of repression ought to endow a person with a prodigious memory which would thenceforth forget nothing. No doubt repression plays a part, but it is not the only factor. If what we call a bad memory were always only the result of repression, those who enjoy an excellent memory ought never to suffer from repression, nor in consequence be neurotic. But experience shows that this is not the case at all. There are certainly cases of abnormally bad memory where it is obvious that the lion's share must be attributed to repression, but these are relatively rare.

[204] 445   We therefore affirm that in addition to the repressed material the unconscious contains all those psychic components that have fallen below the threshold, as well as subliminal sense-perceptions. Moreover, we know, from abundant experience as well as for theoretical reasons, that besides this the unconscious contains all the material that has *not yet* reached the threshold of consciousness. These are the seeds of future conscious con-

tents. Equally we have every reason to suppose that the unconscious is never quiescent in the sense of being inactive, but presumably is ceaselessly engaged in the grouping and regrouping of so-called unconscious fantasies. This activity should be thought of as relatively autonomous only in pathological cases; normally it is co-ordinated with consciousness in a compensatory relationship.

205] 446   It is to be assumed that all these contents are of a personal nature in so far as they are acquired during the individual's life. Since this life is limited, the number of acquired contents in the unconscious must also be limited. This being so, it might be thought possible to empty the unconscious either by analysis or by making a complete inventory of the unconscious contents, on the ground that the unconscious cannot produce anything more than what is already known and assimilated into consciousness. We should also have to suppose, as we have said, that if one could arrest the descent of conscious contents into the unconscious by doing away with repression, unconscious productivity would be paralysed. This is possible only to a very limited extent, as we know from experience. We urge our patients to hold fast to repressed contents that have been re-associated with consciousness, and to assimilate them into their plan of life. But this procedure, as we may daily convince ourselves, makes no impression on the unconscious, since it calmly goes on producing apparently the same infantile-sexual fantasies which, according to the earlier theory, should be the effects of personal repressions. If in such cases the analysis be continued systematically, one uncovers little by little a medley of incompatible wish-fantasies of a most surprising composition. Besides all the sexual perversions one finds every conceivable kind of criminality, as well as the noblest deeds and the loftiest ideas imaginable, the existence of which one would never have suspected in the subject under analysis.

228] 447   By way of example I would like to recall the case of a schizophrenic patient of Maeder's, who used to declare that the world was his picture-book.[2] He was a wretched locksmith's apprentice who fell ill at an early age and had never been blessed with much intelligence. This notion of his, that the world was

2 Maeder, "La Langue d'un aliéné," *Archives de Psychologie*, IX, 212.

his picture-book, the leaves of which he was turning over as he looked around him, is exactly the same as Schopenhauer's "world as will and idea," but expressed in primitive picture language. His vision is just as sublime as Schopenhauer's, the only difference being that with the patient it remained at an embryonic stage, whereas in Schopenhauer the same idea is transformed from a vision into an abstraction and expressed in a language that is universally valid.

[229] 448   It would be quite wrong to suppose that the patient's vision had a personal character and value, for that would be to endow the patient with the dignity of a philosopher. But, as I have indicated, he alone is a philosopher who can transmute a vision born of nature into an abstract idea, thereby translating it into a universally valid language. Schopenhauer's philosophical conception represents a personal value, but the vision of the patient is an impersonal value, a merely natural growth, the proprietary right to which can be acquired only by him who abstracts it into an idea and expresses it in universal terms. It would, however, be wrong to attribute to the philosopher, by exaggerating the value of his achievement, the additional merit of having actually created or invented the vision itself. It is a primordial idea that grows up quite as naturally in the philosopher and is simply a part of the common property of mankind, in which, in principle, everyone has a share. The golden apples drop from the same tree, whether they be gathered by a locksmith's apprentice or by a Schopenhauer.

[218] 449   These primordial ideas, of which I have given a great many examples in my work on libido,[3] oblige one to make, in regard to unconscious material, a distinction of quite a different character from that between "preconscious" and "unconscious" or "subconscious" and "unconscious." The justification for these distinctions need not be discussed here. They have their specific value and are well worth elaborating further as points of view. The fundamental distinction which experience has forced upon me claims to be no more than that. It should be evident from the foregoing that we have to distinguish in the unconscious a layer which we may call the *personal unconscious*. The contents of this layer are of a personal nature in so far as they have the character partly of acquisitions derived from the indi-

[3] *Psychology of the Unconscious.*

vidual's life and partly of psychological factors[4] which could just as well be conscious.

[218] 450   It can readily be understood that incompatible psychological elements are liable to repression and therefore become unconscious. But this implies the possibility, on the other hand, of making and keeping the repressed contents conscious once they have been recognized. We recognize them as personal contents because their effects, or their partial manifestation, or their source can be discovered in our personal past. They are integral components of the personality, they belong to its inventory, and their loss to consciousness produces an inferiority in one respect or another. This inferiority has the psychological character not so much of an organic lesion or an inborn defect as of a lack which gives rise to a feeling of moral resentment. The sense of moral inferiority always indicates that the missing element is something which, to judge by this feeling about it, really ought not to be missing, or which could be made conscious if only one took sufficient trouble. The moral inferiority does not come from a collision with the generally accepted and, in a sense, arbitrary moral law, but from the conflict with one's own self, which for reasons of psychic equilibrium demands that the deficit be redressed. Whenever a sense of moral inferiority appears, it indicates not only a need to assimilate an unconscious component, but also the possibility of such assimilation. In the last resort it is a man's moral qualities which force him, either through direct recognition of the need or indirectly through a painful neurosis, to assimilate his unconscious self and keep himself fully conscious. Whoever progresses along this path of self-realization must inevitably bring into consciousness the contents of his personal unconscious, thus enlarging considerably the scope of his personality.

2. *Phenomena Resulting from the Assimilation of the Unconscious*

[221] 451   The process of assimilating the unconscious gives rise to some very remarkable phenomena. It produces in some patients

---

[4] For instance, repressed wishes or tendencies that are incompatible with the moral or aesthetic sentiments of the subject.

an unmistakable and often unpleasant increase of self-confidence and conceit: they are full of themselves, they know everything, they imagine themselves to be fully informed of everything concerning their unconscious, and are persuaded that they understand perfectly everything that comes out of it. At every interview with the doctor they get more and more above themselves. Others on the contrary feel themselves more and more crushed under the contents of the unconscious, they lose their self-confidence and abandon themselves with dull resignation to all the extraordinary things that the unconscious produces. The former, overflowing with feelings of their own importance, assume a responsibility for the unconscious that goes much too far, beyond all reasonable bounds; the others finally give up all sense of responsibility, overcome by a sense of the powerlessness of the ego against the fate working through the unconscious.

[222] 452   If we analyse these two modes of reaction more deeply, we find that the optimistic self-confidence of the first conceals a profound sense of impotence, for which their conscious optimism acts as an unsuccessful compensation; while the pessimistic resignation of the others masks a defiant will to power, far surpassing in cocksureness the conscious optimism of the first type.

[224] 453   Adler has employed the term "godlikeness" to characterize certain basic features of neurotic power psychology. If I likewise borrow the same term from *Faust*, I use it here more in the sense of that well known passage where Mephisto writes "Eritis sicut Deus, scientes bonum et malum" in the student's album, and makes the following aside:

> Just follow the old advice
> Of my cousin the snake.
> There'll come a time when your godlikeness
> Will make you quiver and quake.[5]

454   Godlikeness is certainly not a scientific concept, although it aptly characterizes the psychological state in question. It has yet to be seen whence this attitude arises and why it deserves the name of godlikeness. As the term indicates, the abnormality of the patient's condition consists in his attributing to himself qualities or values which obviously do not belong to him, for to

5 *Faust*, Part I, 3rd scene in Faust's study.

be "godlike" is to be like a spirit superior to the spirit of man.

[235] 455   If, with a psychological aim in view, we dissect this notion of godlikeness, we find that the term comprises not only the dynamic phenomenon I have discussed in my book on libido, but also a certain psychic function having a collective character supraordinate to the individual mentality. Just as the individual is not merely a unique and separate being, but is also a social being, so the human mind is not a self-contained and wholly individual phenomenon, but also a collective one. And just as certain social functions or instincts are opposed to the egocentric interests of the individual, so certain functions or tendencies of the human mind are opposed, by their collective nature, to the personal mental functions.[6] The reason for this is that every man is born with a brain that is highly differentiated. This makes him capable of a wide range of mental functioning which is neither developed ontogenetically nor acquired. But, inasmuch as human brains are uniformly differentiated, the mental functioning thereby made possible is collective and universal. This explains, for example, the interesting fact that the unconscious processes of the most widely separated peoples and races show a quite remarkable correspondence, which displays itself, among other things, in the extraordinary but well-authenticated analogies between the forms and motifs of autochthonous myths.

[235] 456   The universal similarity of human brains leads to the universal possibility of a uniform mental functioning. This functioning is the *collective psyche*. This can be subdivided into the *collective mind* and the *collective soul*.[7] Inasmuch as there are differentiations corresponding to race, tribe, and even family, there is also a collective psyche limited to race, tribe, and family over and above the "universal" collective psyche. To borrow an

---

[6] This conflict arises, for instance, when it is a question of subordinating personal desires or opinions to social laws. Cf. Rousseau, *Emile*, Book I: "What can one do . . . when, instead of educating a man for himself, people want to educate him for others? Harmony is then impossible. Obliged to fight either against nature or against the social institutions, one has to choose between making a man or a citizen; for one cannot make the one and the other at the same time."

[7] By the collective mind I mean collective thinking; by the collective soul collective feeling; and by the collective psyche the collective psychological functions as a whole.

expression from Pierre Janet, the collective psyche comprises the *parties inférieures* of the mental functions, that is to say those deep-rooted, well-nigh automatic portions of the individual psyche which are inherited and are to be found everywhere, and are thus impersonal or suprapersonal. Consciousness plus the personal unconscious constitutes the *parties supérieures* of the mental functions, those portions, therefore, that are developed ontogenetically and acquired as a result of personal differentiation.

[235] 457   Consequently, the individual who annexes the unconscious heritage of the collective psyche to what has accrued to him in the course of his ontogenetic development enlarges the scope of his personality in an illegitimate way and suffers the consequences. In so far as the collective psyche comprises the *parties inférieures* of the mental functions and thus forms the basis of every personality, it has the effect of crushing and devaluing the latter. This shows itself in the aforementioned stifling of self-confidence and in an unconscious heightening of the ego's importance to the point of a pathological will to power. On the other hand, in so far as the collective psyche is supraordinate to the personality, being the matrix of all personal differentiations and the mental function common to all individuals, it will have the effect, if annexed to the personality, of producing a hypertrophy of self-confidence, which in turn is compensated by an extraordinary sense of inferiority in the unconscious.

[237] 458   If, through assimilation of the unconscious, we make the mistake of including the collective psyche in the inventory of personal mental functions, a dissolution of the personality into its paired opposites inevitably follows. Besides the pair of opposites already discussed, megalomania and the sense of inferiority, which are so painfully evident in neurosis, there are many others, from which I will single out only the specifically moral pair of opposites, namely good and evil (*scientes bonum et malum!*). The formation of this pair goes hand in hand with the increase and diminution of self-confidence. The specific virtues and vices of humanity are contained in the collective psyche like everything else. One man arrogates collective virtue to himself as his personal merit, another takes collective vice as his personal guilt. Both are as illusory as the megalomania and the inferiority, because the imaginary virtues and the imaginary wickedness

276

are simply the moral pair of opposites contained in the collective psyche, which have become perceptible or have been rendered conscious artificially. How much these paired opposites are contained in the collective psyche is exemplified by primitives: one observer will extol the greatest virtues in them, while another will record the very worst impressions of the selfsame tribe. For the primitive, whose personal differentiation is, as we know, only just beginning, both judgments are true, because his mentality is essentially collective. He is still more or less identical with the collective psyche, and for that reason shares equally in the collective virtues and vices without any personal attribution and without inner contradiction. The contradiction arises only when the personal development of the mind begins, and when reason discovers the irreconcilable nature of the opposites. The consequence of this discovery is the conflict of repression. We want to be good, and therefore must repress evil; and with that the paradise of the collective psyche comes to an end.

[237] 459   Repression of the collective psyche was absolutely necessary for the development of the personality, since collective psychology and personal psychology exclude one another up to a point. History teaches us that whenever a psychological attitude acquires a collective value, schisms begin to break out. Nowhere is this more evident than in the history of religion. A collective attitude is always a threat to the individual, even when it is a necessity. It is dangerous because it is very apt to check and smother all personal differentiation. It derives this characteristic from the collective psyche, which is itself a product of the psychological differentiation of the powerful gregarious instinct in man. Collective thinking and feeling and collective effort are relatively easy in comparison with individual functioning and performance; and from this may arise, all too easily, a dangerous threat to the development of personality through enfeeblement of the personal function. The damage done to the personality is compensated—for everything is compensated in psychology—by a compulsive union and unconscious identity with the collective psyche.

[240] 460   There is now a danger that in the analysis of the unconscious the collective and the personal psyche may be fused together, with, as I have intimated, highly unfortunate results. These results are injurious both to the patient's life-feeling and

to his fellow men, if he has any power at all over his environment. Through his identification with the collective psyche he will infallibly try to force the demands of his unconscious upon others, for identity with the collective psyche always brings with it a feeling of universal validity—"godlikeness"—which completely ignores all differences in the psychology of his fellows.

461   The worst abuses of this kind can be avoided by a clear understanding and appreciation of the fact that there are differently oriented psychological types whose psychology cannot be forced into the mould of one's own type. It is hard enough for one type completely to understand another type, but perfect understanding of another individuality is totally impossible. Due regard for the individuality of another is not only advisable but absolutely essential in analysis if the development of the patient's personality is not to be stifled. Here it is to be observed that, for one type of individual, to show respect for another's freedom is to grant him freedom of action, while for another it is to grant him freedom of thought. In analysis both must be safeguarded so far as the analyst's own self-preservation permits him to do so. An excessive desire to understand and enlighten is just as useless and injurious as a lack of understanding.

[241] 462   The collective instincts and fundamental forms of thinking and feeling brought to light by analysis of the unconscious constitute, for the conscious personality, an acquisition which it cannot assimilate completely without injury to itself.[8] It is

---

[8] Here I would pause to remark that I intentionally abstain from discussing the question of how this problem presents itself from the point of view of the psychology of types. A special and somewhat complicated study would be required to formulate this in the language of type psychology. I must content myself here with indicating the difficulties that such a task would involve. The word "person," for instance, signifies one thing to the introvert and another to the extravert. During childhood the conscious function of adaptation to reality is archaic and collective, but it soon acquires a personal character which it may maintain henceforth if the individual feels no particular need to develop his type towards the ideal. If such an eventuality arises, the function of adaptation to reality may attain a perfection which pretends to universal validity, and therefore bears a *collectivistic* character as contrasted with its primitive *collective* character. To pursue this terminology, the *collective psyche* would be identical with the "herd soul" in the individual, whereas a *collectivistic* psychology would represent a highly differentiated attitude to society.

Now in the introvert the conscious function of adaptation to reality is *thinking*, which in the early stages of development is personal, but which tends to acquire a

278

therefore of the utmost importance in practical treatment to keep the goal of the individual's development constantly in view. For, if the collective psyche is taken to be the personal possession of the individual or as a personal burden, it will result in a distortion or an overloading of the personality which is very difficult to deal with. Hence it is imperative to make a clear distinction between the personal unconscious and the contents of the collective psyche. This distinction is far from easy, because the personal grows out of the collective psyche and is intimately bound up with it. So it is difficult to say exactly what contents are to be called personal and what collective. There is no doubt, for instance, that archaic symbolisms such as we frequently find in fantasies and dreams are collective factors. All basic instincts and basic forms of thinking and feeling are collective. Everything that all men agree in regarding as universal is collective, likewise everything that is universally understood, universally found, universally said and done. On closer examination one is always astonished to see how much of our so-called individual psychology is really collective. So much, indeed, that the individual traits are completely overshadowed by it. Since, however, individuation is an ineluctable psychological necessity, we can see from the ascendency of the collective what very special attention must be paid to this delicate plant "individuality" if it is not to be completely smothered.

[242] 463   Human beings have one faculty which, though it is of the greatest utility for collective purposes, is most pernicious for individuation, and that is the faculty of imitation. Collective psy-

---

general character of a collectivistic nature, while his *feeling* remains markedly personal in so far as it is conscious, and collective-archaic in so far as it is unconscious or is repressed. In the extravert, precisely the reverse happens. Besides this important difference there is another, and one which is much more profound, between the role and meaning of the "person" for the extravert and for the introvert. The whole endeavour of the introvert is directed towards preserving the integrity of his ego, which makes him assume an attitude towards his own person entirely different from that of the extravert, whose adaptation is made through feeling, even at the cost of his own person. These observations show what extraordinary difficulties we should have to surmount if we wished to consider our problem from the angle of type psychology, and justify us in abstaining from the attempt.

[This theme was greatly developed in *Psychological Types,* where the identification of thinking with introversion and feeling with extraversion was given up.—EDITORS.]

chology cannot dispense with imitation, for without it all mass organizations, the State and the social order, are simply impossible. Society is organized, indeed, less by law than by the propensity to imitation, implying equally suggestibility, suggestion, and mental contagion. But we see every day how people use, or rather abuse, the mechanism of imitation for the purpose of personal differentiation: they are content to ape some eminent personality, some striking characteristic or mode of behaviour, thereby achieving an outward distinction from the circle in which they move. We could almost say that as a punishment for this the uniformity of their minds with those of their neighbours, already real enough, is still further increased until it becomes an unconscious enslavement to their surroundings. As a rule these specious attempts at differentiation stiffen into a pose, and the imitator remains at the same level as he always was, only several degrees more sterile than before. To find out what is truly individual in ourselves, profound reflection is needed; and suddenly we realize how uncommonly difficult the discovery of individuality is.

3. *The Persona as a Segment of the Collective Psyche*

[243] 464   Here we come to a problem which, if overlooked, is liable to cause the greatest confusion. It will be remembered that in the analysis of the personal unconscious the first things to be added to consciousness are the personal contents, and I suggested that these contents, which have been repressed but are capable of being made conscious again, should be called the *personal unconscious.* I also showed that to annex the deeper layers of the unconscious, which I have called the *impersonal unconscious,* produces an enlargement of the personality leading to the state of "godlikeness." This state is reached by simply continuing the analytical work which has restored to consciousness the repressed portions of the personality. By continuing the analysis we add to the personal consciousness certain fundamental, general, and impersonal characteristics of humanity, thereby bringing about the condition I have described, which might be

280

regarded as one of the disagreeable consequences of analysis.[9]

[245] 465   From this point of view the conscious personality looks to us like a more or less arbitrary segment of the collective psyche. It owes its existence simply to the fact that it is from the outset unconscious of these fundamental and universal characteristics of humanity, and in addition has repressed, more or less arbitrarily, psychic or characterological elements of which it could just as well be conscious, in order to build up that segment of the collective psyche which we call the *persona*. The term *persona* is a very appropriate expression for this, for originally it meant the mask once worn by actors to indicate the role they played. If we endeavour to draw a precise distinction between what psychic material should be considered personal, and what impersonal, we soon find ourselves in the greatest dilemma, for by definition we have to say of the persona's contents what we have said of the impersonal unconscious, namely, that they are collective. It is only because the persona represents a more or less arbitrary and fortuitous segment of the collective psyche that we can make the mistake of regarding it *in toto* as something individual. It is, as its name implies, only the mask worn by the collective psyche, a mask that *feigns individuality,* making others and oneself believe that one is individual, whereas one is simply acting a role through which the collective psyche speaks.

[246] 466   When we analyse the persona we strip off the mask, and discover that what seemed to be individual is at bottom collective. We thus trace the "petty god of this world" back to his origin in the universal god who is a personification of the collective psyche. Whether we reduce the personality to the fundamental instinct of sexuality, like Freud, or to the ego's elementary will to power, like Adler, or to the general principle of the collective psyche which embraces both the Freudian and the Adlerian principles, we arrive at the same result: the dissolution of

[9] In a certain sense this feeling of "godlikeness" exists *a priori,* even before analysis, not only in the neurotic but also in the normal person, the only difference being that the normal individual is effectively shielded from any perception of his unconscious, while the neurotic is less and less so. On account of his quite peculiar sensibility, the latter participates to a greater extent in the life of the unconscious than does the normal person. Consequently, "godlikeness" manifests itself more clearly in the neurotic and it is heightened still further by the realization of unconscious contents through analysis.

the personality in the collective. That is why, in any analysis that is pushed far enough, there comes a moment when the subject experiences that feeling of "godlikeness" of which we have spoken.

[250] 467   This condition frequently announces itself by very peculiar symptoms, as for example dreams in which the dreamer is flying through space like a comet, or feels that he is the earth, the sun, or a star, or that he is of immense size, or dwarfishly small, or that he is dead, is in a strange place, is a stranger to himself, confused, mad, etc. He may also experience body-sensations, such as being too large for his skin, or too fat; or hypnagogic sensations of falling or rising endlessly, of the body growing larger, or of vertigo. Psychologically this state is marked by a peculiar disorientation in regard to one's own personality; one no longer knows who one is, or one is absolutely certain that one actually is what one seems to have become. Intolerance, dogmatism, self-conceit, self-depreciation, and contempt for "people who have not been analysed," and for their views and activities, are common symptoms. Often enough I have observed an increase in the liability to physical illness, but only when the patients relish their condition and dwell on it too long.

[251] 468   The forces that burst out of the collective psyche are confusing and blinding. One result of the dissolution of the persona is the release of fantasy, which is apparently nothing less than the specific activity of the collective psyche. This outburst of fantasy throws up into consciousness materials and impulses whose existence one had never before suspected. All the treasures of mythological thinking and feeling are unlocked. It is not always easy to hold one's own against such an overwhelming impression. This phase must be reckoned one of the real dangers of analysis, a danger that ought not to be minimized.

469   It will readily be understood that this condition is so insupportable that one would like to put an end to it as speedily as possible, since the analogy with mental derangement is too close. As we know, the commonest form of insanity, dementia praecox or schizophrenia, consists essentially in the fact that the unconscious in large measure ousts and supplants the function of the conscious mind. The unconscious usurps the reality function and substitutes its own reality. Unconscious thoughts become audible as voices, or are perceived as visions or body-hallucina-

tions, or they manifest themselves in senseless, unshakable judgments upheld in the face of reality.

470   In a similar but not quite identical manner the unconscious is pushed into consciousness when the persona is dissolved in the collective psyche. The one difference between this state and that of mental alienation is that here the unconscious is brought to the surface with the help of conscious analysis—at least, this is how things go at the beginning of an analysis, when powerful cultural resistances to the unconscious have still to be overcome. Later, when the barriers built up by the years have been broken down, the unconscious intrudes spontaneously, and sometimes irrupts into the conscious mind like a torrent. In this phase the analogy with mental derangement is very close. [In the same way, the moments of inspiration in a genius often bear a decided resemblance to pathological states.] But it would be real insanity only if the contents of the unconscious became a reality that took the place of conscious reality; in other words, if they were believed in without reserve. [Actually, one can believe in the contents of the unconscious without this amounting to insanity in the proper sense, even though actions of an unadapted nature may be performed on the basis of such convictions. Paranoid delusions, for instance, do not depend on belief—they appear to be true *a priori* and have no need of belief in order to lead an effective and valid existence. In the cases we are discussing the question is still open whether belief or criticism will triumph. This alternative is not found in genuine insanity.]

4. *Attempts to Free the Individuality from the Collective Psyche*

a. THE REGRESSIVE RESTORATION OF THE PERSONA

471   The unbearable state of identity with the collective psyche drives the patient, as we have said, to some radical solution. Two ways are open to him for getting out of the condition of "godlikeness." The first possibility is to try to re-establish regressively the previous persona by attempting to control the unconscious through the application of a reductive theory—by declaring, for instance, that it is "nothing but" repressed and long overdue

infantile sexuality which would really be best replaced by the normal sexual function. This explanation is based on the undeniably sexual symbolism of the language of the unconscious and on its concretistic interpretation. Alternatively the power theory may be invoked and, relying on the equally undeniable power tendencies of the unconscious, one may interpret the feeling of "godlikeness" as "masculine protest," as the infantile desire for domination and security. Or one may explain the unconscious in terms of the archaic psychology of primitives, an explanation that would not only cover both the sexual symbolism and the "godlike" power strivings that come to light in the unconscious material but would also seem to do justice to its religious, philosophical, and mythological aspects.

472   In each case the conclusion will be the same, for what it amounts to is a repudiation of the unconscious as something everybody knows to be useless, infantile, devoid of sense, and altogether impossible and obsolete. After this devaluation, there is nothing to be done but shrug one's shoulders resignedly. To the patient there seems to be no alternative, if he is to go on living rationally, but to reconstitute, as best he can, that segment of the collective psyche which we have called the persona, and quietly give up analysis, trying to forget if possible that he possesses an unconscious. He will take Faust's words to heart:

[257]   This earthly circle I know well enough.
             Towards the Beyond the view has been cut off;
             Fool—who directs that way his dazzled eye,
             Contrives himself a double in the sky!
             Let him look round him here, not stray beyond;
             To a sound man this world must needs respond.
             To roam into eternity is vain!
             What he perceives, he can attain.
             Thus let him walk along his earthlong day;
             Though phantoms haunt him, let him go his way,
             And, moving on, to weal and woe assent—
             He at each moment ever discontent.[10]

[258] 473   Such a solution would be perfect if a man were really able to shake off the unconscious, drain it of libido and render it inactive. But experience shows that it is not possible to drain the

10 *Faust,* trans. by MacNeice, Part II, Act V, p. 283.

energy from the unconscious: it remains active, for it not only contains but is itself the source of libido from which all the psychic elements flow into us—the thought-feelings or feeling-thoughts, the still undifferentiated germs of formal thinking and feeling. It is therefore a delusion to think that by some kind of magical theory or method the unconscious can be finally emptied of libido and thus, as it were, eliminated. One may for a while play with this delusion, but the day comes when one is forced to say with Faust:

> But now such spectredom so throngs the air
> That none knows how to dodge it, none knows where.
> Though one day greet us with a rational gleam,
> The night entangles us in webs of dream.
> We come back happy from the fields of spring—
> And a bird croaks. Croaks what? Some evil thing.
> Enmeshed in superstition night and morn,
> It forms and shows itself and comes to warn.
> And we, so scared, stand without friend or kin,
> And the door creaks—and nobody comes in.
> Anyone here?
> CARE: The answer should be clear.
> FAUST: And you, who are you then?
> CARE: I am just here.
> FAUST: Take yourself off!
> CARE: This is where I belong.
> FAUST: Take care, Faust, speak no magic spell, be strong.
> CARE: Unheard by the outward ear
> In the heart I whisper fear;
> Changing shape from hour to hour
> I employ my savage power.[11]

[258] 474   The unconscious cannot be analysed to a finish and brought to a standstill. Nothing can deprive it of its power for any length of time. To attempt to do so by the method described is to deceive ourselves, and is nothing but ordinary repression in a new guise.

[258] 475   Mephistopheles leaves an avenue open which should not be overlooked, since it is a real possibility for some people. He tells Faust, who is sick of the "madness of magic" and would gladly escape from the witch's kitchen:

[11] Ibid., pp. 281f. (modified).

Right. There is one way that needs
No money, no physician, and no witch.
Pack up your things and get back to the land
And there begin to dig and ditch;
Keep to the narrow round, confine your mind,
And live on fodder of the simplest kind,
A beast among the beasts; and don't forget
To use your own dung on the crops you set.[12]

[Anyone who finds it possible to live this kind of life will never be in danger of coming to grief in either of the two ways we are discussing, for his nature does not compel him to tackle a problem that is beyond his powers. But if ever the great problem should be thrust upon him, this way out will be closed.]

b. IDENTIFICATION WITH THE COLLECTIVE PSYCHE

[260] 476   The second way leads to identification with the collective psyche. This amounts to an acceptance of "godlikeness," but now exalted into a system. That is to say, one is the fortunate possessor of *the* great truth which was only waiting to be discovered, of the eschatological knowledge which spells the healing of the nations. This attitude is not necessarily megalomania in direct form, but in the milder and more familiar form of prophetic inspiration and desire for martyrdom. For weak-minded persons, who as often as not possess more than their fair share of ambition, vanity, and misplaced naïveté, the danger of yielding to this temptation is very great. Access to the collective psyche means a renewal of life for the individual, no matter whether this renewal is felt as pleasant or unpleasant. Everybody would like to hold fast to this renewal: one man because it enhances his life-feeling, another because it promises a rich harvest of knowledge. Therefore both of them, not wishing to deprive themselves of the great treasures that lie buried in the collective psyche, will strive by every means possible to maintain their newly won connection with the primal source of life.[13] Identifi-

---

12 Ibid., Part I, p. 67 (modified).
13 I would like to call attention here to an interesting remark of Kant's. In his lectures on psychology (*Vorlesungen über Psychologie*) he speaks of the "treasure lying within the field of dim representations, that deep abyss of human knowledge forever beyond our reach." This treasure, as I have demonstrated in my

cation would seem to be the shortest road to this, for the dissolution of the persona in the collective psyche positively invites one to plunge into that "ocean of divinity" and blot out all memory in its embrace. This piece of mysticism is innate in all better men as the "longing for the mother," the nostalgia for the source from which we came.

[261] 477   As I have shown in my book on libido, there lie at the root of the regressive longing, which Freud conceives as "infantile fixation" or the "incest wish," a specific value and a specific need which are made explicit in myths. It is precisely the strongest and best among men, the heroes, who give way to their regressive longing and purposely expose themselves to the danger of being devoured by the monster of the maternal abyss. But if a man is a hero, he is a hero because, in the final reckoning, he did not let the monster devour him, but subdued it, not once but many times. Victory over the collective psyche alone yields the true value—the capture of the hoard, the invincible weapon, the magic talisman, or whatever it be that the myth deems most desirable. Anyone who identifies with the collective psyche—or, in mythological terms, lets himself be devoured by the monster— and vanishes in it, attains the treasure that the dragon guards, but he does so in spite of himself and to his own greatest harm.

478   [The danger, therefore, of falling victim to the collective psyche by identification is not to be minimized. Identification is a retrograde step, one more stupidity has been committed, and on top of that the principle of individuation is denied and repressed under the cloak of the individual deed and in the nebulous conceit that one has discovered what is truly one's own. In reality one has not discovered one's own at all, but rather the eternal truths and errors of the collective psyche. In the collective psyche one's true individuality is lost.]

479   Identification with the collective psyche is thus a mistake that, in another form, ends as disastrously as the first way, which led to the separation of the persona from the collective psyche.

Psychology of the Unconscious, is the aggregate of all those primordial images in which the libido is invested, or rather, which are self-representations of the libido.

5. *Fundamental Principles in the Treatment of Collective Identity*

480   In order to solve the problem presented by the assimilation of the collective psyche, and to find a practical method of treatment, we have first of all to take account of the error of the two procedures we have just described. We have seen that neither the one nor the other can lead to good results.

481   The first, by abandoning the vital values in the collective psyche, simply leads back to the point of departure. The second penetrates directly into the collective psyche, but at the price of losing that separate human existence which alone can render life supportable and satisfying. Yet each of these ways proffers absolute values that should not be lost to the individual.

482   The mischief, then, lies neither with the collective psyche nor with the individual psyche, but in allowing the one to exclude the other. The disposition to do this is encouraged by the *monistic tendency,* which always and everywhere looks for a *unique* principle. Monism, as a general psychological tendency, is a characteristic of all civilized thinking and feeling, and it proceeds from the desire to set up one function or the other as the supreme psychological principle. The introverted type knows only the principle of *thinking,* the extraverted type only that of *feeling.*[14] This psychological monism, or rather monotheism, has the advantage of simplicity but the defect of one-sidedness. It implies on the one hand exclusion of the diversity and rich reality of life and the world, and on the other the practicality of realizing the ideals of the present and the immediate past, but it holds out no real possibility of human development.

483   The disposition to exclusiveness is encouraged no less by *rationalism.* The essence of this consists in the flat denial of whatever is opposed to one's own way of seeing things either from the logic of the intellect or from the logic of feeling. It is equally monistic and tyrannical in regard to reason itself. We ought to be particularly grateful to Bergson for having broken a lance in defence of the irrational. Although it may not be at all to the taste of the scientific mind, psychology will nonetheless have to

14 [A view abandoned later. Cf. n. 8 supra.—EDITORS.]

recognize a plurality of principles and accommodate itself to them. It is the only way to prevent psychology from getting stranded. In this matter we owe a great deal to the pioneer work of William James.

484 With regard to individual psychology, however, science must waive its claims. To speak of a science of individual psychology is already a contradiction in terms. It is only the collective element in the psychology of an individual that constitutes an object for science; for the individual is by definition something unique that cannot be compared with anything else. A psychologist who professes a "scientific" individual psychology is simply denying individual psychology. He exposes his individual psychology to the legitimate suspicion of being merely his own psychology. The psychology of every individual would need its own manual, for the general manual can deal only with collective psychology.

485 These remarks are intended as a prelude to what I have to say about the handling of the aforesaid problem. The fundamental error of both procedures consists in identifying the subject with one side or the other of his psychology. His psychology is as much individual as collective, but not in the sense that the individual ought to merge himself in the collective, nor the collective in the individual. We must rigorously separate the concept of the individual from that of the persona, for the persona *can* be entirely dissolved in the collective. But the individual is precisely that which can never be merged with the collective and is never identical with it. That is why identification with the collective and voluntary segregation from it are alike synonymous with disease.

486 It is simply impossible to effect a clear division of the individual from the collective, and even if it were possible it would be quite pointless and valueless for our purpose. It is sufficient to know that the human psyche is both individual and collective, and that its well-being depends on the natural co-operation of these two apparently contradictory sides. Their union is essentially an irrational life process that can, at most, be described in individual cases, but can neither be brought about, nor understood, nor explained rationally.[15]

15 [This paragraph, though included in the earliest draft of the German MS, was omitted from the earlier French and English translations.—EDITORS.]

487   If I may be forgiven a humorous illustration of the starting-point for the solution of our problem, I would cite Buridan's ass between the two bundles of hay. Obviously his question was wrongly put. The important thing was not whether the bundle on the right or the one on the left was the better, or which one he ought to start eating, but what he wanted in the depths of his being—which did he feel pushed towards? The ass wanted the object to make up his mind for him.

488   What is it, at this moment and in this individual, that represents the natural urge of life? That is the question.

489   That question neither science, nor worldly wisdom, nor religion, nor the best of advice can resolve for him. The resolution can come solely from absolutely impartial observation of those psychological germs of life which are born of the natural collaboration of the conscious and the unconscious on the one hand and of the individual and the collective on the other. Where do we find these germs of life? One man seeks them in the conscious, another in the unconscious. But the conscious is only one side, and the unconscious is only its reverse. We should never forget that dreams are the compensators of consciousness. If it were not so, we would have to regard them as a source of knowledge superior to consciousness: we should then be degraded to the mental level of fortune tellers and would be obliged to accept all the futility of superstition, or else, following vulgar opinion, deny any value at all to dreams.

490   It is in *creative fantasies* that we find the unifying function we seek. All the functions that are active in the psyche converge in fantasy. Fantasy has, it is true, a poor reputation among psychologists, and up to the present psychoanalytic theories have treated it accordingly. For Freud as for Adler it is nothing but a "symbolic" disguise for the basic drives and intentions presupposed by these two investigators. As against these opinions it must be emphasized—not on theoretical grounds but essentially for practical reasons—that although fantasy can be causally explained and devalued in this way, it nevertheless remains the creative matrix of everything that has made progress possible for humanity. Fantasy has its own irreducible value, for it is a psychic function that has its roots in the conscious and the unconscious alike, in the individual as much as in the collective.

491   Whence has fantasy acquired its bad reputation? Above all from the circumstance that it cannot be taken literally. *Concretely* understood, it is worthless. If it is understood *semiotically*, as Freud understands it, it is interesting from the scientific point of view; but if it is understood *hermeneutically*, as an authentic symbol, it acts as a signpost, providing the clues we need in order to carry on our lives in harmony with ourselves.

492   The symbol is not a sign that disguises something generally known.[16] Its meaning resides in the fact that it is an attempt to elucidate, by a more or less apt analogy, something that is still entirely unknown or still in the process of formation.[17] If we reduce this by analysis to something that is generally known, we destroy the true value of the symbol; but to attribute hermeneutic significance to it is consistent with its value and meaning.

493   The essence of hermeneutics, an art widely practised in former times, consists in adding further analogies to the one already supplied by the symbol: in the first place subjective analogies produced at random by the patient, then objective analogies provided by the analyst out of his general knowledge. This procedure widens and enriches the initial symbol, and the final outcome is an infinitely complex and variegated picture the elements of which can be reduced to their respective *tertia comparationis*. Certain lines of psychological development then stand out that are at once individual and collective. There is no science on earth by which these lines could be proved "right"; on the contrary, rationalism could very easily prove that they are wrong. Their validity is proved by their intense value for life. And that is what matters in practical treatment: that human beings should get a hold on their own lives, not that the principles by which they live should be proved rationally to be "right."

494   [This view will seem the only acceptable one to the man of our time who thinks and feels scientifically, but not to the extraordinarily large number of so-called educated people for whom science is not a principle of intellectual ethics superior to their own minds, but rather a means of corroborating their inner ex-

---

[16] A disguise, that is, for the basic drive or elementary intention.
[17] Cf. Silberer, *Problems of Mysticism and Its Symbolism;* also my *Symbols of Transformation* and "The Content of the Psychoses"

periences and giving them general validity. No one who is concerned with psychology should blind himself to the fact that besides the relatively small number of those who pay homage to scientific principles and techniques, humanity fairly swarms with adherents of quite another principle. It is entirely in keeping with the spirit of our present-day culture that one can read in an encyclopaedia, in an article on astrology, the following remark: "One of its last adherents was I. W. Pfaff, whose *Astrologie* (Bamberg, 1816) and *Der Stern der Drei Weisen* (1821) must be called strange anachronisms. Even today, however, astrology is still highly regarded in the East, particularly in Persia, India, and China." One must be smitten with blindness to write such a thing nowadays. The truth is that astrology flourishes as never before. There is a regular library of astrological books and magazines that sell for far better than the best scientific works. The Europeans and Americans who have horoscopes cast for them may be counted not by the hundred thousand but by the million. Astrology is a flourishing industry. Yet the encyclopaedia can say: "The poet Dryden (d. 1701) still had horoscopes cast for his children." Christian Science, too, has swamped Europe and America. Hundreds and thousands of people on both sides of the Atlantic swear by theosophy and anthroposophy, and anyone who believes that the Rosicrucians are a legend of the dim bygone has only to open his eyes to see them as much alive today as they ever were. Folk magic and secret lore have by no means died out. Nor should it be imagined that only the dregs of the populace fall for such superstitions. We have, as we know, to climb very high on the social scale to find the champions of this other principle.]

495   [Anyone who is interested in the real psychology of man must bear such facts in mind. For if such a large percentage of the population has an insatiable need for this counterpole to the scientific spirit, we can be sure that the collective psyche in every individual—be he never so scientific—has this psychological requirement in equally high degree. A certain kind of "scientific" scepticism and criticism in our time is nothing but a misplaced compensation of the powerful and deep-rooted superstitious impulses of the collective psyche. We have seen from experience that extremely critical minds have succumbed completely to this demand of the collective psyche, either directly,

or indirectly by making a fetish of their particular scientific theory.] [18]

496   Faithful to the spirit of scientific superstition, someone may now begin to talk about *suggestion*. But we ought to have realized long ago that a suggestion is not accepted unless it is agreeable to the person concerned. Unless it is acceptable, all suggestion is futile; otherwise the treatment of neurosis would be an extremely simple affair: one would merely have to suggest the state of health. This pseudo-scientific talk about suggestion is based on the unconscious superstition that suggestion is possessed of some self-generated magical power. No one succumbs to suggestion unless from the very bottom of his heart he is willing to comply with it.

497   By means of the hermeneutic treatment of fantasies we arrive, in theory, at a synthesis of the individual with the collective psyche; but in practice one indispensable condition remains to be fulfilled. It belongs essentially to the regressive nature of the neurotic—and this is something he has also learnt in the course of his illness—never to take himself or the world seriously, but always to rely first on one doctor and then on another, by this or that method, and in such and such circumstances, to cure him, without any serious cooperation on his part. Now, no dog can be washed without getting wet. Without the complete willingness and absolute seriousness of the patient, no recovery is possible. There are no magical cures for neurosis. The moment we begin to map out the lines of advance that are symbolically indicated, the patient himself must proceed along them. If he shirks this by his own deceit, he automatically precludes any cure. He must in very truth take the way of the individual lifeline he has recognized as his own, and continue along it until such time as an unmistakable reaction from the unconscious tells him that he is on the wrong track.

498   He who does not possess this moral function, this loyalty to himself, will never get rid of his neurosis. But he who has this capacity will certainly find the way to cure himself.

18 [In *Gesammelte Werke*, vol. 7, these additions (pars. 494–95) follow par. 477. There is, however, no indication in the holograph MS that they belong there—or indeed anywhere else, since they were written on a separate slip of paper. We have therefore placed them where they seem to have a greater relevance to the context.—Editors.]

499   Neither the doctor nor the patient, therefore, should let himself slip into the belief that analysis by itself is sufficient to remove a neurosis. That would be a delusion and a deception. Infallibly, in the last resort, it is the moral factor that decides between health and sickness.

500   The construction of "life-lines" reveals to consciousness the ever-changing direction of the currents of libido. These life-lines are not to be confused with the "guiding fictions" discovered by Adler, for the latter are nothing but arbitrary attempts to cut off the persona from the collective psyche and lend it an independent existence. One might rather say that the guiding fiction is an unsuccessful attempt to construct a life-line. Moreover—and this shows the uselessness of the fiction—such a line as it does produce persists far too long; it has the tenacity of a cramp.

501   The life-line constructed by the hermeneutic method is, on the contrary, temporary, for life does not follow straight lines whose course can be predicted far in advance. "All truth is crooked," says Nietzsche. These life-lines, therefore, are never general principles or universally accepted ideals, but points of view and attitudes that have a provisional value. A decline in vital intensity, a noticeable loss of libido, or, on the contrary, an upsurge of feeling indicate the moment when one line has been quitted and a new line begins, or rather ought to begin. Sometimes it is enough to leave the unconscious to discover the new line, but this attitude is not to be recommended to the neurotic under all circumstances, although there are indeed cases where this is just what the patient needs to learn—how to put his trust in so-called chance. However, it is not advisable to let oneself drift for any length of time; a watchful eye should at least be kept on the reactions of the unconscious, that is, on dreams, which indicate like a barometer the one-sidedness of our attitude.[19] Unlike other psychologists, I therefore consider it necessary for the patient to remain in contact with his unconscious,

[19] One should not look for any moral function in this signification of dreams, and I am not suggesting that there is one. Nor is the function of the dream "teleological" in the philosophic sense of the word—that is, of having a final end, still less of projecting a goal. I have often pointed out that the function of dreams is above all compensatory, in that they represent the subliminal elements constellated by the actual situation of the conscious mind. There is no moral intention in that, nor anything teleological whatsoever; it is simply a phenomenon that ought, in the first place, to be understood causally. However,

even after analysis, if he wishes to avoid a relapse.[20] I am persuaded that the true end of analysis is reached when the patient has gained an adequate knowledge of the methods by which he can maintain contact with the unconscious, and has acquired a psychological understanding sufficient for him to discern the direction of his life-line at the moment. Without this his conscious mind will not be able to follow the currents of libido and consciously sustain the individuality he has achieved. A patient who has had any serious neurosis needs to be equipped in this way if he is to persevere in his cure.

502   Analysis, thus understood, is by no means a therapeutic method of which the medical profession holds a monopoly. It is an art, a technique, a science of psychological life, which the patient, when cured, should continue to practise for his own good and for the good of those amongst whom he lives. If he understands it in this way, he will not set himself up as a prophet, nor as a world reformer; but, with a sound sense of the general good, he will profit by the knowledge he has acquired during treatment, and his influence will make itself felt more by the example of his own life than by any high discourse or missionary propaganda.

[ADDENDUM] [21]

503   [I am well aware that this discussion has landed me on perilous ground. It is virgin territory which psychology has still to conquer, and I am obliged to do pioneer work. I am painfully

---

it would be doing violence to the psyche to consider it from the causal angle alone. One not only can, but one *must* envisage it from the standpoint of finality—causality is itself a point of view—in order to discover to what purpose just these given elements are grouped together. This is not to say that the final meaning, in the sense of an end given *a priori,* pre-existed in the preliminary stages of the phenomenon we are discussing. According to the theory of knowledge it is evidently not possible, from the indubitably final meaning of biological mechanisms, to deduce the pre-existent fixation of a final end. But while thus legitimately abandoning a teleological conclusion it would be weak-minded to sacrifice also the point of view of finality. All one can say is that things happen as if there were a fixed final aim. In psychology one ought to be as wary of believing absolutely in causality as of an absolute belief in teleology.

20 This is not to say that he should adapt himself simply to the unconscious and not to the world of reality.

21 [In the German *Urtext,* pars. 504–506 followed par. 485, and appeared in that

conscious of the inadequacy of many of my formulations, though unfortunately this knowledge is of little avail when it comes to improving on them. I must therefore beg the reader not to be put off by the shortcomings of my presentation, but to try to feel his way into what I am endeavouring to describe. I would like to say a few words more about the concept of individuality in relation to the personal and the collective in order to clarify this central problem.

504   As I have already pointed out, individuality reveals itself primarily in the particular selection of those elements of the collective psyche which constitute the persona. These components, as we have seen, are not individual but collective. It is only their combination, or the selection of a group already combined in a pattern, that is individual. Thus we have an individual nucleus which is covered by the personal mask. It is in the particular differentiation of the persona that the individuality exhibits its resistance to the collective psyche. By analysing the persona we confer a greater value on the individuality and thus accentuate its conflict with the collectivity. This conflict consists, of course, in a psychological opposition within the subject. The dissolution of the compromise between the two halves of a pair of opposites renders their activity more intense. In purely unconscious, natural life this conflict does not exist, despite the fact that purely physiological life has to satisfy individual and collective requirements equally. The natural and unconscious attitude is harmonious. The body, its faculties, and its needs furnish of their own nature the rules and limitations that prevent any excess or disproportion. But because of its one-sidedness, which is fostered by conscious and rational intention, a differentiated psychological function always tends to disproportion. The body also forms the basis of what we might call the mental individuality, which is, as it were, an expression of corporeal individuality and can never come into being unless the rights of the body are acknowledged. Conversely, the body cannot thrive unless the

position in the earlier French and English translations. At the time of the first revision, however, they were incorporated in this addendum, which was not included in the 1928 version. Pars. 507 (sec. 6), 508, and 521 are of particular interest as they contain what appears to be the first formulation of the anima and animus in Jung's writings. For purposes of comparison, the first and second versions of the concluding summary are given in full.—EDITORS.]

mental individuality is accepted. At the same time, it is in the body that the individual is in the highest degree similar to other individuals, although each individual body is distinguishable from all other bodies. Equally, every mental or moral individuality differs from all the others, and yet is so constituted as to render every man equal to all other men. Every living being that is able to develop itself individually, without constraint, will best realize, by the very perfection of its individuality, the ideal type of its species, and by the same token will achieve a collective value.

505   The persona is always identical with a *typical* attitude dominated by a single psychological function, for example, by thinking, feeling, or intuition. This one-sidedness necessarily results in the relative repression of the other functions. In consequence, the persona is an obstacle to the individual's development. The dissolution of the persona is therefore an indispensable condition for individuation. It is, however, impossible to achieve individuation by conscious intention, because conscious intention invariably leads to a typical attitude that excludes whatever does not fit in with it. The assimilation of unconscious contents leads, on the contrary, to a condition in which conscious intention is excluded and is supplanted by a process of development that seems to us irrational. This process alone signifies individuation, and its product is individuality as we have just defined it: particular and universal at once. So long as the persona persists, individuality is repressed, and hardly betrays its existence except in the choice of its personal accessories—by its actor's wardrobe, one might say. Only when the unconscious is assimilated does the individuality emerge more clearly, together with the psychological phenomenon which links the ego with the non-ego and is designated by the word *attitude*. But this time it is no longer a typical attitude but an individual one.

506   The paradox in this formulation arises from the same root as the ancient dispute about universals. The proposition: *animal nullumque animal genus est* makes the fundamental paradox clear and intelligible. The *realia*—these are the particular, the individual; the *universalia* exist psychologically, but are based on a real resemblance between particulars. Thus the individual is that particular thing which possesses in greater or lesser degree the qualities upon which we base the general conception of

"collectivity"; and the more individual it is, the more it develops those qualities which are fundamental to the collective conception of humanity.

507   In the hope of unravelling these tangled problems, I would like to emphasize the architectonics of the factors to be considered. We have to do with the following fundamental concepts:

1. *The world of consciousness and reality.* By this is meant those contents of consciousness which consist of perceived images of the world, and of our conscious thoughts and feelings about it.

2. *The collective unconscious.* By this is meant that part of the unconscious which consists on the one hand of unconscious perceptions of external reality and, on the other, of all the residues of the phylogenetic perceptive and adaptive functions. A reconstruction of the unconscious view of the world would yield a picture showing how external reality has been perceived from time immemorial. The collective unconscious contains, or is, an historical mirror-image of the world. It too is a world, but a world of images.

3. Since the world of consciousness, like the world of the unconscious, is to a large extent collective, these two spheres together form the *collective psyche* in the individual.

4. The collective psyche must be contrasted with a fourth concept, namely, the concept of *individuality.* The individual stands, as it were, between the conscious part of the collective psyche and the unconscious part. He is the reflecting surface in which the world of consciousness can perceive its own unconscious, historical image, even as Schopenhauer says that the intellect holds up a mirror to the universal Will. Accordingly, the individual would be a point of intersection or a dividing line, neither conscious nor unconscious, but a bit of both.

5. The paradoxical nature of the psychological individual must be contrasted with that of the *persona.* The persona is conscious all round, so to speak, or is at least capable of becoming so. It represents a compromise formation between external reality and the individual. In essence, therefore, it is a function for adapting the individual to the real world. The persona thus occupies a place midway between the real world and individuality.

6. Beyond individuality, which appears to be the innermost core of ego-consciousness and of the unconscious alike, we find

the collective unconscious. The place between the individual and the collective unconscious, corresponding to the persona's position between the individual and external reality, appears to be empty. Experience has taught me, however, that here too a kind of persona exists, but a persona of a compensatory nature which (in a man) could be called the *anima*. The anima would thus be a compromise formation between the individual and the unconscious world, that is, the world of historical images, or "primordial images." We frequently meet the anima in dreams, where it appears as a feminine being in a man, and as a man (*animus*) in a woman. A good description of the anima figure can be found in Spitteler's *Imago*. In his *Prometheus and Epimetheus* she appears as the soul of Prometheus, and in his *Olympian Spring* as the soul of Zeus.

508   To the degree that the ego identifies with the persona, the anima, like everything unconscious, is projected into the real objects of our environment. She is regularly to be found, therefore, in the woman we are in love with. This can be seen easily enough from the expressions we use when in love. The poets, too, have supplied a good deal of evidence in this respect. The more normal a person is, the less will the daemonic qualities of the anima appear in the objects of his immediate environment. They are projected upon more distant objects, from which no immediate disturbance is to be feared. But the more sensitive a person is, the closer these daemonic projections will come, until in the end they break through the family taboo and produce the typical neurotic complications of a family romance.

509   If the ego identifies with the persona, the subject's centre of gravity lies in the unconscious. It is then practically identical with the collective unconscious, because the whole personality is collective. In these cases there is a strong pull towards the unconscious and, at the same time, violent resistance to it on the part of consciousness because the destruction of conscious ideals is feared.

510   In certain cases, found chiefly among artists or highly emotional people, the ego is localized not in the persona (the function of relationship to the real world) but in the anima (the function of relationship to the collective unconscious). Here individual and persona are alike unconscious. The collective unconscious then intrudes into the conscious world, and a large

part of the real world becomes an unconscious content. Such persons have the same daemonic fear of reality as ordinary people have of the unconscious.]

6. *Summary*
[FIRST VERSION]

511   *A.* We have to divide psychological material into *conscious* and *unconscious* contents.

1. The *conscious* contents are in part *personal* inasmuch as their general validity is not recognized, and in part *impersonal*, that is, *collective*, inasmuch as their general validity is recognized.

2. The *unconscious* contents are in part *personal* inasmuch as they consist of personal material that was once conscious but was then repressed, and whose general validity is therefore not recognized when it becomes conscious again. They are *impersonal* inasmuch as the material is recognized as having general validity, and of which it is impossible to prove any anterior or even relative consciousness.

512   *B. The Composition of the Persona.*

1. The conscious personal contents constitute the conscious personality, the *conscious* ego.

2. The unconscious personal contents constitute the *self*, the *unconscious or subconscious* ego.

3. The conscious and unconscious contents of a personal nature constitute the *persona*.

513   *C. The Composition of the Collective Psyche.*

1. The conscious and unconscious contents of an *impersonal* or *collective* nature constitute the psychological *non-ego*, the *object-imago*. These contents may appear in analysis as projections of feelings or judgments, but they are *a priori* collective and are identical with the object-imago; that is, they appear to be qualities of the object, and it is only *a posteriori* that they are recognized as subjective psychological qualities.

2. The persona is a grouping of conscious and unconscious contents which is opposed as ego to the non-ego. A general comparison of the personal contents belonging to different individuals shows the surprising resemblance between them, which may even amount to identity, and largely cancels out the *individual* nature of the personal contents as well as of the persona. To this extent the persona must be considered a segment and also a constituent of the collective psyche.

3. The collective psyche is thus composed of the object-imago and the persona.

514   *D. Individuality.*

1. Individuality manifests itself partly as the principle which selects and sets limits to contents that are recognized as personal.

2. Individuality is the principle which makes possible, and if need be compels, a progressive differentiation from the collective psyche.

3. Individuality manifests itself partly as an obstacle to collective functioning, and partly as resistance to collective thinking and feeling.

4. Individuality is that which is peculiar and unique in a given combination of collective psychological elements.

5. Individuality corresponds to the systole, and collective psychology to the diastole, of the movement of libido.

515   *E.* The conscious and unconscious contents are subdivided into those that are *individual* and those that are *collective*.

1. A content whose developmental tendency is towards differentiation from the collective is individual.

2. A content whose developmental tendency is towards a general value is collective.

3. There are insufficient criteria by which to determine whether a given content is purely individual or purely collective, for individuality is very difficult to determine, although always and everywhere present.

4. The life-line of an individual is the resultant of the individual and collective tendencies of the psychological process at a given moment.

[SECOND VERSION]

516   *A.* We have to divide psychological material into *conscious* and *unconscious* contents.

    1. The *conscious* contents are in part *personal* inasmuch as their general validity is not recognized, and in part *impersonal,* that is, *collective,* inasmuch as their general validity is recognized.

    2. The *unconscious* contents are in part *personal* inasmuch as they consist of personal material that was once conscious but was then repressed, and whose general validity is therefore not recognized when it becomes conscious again. They are *impersonal* inasmuch as the material is recognized as having general validity, and of which it is impossible to prove any anterior or even relative consciousness.

517   *B. The Composition of the Persona.*

    1. The conscious personal contents constitute the conscious persona[lity], the *conscious* ego.

    2. The unconscious personal contents are combined with the germs of the still undeveloped individuality and with the collective unconscious. All these elements appear in combination with the repressed personal contents (i.e., the personal unconscious), and, when assimilated by consciousness, dissolve the persona into the collective material.

518   *C. The Composition of the Collective Psyche.*

    1. The conscious and unconscious contents of an *impersonal* or *collective* nature constitute the psychological *non-ego,* the *object-imago.* These materials, in so far as they are unconscious, are *a priori* identical with the object-imago; that is, they appear to be qualities of the object, and it is only *a posteriori* that they are recognized as subjective psychological qualities.

    2. The persona is a *subject-imago,* which, like the object-imago, largely consists of collective material inasmuch as the persona represents a compromise with society, the ego identifying more with the persona than with individuality. The more the ego identifies with the persona, the more the subject

becomes what he appears to be, and is de-individualized.

3. The collective psyche is thus composed of the object-imago and the persona. When the ego is completely identical with the persona, individuality is wholly repressed, and the entire conscious psyche becomes collective. This represents the maximum adaptation to society and the minimum adaptation to one's own individuality.

519   *D. Individuality.*

1. Individuality is that which is unique in the combination of collective elements of the persona and its manifestations.

2. Individuality is the principle of resistance to collective functioning. It makes possible, and if need be compels, differentiation from the collective psyche.

3. Individuality is a developmental tendency constantly aiming at differentiation and separation from the collective.

4. A distinction must be made between *individuality* and the *individual*. The individual is determined on the one hand by the principle of uniqueness and distinctiveness, and on the other by the society to which he belongs. He is an indispensable link in the social structure.

5. Development of individuality is simultaneously a development of society. Suppression of individuality through the predominance of collective ideals and organizations is a moral defeat for society.

6. The development of individuality can never take place through personal relationships alone, but requires a *psychic* relationship to the collective unconscious.

520   *E. The Collective Unconscious.*

1. The collective unconscious is the unconscious portion of the collective psyche. It is the unconscious object-imago.

2. The collective unconscious is composed of:

    a. Subliminal perceptions, thoughts and feelings that were not repressed because of their incompatibility with personal values, but were subliminal from the start because of their low stimulus value or low libido investment.

    b. Subliminal vestiges of archaic functions that exist *a priori* and can be brought back into function at any time through an accumulation of libido. These vestiges are not merely formal but have the dynamic nature of instincts. They represent the primitive and the animal in civilized man.

    c. Subliminal combinations in symbolic form, not yet capable of becoming conscious.

    3. An actual content of the collective unconscious always consists of an amalgamation of the elements enumerated in *a–c,* and its expression varies accordingly.

    4. The collective unconscious always appears projected on a conscious [external] object.

    5. The collective unconscious in individual A bears a greater resemblance to the collective unconscious in individual B than the conscious ideas in the minds of A and B do to one another.

    6. The most important contents of the collective unconscious appear to be "primordial images," that is, unconscious collective ideas (mythical thinking) and vital instincts.

    7. So long as the ego is identical with the persona, individuality forms an essential content of the collective unconscious. In the dreams and fantasies of men it begins by appearing as a masculine figure, and in those of women as a feminine figure. Later it shows hermaphroditic traits which characterize its intermediate position. (Good examples in Meyrink's *Golem* and in the *Walpurgisnacht.*)

521   *F. The Anima.*

    1. The anima is an unconscious subject-imago analogous to the persona. Just as the persona is the image of himself which the subject presents to the world, and which is seen by the world, so the anima is the image of the subject in his relation to the collective unconscious, or an expression of unconscious collective contents unconsciously constellated by him. One could also say: the anima is the face of the subject as seen by the collective unconscious.

    2. If the ego adopts the standpoint of the anima, adaptation to reality is severely compromised. The subject is fully adapted to the collective unconscious but has no adaptation to reality. In this case too he is de-individualized.

BIBLIOGRAPHY

BIBLIOGRAPHY

ADLER, ALFRED. *The Neurotic Constitution.* Translated by B. Glueck and J. E. Lind. London, 1921. (Original: *Über den nervösen Charakter.* Wiesbaden, 1912.)

AIGREMONT, DR., pseud. (Siegmar Baron von Schultze-Galléra). *Fuss- und Schuhsymbolik und -Erotik.* Leipzig, 1909.

BENNET, E. A. *What Jung Really Said.* London, 1966.

BENOÎT, PIERRE. *Atlantida.* Translated by Mary C. Tongue and Mary Ross. New York, 1920. (Original: *L'Atlantide.* Paris, 1920.)

BERNHEIM, HIPPOLYTE. *De la suggestion et de ses applications à la thérapeutique.* Paris, 1886. (Translated by Sigmund Freud as *Die Suggestion und ihre Heilwirkung,* 1888.)

BLEULER, EUGEN. "Dementia praecox oder die Gruppe der Schizophrenien," in *Handbuch der Psychiatrie,* ed. G. Aschaffenburg (Leipzig, 1911). (Translated by J. Zinkin as *Dementia Praecox or the Group of Schizophrenias,* New York, 1950.)

———. "Die Psychoanalyse Freuds," *Jahrbüch für psychoanalytische und psychopathologische Forschungen* (Leipzig and Vienna), II (1910), 623–730.

BREUER, JOSEF, and FREUD, SIGMUND. *Studies on Hysteria.* Translated by James and Alix Strachey. *Standard Edition of the Complete Psychological Works of Sigmund Freud,* vol. 2. London, 1955.

DAUDET, LÉON. *L'Hérédo.* Paris, 1916.

FECHNER, G. T. *Elemente der Psychophysik.* Leipzig, 1860.

FERRERO, GUGLIELMO. *Les Lois psychologiques du symbolisme.* Paris, 1895. (Original: *I simboli in rapporto alla storia e filosofia del diritto alla psicologia e alla sociologia.* Turin, 1893.)

FLOURNOY, THÉODORE. "Automatisme téléologique antisuicide: un cas de suicide empêché par une hallucination," *Archives de psychologie* (Geneva), VII (1907), 113–37.

———. *Des Indes à la planète Mars: Étude sur un cas de somnambulisme avec glossolalie.* Paris and Geneva, 1900. (Translation: *From India to the Planet Mars.* Trans. by D. B. Vermilye. New York, 1900.)

FOREL, AUGUST. *The Sexual Question.* Translated from the second

German edition by C. F. Marshall. New York, 1925. (Original: *Die sexuelle Frage*. Munich, 1905; 2nd edn., 1906.)

FREUD, SIGMUND. "Beyond the Pleasure Principle." Translated by James Strachey. *Standard Edition*, vol. 18 (1955), pp. 3–64.

——. *The Interpretation of Dreams*. Translated by James Strachey. *Standard Edition*, vols. 4 and 5 (1953).

——. "Leonardo da Vinci and a Memory of His Childhood." Translated by Alan Tyson. *Standard Edition*, vol. 11 (1957), pp. 63–137.

——. "An Outline of Psycho-Analysis." Translated by James Strachey. *Standard Edition*, vol. 23 (1946), pp. 141–207.

——. *The Standard Edition of the Complete Psychological Works*. Translated from the German under the general editorship of James Strachey, in collaboration with Anna Freud, assisted by Alix Strachey and Alan Tyson. London, 1953– . 24 vols.

——. *Early Psycho-Analytic Publications*. Translated by James Strachey and others. *Standard Edition*, vol. 3 (1962).

——. "Three Essays on the Theory of Sexuality." Translated by James Strachey. *Standard Edition*, vol. 7 (1953), pp. 125–243.

——. *Totem and Taboo*. Translated by James Strachey. *Standard Edition*, vol. 13 (1955), pp. 1–161.

——. See also BREUER.

FROBENIUS, LEO. *Das Zeitalter des Sonnengottes*. Vol. I (no more published). Berlin, 1904.

GANZ, HANS. *Das Unbewusste bei Leibniz in Beziehung zu modernen Theorien*. Zurich, 1917.

[GOETHE, JOHANN WOLFGANG VON.] *Geothe's Faust, Parts I and II*. An abridged version translated by Louis MacNeice. London and New York, 1951.

——. "Die Geheimnisse." In *Werke* (Gedenkausgabe), edited by Ernst Beutler. Zurich, 1948–54. 24 vols. (Vol. III, pp. 273–83.)

HAGGARD, SIR HENRY RIDER. *She*. London, 1887.

HELM, GEORG. *Die Energetik nach ihrer geschichtlichen Entwickelung*. Leipzig, 1898.

HOFFMANN, ERNST THEODORE WILHELM (Amadeus). *The Devil's Elixir*. (Trans. anon.) Edinburgh, 1824. 2 vols.

HUBERT, HENRI, and MAUSS, MARCEL. *Mélanges d'histoire des religions*. Paris, 1909.

I Ching, or the Book of Changes. The German translation by Richard Wilhelm rendered into English by Cary F. Baynes. New

York (Bollingen Series XIX) and London, 1950. 2 vols. (1 vol. edn., 1961.)

JAMES, WILLIAM. *Pragmatism.* London and Cambridge, Mass., 1907.

——. *The Varieties of Religious Experience.* London and Cambridge, Mass., 1902.

JANET, PIERRE. *L'Automatisme psychologique.* Paris, 1889.

——. *Névroses et idées fixes.* Paris, 1898. 2 vols.

——. *Les Névroses.* (Bibliothèque de philosophie scientifique.) Paris, 1909.

JUNG, CARL GUSTAV. *The Archetypes and the Collective Unconscious.* In: *Collected Works,** vol. 9, i.

——. "The Archetypes of the Collective Unconscious." In: *Collected Works,** vol. 9, i.

——. "Brother Klaus." In: *Collected Works,** vol. 11.

——. *Collected Papers on Analytical Psychology.* Edited by Constance E. Long; translated by various persons. London and New York, 1916; 2nd edn., 1917.

——. Commentary on *The Secret of the Golden Flower.* In: *Collected Works,** vol. 13. (Alternative source: Wilhelm and Jung, *The Secret of the Golden Flower,* q.v.)

——. "The Concept of the Collective Unconscious." In: *Collected Works,** vol. 9, i.

——. "Concerning the Archetypes, with Special Reference to the Anima Concept." In: *Collected Works,** vol. 9, i.

——. "The Content of the Psychoses." In: *Collected Works,** vol. 3.

——. *Freud and Psychoanalysis. Collected Works,* vol. 4.

——. "General Aspects of Dream Psychology." In: *Collected Works,** vol. 8.

——. "Instinct and the Unconscious." In: *Collected Works,** vol. 8.

——. *Mysterium Coniunctionis. Collected Works,** vol. 14.

——. "On Psychic Energy." In: *Collected Works,** vol. 8.

——. "On the Psychology and Pathology of So-Called Occult Phenomena." In: *Collected Works,** vol. 1.

——. "Paracelsus as a Spiritual Phenomenon." In: *Collected Works,** vol. 13.

——. *The Practice of Psychotherapy. Collected Works,** vol. 16. (2nd edn., 1966.)

* For details of the *Collected Works* of C. G. Jung, see list at end of this volume.

———. "Preface to the Second Edition of *Collected Papers on Analytical Psychology*." In: *Collected Works*,* vol. 4.

———. "The Psychological Aspects of the Kore." In: *Collected Works*,* vol. 9, i.

———. "The Psychological Foundations of Belief in Spirits." In: *Collected Works*,* vol. 8.

———. *Psychological Types. Collected Works*,* vol. 6. (Alternative source: Translation by H. Godwin Baynes. London and New York, 1923.)

———. *Psychology and Alchemy. Collected Works*,* vol. 12.

———. "The Psychology of Dementia Praecox." In: *Collected Works*,* vol. 3.

———. "On Psychological Understanding." In: *Collected Works*,* vol. 3.

———. "Psychology and Religion." In: *Collected Works*,* vol. 11.

———. "The Realities of Practical Psychotherapy." In: *Collected Works*,* vol. 16, 2nd edn.

———. "A Review of the Complex Theory." In: *Collected Works*,* vol. 8.

———. "The Role of the Unconscious." In: *Collected Works*,* vol. 10.

———. "Sigmund Freud in His Historical Setting." In: *Collected Works*,* vol. 15.

———. "The Stages of Life." In: *Collected Works*,* vol. 8.

———. "The Structure of the Psyche." In: *Collected Works*,* vol. 8.

———. *Studies in Word Association. Collected Works*,* vol. 2. (Alternative source: Translation by M. D. Eder, London, 1918; New York, 1919.)

———. "A Study in the Process of Individuation." In: *Collected Works*,* vol. 9, i.

———. *Symbols of Transformation. Collected Works*,* vol. 5.

———. "The Theory of Psychoanalysis." In: *Collected Works*,* vol. 4.

———. "The Transcendent Function." In: *Collected Works*,* vol. 8.

———. *Wandlungen und Symbole der Libido*. Ein Beitrag zur Entwicklungsgeschichte des Denkens. Leipzig and Vienna, 1912. For translation, see: *Psychology of the Unconscious*. Translated by Beatrice M. Hinkle. New York, 1916; London, 1917. (Subsequently replaced by *Symbols of Transformation*, q.v.)

JUNG, EMMA. "On the Nature of the Animus." Translated by Cary

* For details of the *Collected Works* of C. G. Jung, see list at end of this volume.

F. Baynes, in: *Animus and Anima*. New York (Analytical Psychology Club), 1957.

KANT, IMMANUEL. *Vorlesungen über Psychologie*. Leipzig, 1889.

KUBIN, ALFRED. *Die andere Seite*. Munich, 1908.

LEHMANN, FRIEDRICH RUDOLF. *Mana*. Leipzig, 1922.

LIÉBEAULT, AMBROISE AUGUSTE. *Du sommeil et des états analogues considérés au point de vue de l'action du moral sur le physique*. Paris, 1866.

LONGFELLOW, HENRY WADSWORTH. *The Song of Hiawatha*. Boston, 1855.

LOVEJOY, ARTHUR O. "The Fundamental Concept of the Primitive Philosophy." *The Monist* (Chicago), XVI (1906), 357–82.

MAEDER, ALFRED. "La Langue d'un aliéné." *Archives de psychologie* (Geneva), IX (1910), 208–216.

——. "Psychologische Untersuchungen an Dementia-Praecox-Kranken," *Jahrbuch für psychoanalytische und psychopathologische Forschungen* (Leipzig and Vienna), II (1910), 185–245.

MAYER, ROBERT. *Kleinere Schriften und Briefe*. Stuttgart, 1893.

MEYRINK, GUSTAV. *Der Golem*. Leipzig, 1915. For translation, see: *The Golem*. Translated by Madge Pemberton. London, 1928.

——. *Fledermäuse: 7 Geschichten*. Leipzig, 1916.

NELKEN, JAN. "Analytische Beobachtungen über Phantasien eines Schizophrenen," *Jahrbuch für psychoanalytische und psychopathologische Forschungen* (Leipzig and Vienna), IV (1912), 504–62.

NERVAL, GÉRARD DE (LABRUNIE DE). "Aurélia." In: *Le Rêve et la vie*. Paris, 1855. (Pp.1–129.) For translation, see: *Aurelia*. Translated by Richard Aldington. London, 1932.

OSTWALD, WILHELM. *Grosse Männer*. Leipzig, 1910.

——. *Die Philosophie der Werte*. Leipzig, 1913.

PFAFF, JOHANN WILHELM ANDREAS. *Astrologie*. Nurnberg, 1816.

——. *Der Stern der Drei Weisen*. 1821.

ROUSSEAU, JEAN-JACQUES. *Emile, ou L'Education*. Amsterdam and The Hague, 1762. 4 vols. For translation, see: *Emile*. Translated by Barbara Foxley. London and New York (Everyman's Library), 1911.

SEMON, RICHARD WOLFGANG. *Die Mneme als erhaltendes Prinzip im Wechsel des organischen Geschehens*. Leipzig, 1904. For translation, see: *The Mneme*. Translated by Louis Simon. London and New York, 1921.

SILBERER, HERBERT. *Problems of Mysticism and Its Symbolism.* Translated by Smith Ely Jelliffe. New York, 1917.

SÖDERBLOM, NATHAN. *Das Werden des Gottesglaubens.* Leipzig, 1916. (Original: *Gudstrons uppkomst.* Stockholm, 1914.)

SPIELREIN, SAVINA. "Die Destruktion als Ursache des Werdens," *Jahrbuch für psychoanalytische und psychopathologische Forschungen* (Leipzig and Vienna), IV (1912), 465–503.

——. *Spiritual Disciplines.* Translated by Ralph Manheim and R. F. C. Hull. (Papers from the Eranos Yearbooks, 4.) New York (Bollingen Series XXX:4) and London, 1960.

SPITTELER, CARL. *Imago.* Jena, 1919.

——. *Olympischer Frühling: Epos.* Leipzig, 1900–1905. 4 parts.

——. *Prometheus und Epimetheus.* Jena, 1920. For translation, see: *Prometheus and Epimetheus.* Translated by James Fullarton Muirhead. London, 1931.

TACITUS, PUBLIUS CORNELIUS. *Dialogus: Agricola: Germania.* Translated by Sir William Peterson and Maurice Hutton. (Loeb Classical Library.) London and New York, 1920.

WARNECKE, JOHANNES. *Die Religion der Batak.* (Religions-Urkunden der Völker, ed. Julius Boehmer, Part IV, vol. 1.) Leipzig, 1909.

WEBSTER, HUTTON. *Primitive Secret Societies.* New York, 1908.

WELLS, HERBERT GEORGE. *Christina Alberta's Father.* London and New York, 1925.

WILHELM, RICHARD, and JUNG, CARL GUSTAV. *The Secret of the Golden Flower.* Translated by Cary F. Baynes. New edition, London and New York, 1962.

WOLFF, TONI. "Einführung in die Grundlagen der komplexen Psychologie." In: *Die kulturelle Bedeutung der komplexen Psychologie.* Berlin, 1935.

WUNDT, WILHELM. *Grundzüge der physiologischen Psychologie.* Leipzig, 1893. 2 vols. For translation (from 5th German edn., 1902) see: *Principles of Physiological Psychology.* Translated by E. B. Titchener. London, 1904.

INDEX

INDEX

Page numbers in the appendices are printed in italic numerals. To facilitate comparison, identical or similar references in the appendices and in the main Two Essays are printed as follows: "absentmindedness, 11/*249*." A numbered list of Jung's cases is given under his name.

A

abaissement du niveau mental, 215
Abelard, Peter, 54
absentmindedness, 11/*249*
"absolute," meaning of, 235*n*
absoluteness, 235
abyss, maternal, 170/*287*
accidents, 115
Achomawi (Californian tribe), 96*n*
activity of unconscious: autonomous, 128/*271*; instinctive, 162; mythological, 100*n*
adaptation, 55, 56, 149, 154*n*, 204*f*, 209, 278*n*, 279*n*; collective, 58; to collective unconscious, 161; difficulties of, 161; faulty, 199; maximum, to society, *303*; minimum, to individuality, *303*; to reality, *304*
adjustment, 154*n*
Adler, Alfred, 3, 117*f*; Adlerian theory, 165; "arrangement," *see* arrangement(s); and "godlikeness," *140*/*274*; and "guiding fictions," *294*; "masculine protest," *see* masculine/masculinity; "power drive," 165; and power principle, 35, 38,

40, 53, 140/*274*, *281*; reductive method, 59; theory of compensation, 104*n*; theory of fantasy, *290*; theory of neurosis contrasted with Freud's, 35, 40*ff*, 61, *281*; and transference, 165; *The Neurotic Constitution,* 35*n*, 165*n*
adolescence, 107*ff*; *see also* young people
adulthood: entry into, 106; special problems of, 60
aestheticism, 102
aether, 95
affect, 176, 178, 194; release of, 68; state of, 202; world of, 203
affectivity, 94, 202
Africa, 205; *see also* Elgon; Kavirondos
age, and youth, 76; *see also* life, afternoon of; young people; youth
agoraphobia, 217
Aigremont, Dr. (Baron Siegmar von Schultze-Galléra), *Fuss- und Schuhsymbolik und -Erotik,* 83*n*
aim: cultural, 74; final, *295n*; natural, of man, 74
alchemy, 219*f*, 223; secret of, 220

315

interpretation(s) (*cont.*)
causal-reductive, 83*f;* of dreams, *see* dream(s); hermeneutic, *291;* objective, 84, 88, 90, 98; semiotic, *291;* and settlement with the unconscious, 213; subjective, 84*f,* 88, 90; synthetic (constructive), 85; of transference, 63
interpretive principle, *269*
introjection, 70
introversion, 44, 54*ff;* anima in, 218*f;* in extravert, 56*f;* inferior, 58; neglected, of Western culture, 191; rhythm of, 59
introvert: characteristics, 55; extraversion of, 57*f;* illustration of, 56*f;* and integrity of ego, *278n;* meaning of persona for, *278n;* Promethean, 57; subject and object in, 56*ff;* and thinking, *278n, 288;* unconscious contents in, 225
intuition, 44*n,* *297;* creative, 175; in woman, 188
inversion, 100; of types, 57
irrational, the, 71*f,* 94*f,* *288f; see also* rational
irrationality, 49*f*
irreality, 217
isolation, 200
ivory figure, Japanese, 107

J

James, William, *289; Pragmatism,* 54; *The Varieties of Religious Experience,* 175
Janet, Pierre, 9*f,* 148/*276,* 215; *L'Automatisme psychologique,* 9*n; Les Névroses,* 148; *Névroses et idées fixes,* 9*n*
jealousy, infantile, 23
Jew(s), 107; *see also* circumcision; psychology
Job, 196
Jonah, 99
judgment(s): of animus, 207; intui-

tive, 93; projections of, *300;* senseless, *283*
Jung, Carl Gustav:
CASES IN SUMMARY (*in order of presentation, numbered for reference*):
[1] Young woman, whose hysterical neurosis arose following a trauma. Case leads to problem of predisposition as a cause of the neurosis.—13–18/252*f*
[2] Young married woman with anxiety attacks and hysterical asthma, and background of father fixation; case used to illustrate Adlerian system.—35–40
[3] American business man, aged 45, who became hypochondriacal upon retiring from business; case illustrates factors of disposable energy in relation to energy gradients.—50*f,* 72, 76
[4] Woman, with homosexual attachment, whose dream of crossing a ford and encountering crab is analysed to show critical nature of transition from the personal to the collective unconscious.—81–88, 97–102
[5] Homosexual youth; religious dreams compensate the negative view of his condition.—102–109
[6] Woman, treatment of whom does not succeed until doctor's dream of her.—112*f*
[7] Young girl, a somnambulistic medium; here only referred to (Jung's first published case).—118, 123
[8] Young woman philosophy student with father fixation, in which the father image deepened into the image of God, through it the transference being resolved.—128–35, 156, 158*ff,* 164*ff*
[9] Youth with sentimenal love-fantasy, who intends suicide,

has hallucination of stars, commits crime.—146, 162

[10] Insane patient, in whom refusal of food indicated a suicidal attempt; illustrates importance of previous history.—176*f*

[11] Business man, in conflict with his brother, his dreams illustrating the compensatory function of the unconscious.—179, 180

[12] Young woman, with mother fixation, whose dreams illustrate the compensatory function of the unconscious.—179, 180

[13] Youth, aged 16, with severe compulsion neurosis, who dreams of seeing devil behind him.—181

[14] Young theological student, with religious problem, who dreams of black and white magicians.—181*ff*

[15] Young man, with a psychogenic depression; a dream demonstrates the limits of intellectual insight and the need for inaugurating the fantasy method.—213-9, 230, 232

[16] Woman, whose "vision" leads to her merging in unconscious processes.—221*ff*, 230

WORKS: *The Archetypes and the Collective Unconscious,* 7*n*, 66*n*, 97*n*, 100*n*, 181*n; Die Beziehungen zwischen dem Ich und dem Unbewussten,* 123*f*, 269*n;* "Brother Klaus," 78*n; Collected Papers on Analytical Psychology,* 3*n*, 6*n*, 49*n*, 123, 245*n*, 269*n;* Commentary on *The Secret of the Golden Flower,* 66*n;* "The Concept of the Collective Unconscious," 65*n;* "The Conception of the Unconscious," 123, 269*n;* "Concerning the Archetypes, with Special Reference to the Anima Concept," 189*n;* "The Content of the Psychoses," 123,

29*1n;* "Dream Symbols of the Individuation Process," 7*n; Freud and Psychoanalysis,* 49*n;* "General Aspects of Dreams Psychology," 100*n;* "Instinct and the Unconscious," 116*n; Mysterium Coniunctionis,* 100*n*, 222*n;* "Neue Bahnen der Psychologie," 3 *(see also* "New Paths in Psychology"); "New Paths in Psychology," v, vii, 3*n;* "On Psychic Energy," 47*n*, 53*n;* "On the Psychology and Pathology of So-called Occult Phenomena," 118*n*, 123, 137*n;* "Paracelsus as a Spiritual Phenomenon," 78*n; The Practice of Psychotherapy,* 112*n;* "The Psychological Aspects of the Kore," 189*n;* "The Psychological Foundations of Belief in Spirits," 186*n; Psychological Types,* 5*n*, 6, 44*n*, 54*n*, 57*n*, 58*n*, 100*n*, 134*n*, 138, 147*n*, 154*n*, 155*n*, 189*n*, 196*n*, 279*n; Die Psychologie der unbewussten Prozesse,* 3*n*, 245*n (see also* "The Psychology of the Unconscious Processes"); *Ueber die Psychologie des Unbewussten,* 7*n; Psychology and Alchemy,* 78*n*, 80*n*, 110; "The Psychology of Dementia Praecox," 162*n*, 262*n;* "On Psychological Understanding," 85*n;* "Psychology and Religion," 110; *Psychology of the Unconscious,* 123*n*, 169/275, 272*n*, 287, 291*n;* "The Psychology of the Unconscious Processes," 3*n*, 245*n;* "The Realities of Practical Psychotherapy," 112*n;* "A Review of the Complex Theory," 21*n;* "The Role of the Unconscious," 32*n; The Secret of the Golden Flower,* 110, 124; "Sigmund Freud in His Historical Setting," 28*n;* "The Stages of Life," 74*n;* "La Structure de l'inconscient," 123, 269*n;* "The Structure of the Psyche," 69*n*, 95*n;* "The Structure of the Unconscious," v, vii, 123*n;* "Studies in

persona (cont.)

analysis of, 158/281; as barricade, 175; and collective psyche, 294, 296f; compensatory relationship with anima, 192; composition of, 300, 302; as compromise with society, 302; contents of, 157/281; dazzling, 198; definition of, 192; developed, 198, 199; differentiation from anima, 198; differentiation of, 296; of disciple, 171; disintegration of, 161, 169; dissolution of, see dissolution; no Eastern concept of, 192; and ego, 194; effect on ego, 197; ego's identification with, 193, 195; feminine, 209; function of, 298f; ideal, 195; identical with typical attitude, 297; identification with, 150, 192; in Jung's case [8], 159; as mask of collective psyche, 158; neglected, 199; obstacle to individual development, 297; and personality, 196f; psychology of, 174; regressive restoration of, 163, 166, 168, 283f; as segment of collective psyche, 287; as subject-imago, 302; variety of, 210

personal, 196, 234; attitude, 158; and collective, 296 (see also individual and collective); definition of, 157; tie, 134; unconscious, see unconscious, personal

personality(-ies), 26/267, 58, 110, 151, 232, 238f; anima as, 197, 210; animus as, 210; artificial, 193f (see also persona); birth of, 230; change of, 175f, 219, 221 (see also transformation below); —, pathological, 175; cleavage of, 24; collective, 299; components of, 136/273; and compulsion neurosis, 181; conscious, 83, 124, 154/278, 161, 228, 300, 302; —, a segment of collective psyche, 157/281; dark half of, 96; developing, 104; development, see development; differentiation, 151; diminished, 168;

disintegration, 147; dissociation of, 44; dissolution, see dissolution; distortion of, 154/279; enlargement/extension/widening, 136/273, 143, 148/276, 156/280, 164; in Freud's theory, 127/270; integrity of, 38, 154, 166; and internal parent-imagos, 60; limited, 164; mana-, see mana; mid-point of, 221, 230; modern notion of, 196f; negative side of, 66n; partial, 111; pathological, 32; and personal unconscious, 136/273; renewed, 105; retarded maturation of, 184; and shadow, 53; total, 221, 223; transformations, 146f, 220, 223; "true," 197; weakness of, 147

personification: of anima and animus, 207, 210, 224; of autonomous complex, 196; of part-soul, 90; negative, 224

perversion, 209; sexual, 271

pessimism(-ist), 130, 139/274, 142

Peter, St., denial, 151

Pfaff, I. W.: Astrologie, 292; Der Stern der Drei Weisen, 292

phallic symbolism: of figurine, 107; of foot, 83, 87

philosopher, 144f/272; neurotic, 237

philosophy, 54, 129, 145, 190, 267; causal, 49; Chinese, 183; Gnostic, 66; Indian, 77n, 152n; medieval alchemical, 219f; Oriental, 124f; Platonic, 54; in psychoanalysis, 119; student, case of, see Jung's case [8]; Taoist, 78, 182; see also Stoics

phobias, 194

Phobos, 53

physics, 67; and causality, 49n

physiology, 67, 246

picture-book, world as, 144/271f

platonic friendship, 108

Platonic school of philosophy, 54

pleasure: Carnal, statue of, 265; principle, 42

plurality: of animus, 209; of persons, 207; of principles, 289

THE COLLECTED WORKS OF
C. G. JUNG

T HE PUBLICATION of the first complete edition, in English, of the works of C. G. Jung was undertaken by Routledge and Kegan Paul, Ltd., in England and by Bollingen Foundation in the United States. The American edition is number XX in Bollingen Series, which since 1967 has been published by Princeton University Press. The edition contains revised versions of works previously published, such as *Psychology of the Unconscious*, which is now entitled *Symbols of Transformation*; works originally written in English, such as *Psychology and Religion*; works not previously translated, such as *Aion*; and, in general, new translations of virtually all of Professor Jung's writings. Prior to his death, in 1961, the author supervised the textual revision, which in some cases is extensive. Sir Herbert Read (d. 1968), Dr. Michael Fordham, and Dr. Gerhard Adler compose the Editorial Committee; the translator is R. F. C. Hull (except for Volume 2) and William McGuire is executive editor.

The price of the volumes varies according to size; they are sold separately, and may also be obtained on standing order. Several of the volumes are extensively illustrated. Each volume contains an index and in most a bibliography; the final volume will contain a complete bibliography of Professor Jung's writings and a general index to the entire edition.

In the following list, dates of original publication are given in parentheses (of original composition, in brackets). Multiple dates indicate revisions.

* Published 1957; 2nd edn., 1970.   † Published 1973.

(*continued*)

* Published 1960.   † Published 1961.
‡ Published 1956; 2nd edn., 1967. (65 plates, 43 text figures.)

* Published 1959; 2nd edn., 1968. (Part I: 79 plates, with 29 in colour.)

* Published 1964; 2nd edn., 1970. (8 plates.)
† Published 1958; 2nd edn., 1969.

A Psychological Approach to the Dogma of the Trinity (1942/1948)
Transformation Symbolism in the Mass (1942/1954)
Forewords to White's "God and the Unconscious" and Werblowsky's "Lucifer and Prometheus" (1952)
Brother Klaus (1933)
Psychotherapists or the Clergy (1932)
Psychoanalysis and the Cure of Souls (1928)
Answer to Job (1952)

EASTERN RELIGION

Psychological Commentaries on "The Tibetan Book of the Great Liberation" (1939/1954) and "The Tibetan Book of the Dead" (1935/1953)
Yoga and the West (1936)
Foreword to Suzuki's "Introduction to Zen Buddhism" (1939)
The Psychology of Eastern Meditation (1943)
The Holy Men of India: Introduction to Zimmer's "Der Weg zum Selbst" (1944)
Foreword to the "I Ching" (1950)

*12. PSYCHOLOGY AND ALCHEMY (1944)
Prefatory note to the English Edition ([1951?] added 1967)
Introduction to the Religious and Psychological Problems of Alchemy
Individual Dream Symbolism in Relation to Alchemy (1936)
Religious Ideas in Alchemy (1937)
Epilogue

†13. ALCHEMICAL STUDIES
Commentary on "The Secret of the Golden Flower" (1929)
The Visions of Zosimos (1938/1954)
Paracelsus as a Spiritual Phenomenon (1942)
The Spirit Mercurius (1943/1948)
The Philosophical Tree (1945/1954)

‡14. MYSTERIUM CONIUNCTIONIS (1955-56)
AN INQUIRY INTO THE SEPARATION AND
SYNTHESIS OF PSYCHIC OPPOSITES IN ALCHEMY
The Components of the Coniunctio
The Paradoxa
The Personification of the Opposites
Rex and Regina   (continued)

* Published 1953; 2nd edn., completely revised, 1968. (270 illustrations.)
† Published 1968. (50 plates, 4 text figures.)
‡ Published 1963; 2nd edn., 1970. (10 plates.)

* Published 1966.
† Published 1954; 2nd edn., revised and augmented, 1966. (13 illustrations.)
‡ Published 1954.

The Development of Personality (1934)
Marriage as a Psychological Relationship (1925)

18. MISCELLANY
Posthumous and Other Miscellaneous Works

19. BIBLIOGRAPHY AND INDEX
Complete Bibliography of C. G. Jung's Writings
General Index to the Collected Works

See also:

C. G. JUNG: LETTERS

Selected and edited by Gerhard Adler, in collaboration with Aniela Jaffé.
Translations from the German by R.F.C. Hull.
VOL. 1: 1906–1950*
VOL. 2: 1951–1961

* Published 1973. In the Princeton edition, the *Letters* constitute Bollingen
Series XCV.

†THE FREUD/JUNG LETTERS

The Correspondence between Sigmund Freud and C. G. Jung
Translated by Ralph Manheim and R.F.C. Hull
Edited by William McGuire

†Published 1974. In the Princeton edition, *The Freud/Jung Letters* constitutes
Bollingen Series XCIV.